EVANSTON PUBLIC LIBRARY

3 1192 01387 9661

823.8 Dicke.C Bloom.H
Charles Dickens /

D1762353

DATE DUE

823.8
Dicke.C
Bloom.H

JAN 1 0 2008

Bloom's Classic Critical Views

CHARLES DICKENS

Bloom's Classic Critical Views

Jane Austen

Geoffrey Chaucer

Charles Dickens

Ralph Waldo Emerson

Nathaniel Hawthorne

Herman Melville

Edgar Allan Poe

Walt Whitman

Bloom's Classic Critical Views

CHARLES DICKENS

Edited and with an introduction by
Harold Bloom
Sterling Professor of the Humanities
Yale University

EVANSTON PUBLIC LIBRARY
1703 ORRINGTON AVENUE
EVANSTON, ILLINOIS 60201

Bloom's Classic Critical Views: Charles Dickens

Copyright © 2008 Infobase Publishing

Introduction © 2008 by Harold Bloom

All rights reserved. No part of this publication may be reproduced or utilized in any form or by any means, electronic or mechanical, including photocopying, recording, or by any information storage or retrieval systems, without permission in writing from the publisher. For more information contact:

Bloom's Literary Criticism
An imprint of Infobase Publishing
132 West 31st Street
New York NY 10001

Library of Congress Cataloging-in-Publication Data
Charles Dickens / [edited by] Harold Bloom.
   p. cm. — (Bloom's classic critical views)
  Includes bibliographical references and index.
  ISBN-13: 978-0-7910-9558-4 (acid-free paper)
  ISBN-10: 0-7910-9558-4 (acid-free paper) 1. Dickens, Charles, 1812–1870—Criticism and interpretation. I. Bloom, Harold.

PR4588.C3585 2007
823'.8—dc22
                                                                                        2007019858

Bloom's Literary Criticism books are available at special discounts when purchased in bulk quantities for businesses, associations, institutions, or sales promotions. Please call our Special Sales Department in New York at (212) 967-8800 or (800) 322-8755.

You can find Bloom's Literary Criticism on the World Wide Web at
http://www.chelseahouse.com

Series design by Erika K. Arroyo
Cover design by Takeshi Takahashi
Printed in the United States of America
Bang EJB 10 9 8 7 6 5 4 3 2 1

This book is printed on acid-free paper.

All links and Web addresses were checked and verified to be correct at the time of publication. Because of the dynamic nature of the Web, some addresses and links may have changed since publication and may no longer be valid.

Contents

Series Introduction	ix
Introduction by Harold Bloom	xi
Biography	xiii
Personal	3
Thomas Carlyle (1840)	5
Philip Hone (1842)	6
Richard Henry Dana (1842)	6
Frances Ann Kemble (1842)	7
Nathaniel Hawthorne (1853)	7
Hans Christian Andersen (1857)	8
John Forster (1872–74)	8
Mamie Dickens and Georgina Hogarth (1882)	8
Percy Fitzgerald "Charles Dickens as an Editor" (1882)	9
Thomas Adolphus Trollope (1888)	9
General	11
William Cullen Bryant (1842)	13
Elizabeth Barrett Browning (1843)	14
Edwin P. Whipple "Novels and Novelists: Charles Dickens" (1844)	14
Leigh Hunt "To Charles Dickens" (1849)	17
Mary Russell Mitford (1853)	18
George Eliot (1856)	18
Ralph Waldo Emerson "Literature" (1856)	19
John Ruskin (1856)	19
Peter Bayne "The Modern Novel: Dickens—Bulwer—Thackeray" (1857)	20

Walter Bagehot "Charles Dickens" (1858)	21
David Masson (1859)	38
Walter Savage Landor "Dickens" (1863)	39
Alexander Smith "On Vagabonds" (1863)	40
Henry James (1865)	41
Charles Eliot Norton "Charles Dickens" (1868)	46
F.B. Perkins (1870)	47
George Henry Lewes "Dickens in Relation to Criticism" (1872)	48
Edward FitzGerald (1874)	56
Harriet Martineau (1877)	56
Justin McCarthy (1879–80)	58
Algernon Charles Swinburne "Dickens" (1882)	58
Adolphus William Ward (1882)	59
Anthony Trollope (1883)	61
Edwin P. Whipple "In Dickens-Land" (1887)	63
Robert Louis Stevenson (1888)	64
W.E. Henley "Dickens" (1890)	67
William Dean Howells (1891)	70
W.H. Mallock "Are Scott, Dickens, and Thackeray Obsolete?" (1892)	70
Frederic Harrison "Charles Dickens" (1895)	72
William Samuel Lilly "Dickens" (1895)	80
David Christie Murray (1897)	81
Herbert Paul "The Apotheosis of the Novel" (1897)	83
George Gissing "Humour and Pathos" (1898)	83
Laurence Hutton "Charles Dickens" (1898)	90
Wilbur L. Cross (1899)	91
Richard Burton "The Fundamentals of Fiction" (1902)	91
Algernon Charles Swinburne "Charles Dickens" (1902)	92
Alice Meynell (1903)	103
G.K. Chesterton "On the Alleged Optimism of Dickens" (1906)	113
George Santayana (1921)	125

Works 139

The Pickwick Papers 141
John Wilson Croker "*The Pickwick Papers*" (1837)	141
Richard Grant White "The Styles of Dickens and Disraeli" (1870)	142

S.C. Hall (1883)	142
Margaret Oliphant (1892)	143

Barnaby Rudge 144
Edgar Allan Poe "Charles Dickens" (1841) 144

The Old Curiosity Shop 145
Edgar Allan Poe "Charles Dickens" (1841) 145
Thomas de Quincey (1847) 148
Sara Coleridge (1849) 149
Bret Harte "Dickens in Camp" (1870) 149
George Gissing "Dickens in Memory" (1902) 150

American Notes 152
Henry Wadsworth Longfellow (1842) 152
Thomas Babington Macaulay (1842) 152
James Spedding "Dickens's *American Notes*" (1843) 153
Lord Jeffrey Francis (1852) 154

A Christmas Carol 155
William Makepeace Thackeray "A Box of Novels" (1844) 155
Julia C.R. Dorr "Christmas and Its Literature" (1868) 156

Martin Chuzzlewit 157
Philip Hone (1843) 157
Sara Coleridge (1874) 158
William Dean Howells "Dickens" (1895) 158

David Copperfield 159
Charlotte Brontë (1849) 159
Charles Dickens (1850) 159
William Makepeace Thackeray "Mr. Brown the Elder
    Takes Mr. Brown the Younger to a Club" (1850) 160
Hans Christian Andersen "A Visit to Charles Dickens" (1870) 160
Mowbray Morris "Charles Dickens" (1882) 161
James Russell Lowell (1887) 163
G.K. Chesteron "David Copperfield" (1911) 163

Great Expectations 170
E.S. Dallas (1861) 170
Margaret Oliphant (1862) 174
G.K. Chesterton "Great Expectations" (1911) 177

A Tale of Two Cities 183
Sir James Fitzjames Stephen (1859) 183
G.K. Chesterton "A Tale of Two Cities" (1911) 189

Oliver Twist 195
Queen Victoria (1839) 195
William Makepeace Thackeray (1840) 196
G.K. Chesterton "Oliver Twist" (1911) 198

Hard Times 205
John Ruskin (1860) 205
George Bernard Shaw (1912) 206

Chronology 215

Index 218

Series Introduction

Bloom's Classic Critical Views is a new series presenting a selection of the most important older literary criticism on the greatest authors commonly read in high school and college classes today. Unlike the Bloom's Modern Critical Views series, which for more than twenty years has provided the best contemporary criticism on great authors, Bloom's Classic Critical Views attempts to present the authors in the context of their time and to provide criticism that has proved over the years to be the most valuable to readers and writers. Selections range from contemporary reviews in popular magazines, which demonstrate how a work was received in its own era, to profound essays by some of the strongest critics in the British and American tradition, including Henry James, G.K. Chesterton, Matthew Arnold, and many more.

Some of the critical essays and extracts presented here have appeared previously in other titles edited by Harold Bloom, such as the New Moulton's Library of Literary Criticism. Other selections appear here for the first time in any book by this publisher. All were selected under Harold Bloom's guidance.

In addition, each volume in this series contains a series of essays by a contemporary expert, who comments on the most important critical selections, putting them in context and suggesting how they might be used by a student writer to influence his or her own writing. This series is intended above all for students, to help them think more deeply and write more powerfully about great writers and their works.

Introduction by Harold Bloom

John Ruskin praised Dickens as the master of "stage fire," without adding that most of the fire was stolen from Shakespeare. An extraordinary stage performer, Dickens hypnotized audiences, particularly by his one-man readings in which he played all the parts in many of his most flamboyant novels.

Biographers agree that Dickens's tremendous stage-exertions hastened his death in his fifty-eighth year. Perhaps no other major writer has had a memory so comprehensive as Dickens, who could recall the principal plays of Shakespeare *verbatim*.

The critic Alexander Welsh sees *Dombey and Son* as Dickens's *King Lear*, but perhaps is more persuasive when he finds much of *Hamlet* in *David Copperfield*. In her *Shakespeare and Dickens* (1996), Valerie Gager includes a one hundred and twenty page catalog of Shakespearean allusions in Dickens's fictions. Musing on this, I tend to be a little puzzled, since Dickens's genius for caricature and the grotesque has far more affinity to Ben Jonson and Christopher Marlowe than to the psychological inwardness of Shakespeare's characters. Variety in Dickens's people mostly manifests in the startlingly different modes of the will that they manifest. In Shakespeare, as in ourselves, the will or desire in all has enough of a common element so that we recognize ourselves in others. With Dickens, there are differences *not of degree but of kind* in the wills of his characters. That is scarcely possible in human nature or in Shakespeare, but all things are possible in the "stage fire" of the Dickens world. Nearly everyone in Dickens seems to be part of Freud's myth of frontier concepts straddling the border between mind and body.

As I grow old teaching Shakespeare, I find that his art of representation, richer even than the art of Dante, Chaucer, and Cervantes, is even more impressive in its elliptical qualities. Something always is left out, in a systematic ellipsis that challenges us to put it back in. Why except for a moment in the wings do we never see Antony and Clopatra alone on stage together? Lear and Edmund never exchange a word: why? Does Hamlet not fear that Claudius is his phallic father, rather than King Hamlet, even though the Prince will not say so? Plutarch, the prime source for *Julius Caesar*, says that all Rome believed Brutus to be Caesar's illegitimate son. Is that a (barely) suppressed element in the play? Do Desdemona and Othello ever consummate their marriage, or does she die still a virgin? Why does Edgar punish himself with a disguise beneath the bottom of the social scale? Lear's Fool simply vanishes from the play. There are dozens more ellipses, but I find none in Dickens, or in Jonson and Marlowe. It is as though Dickens, like James Joyce, absorbs the Shakespearean wealth, but unlike Joyce does not seek to explore Shakespeare's deliberate challenges to us.

Of all English novelists, Dickens is the most Hogarthian, which may be why he preferred Tobias Smollett to Samuel Richardson and Henry Fielding. Perhaps Richardson, Henry James, and Joyce in their different ways surpassed aspects of Dickens, but he triumphs over them in his universality, where only Shakespeare and Cervantes can be said to overshadow him.

BIOGRAPHY

Charles Dickens
(1812–1870)

Charles Dickens was born in Landport, Portsmouth, England, on February 7, 1812. The family moved to London in 1814, to Chatham in 1817, and then back to London in 1822. By 1824 increasing financial difficulties led Dickens's parents to put him to work at a shoe-blacking warehouse. Later that same year, his father was briefly imprisoned for debt. Memories of this painful period of his life were to affect much of Dickens's later writing.

After studying at the Wellington House Academy in London from 1824 to 1827, Dickens worked as a solicitor's clerk and then became a reporter for the *Morning Chronicle* from 1834 to 1836.

By 1837 a collection of articles contributed to various periodicals appeared in two volumes as *Sketches by "Boz," Illustrative of Every-Day Life and Every-Day People*. This was followed by the enormously popular *Posthumous Papers of the Pickwick Club*, published in twenty monthly installments, beginning in April 1836, and appearing in book form, as a loosely constructed novel, the following year. Also in 1836 Dickens married Catherine Hogarth. They had ten children by the time they separated in 1858.

Between 1837 and 1839 Dickens published a second novel, *Oliver Twist*, in monthly installments in *Bentley's Miscellany*, a new periodical of which Dickens was the first editor. This was followed in 1838–39 by *Nicholas Nickleby*, another novel that was initially serialized. In 1840 Dickens founded his own weekly, *Master Humphrey's Clock*, which featured serial versions of his novels *The Old Curiosity Shop* and *Barnaby Rudge*. In 1842 he and his wife visited the United States and Canada. After their return, Dickens published *American Notes*, in 1842, a two-volume work that sparked controversy and ire in the United States with its often unflattering portrait of the nation. He then wrote *Martin Chuzzlewit*, a novel set partly in the United States and which appeared in monthly installments between 1843 and 1844.

In 1843 Dickens published *A Christmas Carol,* the first in a series of Christmas books, the others being *The Chimes* (1844), *The Cricket on the Hearth* (1845), *The Battle of Life* (1846), and *The Haunted Man* (1848). In 1846 he founded the Radical *Daily News,* which he briefly edited and which featured his "Pictures of Italy," after the author's visit there in 1844 and again in 1845. During a visit to Switzerland in 1846, Dickens wrote *Dombey and Son,* which appeared in monthly parts between 1846 and 1848. In 1850 he started the periodical *Household Words;* in 1859 it was incorporated into *All the Year Round,* which Dickens edited until his death. Much of his later work was published in these periodicals, including *David Copperfield* (1849–50), *Bleak House* (1852–53), *Hard Times* (1854), *Little Dorrit* (1855–57), *A Tale of Two Cities* (1859), *Great Expectations* (1860–61), and *Our Mutual Friend* (1864–65).

During these years of intense productivity, Dickens also found time to direct amateur theatrical productions, sometimes of his own plays. He also became involved in a variety of philanthropical activities, gave public readings, and in 1867–68 visited the United States for a second time. Dickens died suddenly on June 9, 1870, leaving his last novel, *The Mystery of Edwin Drood,* unfinished. Despite Dickens's great popularity both during and after his own life, it was not until the twentieth century that serious critical studies began to appear. Modern critical opinion has tended to favor the later works, which are more somber and complex, over the earlier ones, which are characterized by boisterous humor and broad caricature.

PERSONAL

In these brief personal reminiscences, Dickens's contemporaries frequently attribute to his person and character qualities that they admire in his fiction. They emphasize his dramatic ability, his good cheer, and his sympathy, much as Victorian readers enthusiastically praised Dickens's humor, his advocacy for the impoverished and forgotten, and his capacity to ventriloquize Londoners from all classes. While there are few direct interpretive keys here to the novels, students writing on voice or on Dickens's narrators will be interested in how seamlessly his friends connected the author with his works.

THOMAS CARLYLE (1840)

Thomas Carlyle, arguably the most widely influential Victorian writer, was the author of numerous essays and books, including *Sartor Resartus*, *The French Revolution* (which Dickens followed closely for *A Tale of Two Cities*), and *Past and Present*. Carlyle's work was noted for its moral seriousness; he and his wife, Jane Welsh Carlyle, also corresponded vigorously with almost the entire Victorian literary establishment.

He is a fine little fellow, Boz, as I think; clear blue intelligent eyes, eyebrows that he arches amazingly, large protrusive rather loose mouth,—a face of the most extreme *mobility*, which he shuttles about, eyebrows, eyes, mouth and all, in a very singular manner while speaking; surmount this with a loose coil of common-coloured hair, and set it on a small compact figure, very small, and dressed rather *a la d'Orsay* than well: this is Pickwick; for the rest a quiet shrewd-looking little fellow, who seems to guess pretty well what he is, and what others are.

—Thomas Carlyle, Letter to John A. Carlyle
(March 17, 1840)

Philip Hone (1842)

Philip Hone is perhaps best remembered for his meticulous diary, which he kept from 1828 until his death. He was a successful merchant and auctioneer and, briefly, mayor of New York City (1826–27).

Arrival of Charles Dickens. Among the passengers in the *Britannia* is Mr. Charles Dickens and his wife. This gentleman is the celebrated "Boz," whose name "rings through the world with loud applause"; the fascinating writer whose fertile imagination and ready pen conceived and sketched the immortal Pickwick, his prince of valets and his bodyguard of choice cronies, who has made us laugh with "Mantalini," and cry with "poor little Nell," caused us to shrink with horror from the effects of lynch law, as administered by the misguided Lord George Gordon, and to listen with unmitigated delight to the ticking of "Master Humphrey's Clock." The visit of this popular writer has been heralded in advance. He was expected by this packet, and I signed three or four days ago, with a number of other persons, a letter to be presented to him on his arrival in this city, giving him a hearty welcome and inviting him to a public dinner, which, from the spirit which appears to prevail on the subject, will be no common affair.

—Philip Hone, *Diary*, January 24, 1842

Richard Henry Dana (1842)

Richard Henry Dana Jr. was best known for his memoirs of life at sea, especially *Two Years Before the Mast* (1840). Dana's treatment of sailors was far more realistic and frank than the norm; Herman Melville identified Dana as a key influence.

Called on Dickens at 10.30 A.M. by appointment, as he leaves at one. He was at breakfast. Sat down with him. He was very agreeable and full of life. He is the *cleverest* man I ever met. I mean he impresses you more with the alertness of his various powers. His forces are all light infantry and light cavalry, and always in marching order. There are not many heavy pieces, but few *sappers and miners,* the scientific corps is deficient, and I fear there is no chaplain in the garrison.

—Richard Henry Dana, *Journal*
(February 5, 1842), cited in Charles Francis Adams,
Richard Henry Dana: A Biography,
1890, Vol. 1, p. 33

Frances Ann Kemble (1842)

Frances Ann ("Fanny") Kemble was a diarist, poet, and actress of note. She was particularly known for her performances of Shakespeare.

I admire and love the man exceedingly, for he has a deep warm heart, a noble sympathy with and respect for human nature, and great intellectual gifts wherewith to make these fine moral ones fruitful for the delight and consolation and improvement of his fellow-beings.

—Frances Ann Kemble, Letter (April 22, 1842),
Records of a Later Life, 1882, p. 318

Nathaniel Hawthorne (1853)

With his writing, Nathaniel Hawthorne forged a rich symbolic and psychologically gripping backstory for the United States out of its own Puritan past. He is best known for such works as *The Scarlet Letter* (1850) and *The House of Seven Gables* (1851), plus his many accomplished short stories.

At a dinner-party at Mr. Holland's last evening, a gentleman, in instance of Charles Dickens's unweariability, said that during some theatrical performances in Liverpool he acted in play and farce, spent the rest of the night making speeches, feasting, and drinking at table, and ended at seven o'clock in the morning by jumping leap-frog over the backs of the whole company.

—Nathaniel Hawthorne,
The English Note-Books, October 22, 1853

Hans Christian Andersen (1857)

Hans Christian Andersen was a Danish writer now remembered almost exclusively as an author of children's fairy tales. Victorian readers also knew Andersen as a travel writer and diarist, as well as a novelist.

Dickens is forty-five years old, cheerful, amiable, noble, and good. However highly I may place him as an author, I must prize him just as highly as an actor in tragedy, as well as in comedy.

—Hans Christian Andersen, Letter to the Grand Duke of Weimar (August 9, 1857)

John Forster (1872-74)

John Forster was an important critic and editor, working at the *Examiner* for two decades. Also a prolific biographer, Forster was ultimately chosen by Dickens to write his life story.

Of his attractive points in society and conversation I have particularised little, because in truth they were himself. Such as they were, they were never absent from him. His acute sense of enjoyment gave such relish to his social qualities that probably no man, not a great wit or a professed talker, ever left, in leaving any social gathering, a blank so impossible to fill up. In quick and varied sympathy, in ready adaptation to every whim or humour, in help to any mirth or game, he stood for a dozen men. If one may say such a thing, he seemed to be always the more himself for being somebody else, for continually putting off his personality. His versatility made him unique.

—John Forster, *The Life of Charles Dickens,* 1872–74, Bk. 11, Ch. 3

Mamie Dickens and Georgina Hogarth (1882)

Mary ("Mamie") Dickens was the eldest daughter of Charles Dickens and author of a memoir, *My Father as I Recall Him* (1885).

In publishing the more private letters, we do so with the view of showing him in his homely, domestic life—of showing how in the midst of his own constant and arduous work, no household matter was considered too trivial to claim his care and attention. He would take as much pains about the hanging of a picture, the choosing of furniture, the superintending any little improvement in the house, as he would about the more serious business of his life; thus carrying out to the very letter his favourite motto of "What is worth doing at all is worth doing well."

—Mamie Dickens, Georgina Hogarth, "Preface" to
The Letters of Charles Dickens, 1882, Vol. 1, p. viii

Percy Fitzgerald
"Charles Dickens as an Editor" (1882)

Percy Hethrington Fitzgerald was a prolific novelist, drama critic, and biographer of theatrical figures. A contributor to *Household Words*, he published a memoir of Dickens in 1914, and many of his earlier works contributed important details about Dickens's circle.

His extraordinary charm of manner, never capriciously changed, the smile and laugh always ready—that sympathy, too, which rises before me, and was really unique—I can call no one to mind that possessed it or possesses it now in the same degree.

—Percy Fitzgerald, "Charles Dickens as an Editor,"
Recreations of a Literary Man, 1882, pp. 31–32

Thomas Adolphus Trollope (1888)

Thomas Adolphus Trollope (1810–92) was the older brother of Anthony Trollope and son of Frances Trollope. A prolific novelist himself, Trollope lived with his mother in Italy for many years.

Dickens was only thirty-three when I first saw him, being just two years my junior. I have said what he appeared to me then. As I knew him afterwards, and to the end of his days, he was a strikingly manly man, not only in appearance but in bearing. The lustrous brilliancy of his eyes was very striking. And I do not think that I have ever seen it noticed, that those wonderful eyes which saw so much and so keenly, were appreciably, though to a very slight degree, near sighted eyes. Very few persons, even among those who knew him well, were aware of this, for Dickens never used a glass. But he continually exercised his vision by looking at distant objects, and making them out as well as he could without any artificial assistance. It was an instance of that force of will in him, which compelled a naturally somewhat delicate frame to comport itself like that of an athlete. Mr. Forster somewhere says of him, 'Dickens's habits were robust, but his health was not.' This is entirely true as far as my observation extends.

Of the general charm of his manner I despair of giving any idea to those who have not seen or known him. This was a charm by no means dependent on his genius. He might have been the great writer he was and yet not have warmed the social atmosphere wherever he appeared with that summer glow which seemed to attend him. His laugh was brimful of enjoyment. There was a peculiar humorous protest in it when recounting or hearing anything specially absurd, as who should say "Pon my soul this is *too* ridiculous! This passes all bounds!' and bursting out afresh as though the sense of the ridiculous overwhelmed him like a tide, which carried all hearers away with it, and which I well remember. His enthusiasm was boundless. It entered into everything he said or did. It belonged doubtless to that amazing fertility and wealth of ideas and feeling that distinguished his genius.

—Thomas Adolphus Trollope, *What I Remember,* 1888

GENERAL

William Cullen Bryant (1842)

In addition to being a poet, William Cullen Bryant was the longtime editor of the *New York Evening Post*. His best-known poem is "Thanatopsis," in which he urges the acceptance of death's role in nature. Bryant identifies Dickens as a kind of American in exile, a writer who both recognizes the democratic "virtues of the mass" and who has triumphed over class obstacles.

His more obvious excellences are of the kind which are easily understood by all classes—by the stable-boy as well as the statesman. His intimate knowledge of character, his familiarity with the language and experience of low life, his genuine humor, his narrative power, and the cheerfulness of his philosophy, are traits that impress themselves on minds of every description. But, besides these, he has many characteristics to interest the higher orders of mind. They are such as to recommend him peculiarly to Americans. His sympathies seek out that class with which American institutions and laws sympathize most strongly. He has found subjects of thrilling interest in the passions, sufferings, and virtues of the mass. As Dr. Channing has said, "he shows that life in its rudest form may wear a tragic grandeur, that, amid follies or excesses provoking laughter or scorn, the moral feelings do not wholly die, and that the haunts of the blackest crime are sometimes lighted up by the presence and influence of the noblest souls." Here we have the secret of the attentions that have been showered upon Mr. Dickens. That they may have been carried too far is possible; yet we are disposed to regard them, even in their excess, with favor. We have so long been accustomed to seeing the homage of the multitude paid to men of mere titles, or military chieftains, that we have grown tired of it. We are glad to see the mind asserting its supremacy, to find its rights more generally recognized. We rejoice that a young man, without birth, wealth, title, or a sword, whose only claims to distinction are in his intellect and heart, is received with a feeling that was formerly rendered only to kings and conquerors. The author, by his genius, has contributed happy moments to the lives of thousands, and it is right that the thousands should recompense him for the gift.

—William Cullen Bryant, *New York Evening Post*
(February 18, 1842), cited in Parke Godwin,
A Biography of William Cullen Bryant, 1883,
Vol. 1, pp. 396–97

Elizabeth Barrett Browning (1843)

A leading Victorian poet, Browning's reputation during her lifetime (1806–61) outstripped that of her husband, Robert Browning. Perhaps best remembered for her love poems, *Sonnets from the Portugese* (1850), Barrett Browning was also a social critic who wrote verse addressing such issues as the role of women, child employment, and slavery.

Do you know that the royal Boz lives close to us, three doors from Mr. Kenyon in Harley Place? The new numbers appear to me admirable, and full of life and blood—whatever we may say to the thick rouging and extravagance of gesture. There is a beauty, a tenderness, too, in the organ scene, which is worthy of the gilliflowers. But my admiration for 'Boz' fell from its 'sticking place,' I confess, a good furlong, when I read Victor Hugo; and my creed is, that, *not* in his tenderness, which is as much his own as his humour, but in his serious powerful Jew-trial scenes, he has followed Hugo closely, and never scarcely looked away from *Les Trois jours d'un condamne*.

—Elizabeth Barrett Browning,
Letter to James Martin (February 6, 1843)

Edwin P. Whipple "Novels and Novelists: Charles Dickens" (1844)

Edwin Percy Whipple was a notable American literary critic who argued for the moral relevance of romantic literary ideals. In this excerpt, Whipple values Dickens's attention to everyday life, including nature, and especially his ability to immerse himself in his characters. Students might profitably contrast this individualizing view of Dickens with writers such as Peter Bayne and David Masson, who see in Dickens a confusion of the general and the particular.

The immediate and almost unprecedented popularity he attained was owing not more to his own genius than to the general contempt for the school he supplanted. After ten years of conventional frippery and foppery, it was a relief to have once more a view of the earth and firmament,—to feel once more one of those touches of nature "which make the whole world kin." Here was a man, at last, with none of the daintiness of genteel society in his manner, belonging to no clique or sect, with sympathies embracing widely varying conditions of humanity, and whose warm heart and observant eye had been collecting from boyhood those impressions of man and nature which afterwards gushed out in exquisite descriptions of natural scenery, or took shape in his Pickwicks, Wellers, Vardens, Pecksniffs, and their innumerable brotherhood.

Dickens, as a novelist and prose poet, is to be classed in the front rank of the noble company to which he belongs. He has revived the novel of genuine practical life, as it existed in the works of Fielding, Smollett, and Goldsmith, but at the same time has given to his materials an individual coloring and expression peculiarly his own. His characters, like those of his great exemplars, constitute a world of their own, whose truth to nature every reader instinctively recognized in connection with their truth to Dickens. Fielding delineates with more exquisite art, standing more as the spectator of his personages, and commenting on their actions with an ironical humor, and a seeming innocence of insight, which pierces not only into but through their very nature, laying bare their inmost unconscious springs of action, and in every instance indicating that he understands them better than they understand themselves. It is this perfection of knowledge and insight which gives to his novels their naturalness, their freedom of movement, and their value as lessons in human nature as well as consummate representations of actual life. Dickens's eye for the forms of things is as accurate as Fielding's, and his range of vision more extended; but he does not probe so profoundly into the heart of what he sees, and he is more led away from the simplicity of truth by a tricksy spirit of fantastic exaggeration. Mentally he is indisputably below Fielding; but in tenderness, in pathos, in sweetness and purity of feeling, in that comprehensiveness of sympathy which springs from a sense of brotherhood with mankind, he is as indisputably above him.

The tendency of Dickens's genius, both in delineating the actual and the imaginary, is to personify, to individualize. This makes his page all alive with character. Not only does he never treat of man in the abstract, but he gives personality to the rudest shows of nature, everything he touches becoming symbolic of human sympathies or antipathies. There is no writer more deficient in generalization. His comprehensiveness is altogether of the heart, but that heart, like the intelligence of Bacon's cosmopolite, is not "an island cut off from other men's lands, but a continent which joins to them." His observation of life thus beginning and ending with individuals, it seems strange that those highly sensitive and patriotic Americans who paid him the compliment of flying into a passion with his peevish remarks on our institutions, should have overlooked the fact that his mind was altogether destitute of the generalizing qualities of a statesman, and that an angry humorist might have made equally ludicrous pictures of any existing society. When his work on America was quoted in the French Chamber of Deputies, M. de Tocqueville ridiculed the notion that any opinions of Mr. Dickens should be referred to in that place as authoritative. There is a great difference between the criticism of a statesman and the laughter of a tourist, especially when the tourist laughs not from his heart, but his bile. The statesman passes over individual peculiarities to seize on general principles, while the whole force of the other lies in the description of individual peculiarities. Dickens, detecting with the nicest tact the foibles of men, and capable of setting forth our Bevans, Colonel Tompkinses, and Jefferson Bricks, in all the comic splendor of humorous exaggeration, is still unqualified to abstract a general idea of national character from his observation of persons. A man immeasurably inferior to him in creative genius might easily excel him in that operation of the mind. Indeed, were Dickens's understanding as comprehensive as his heart, and as vigorous as his fancy, he would come near realizing the ideal of a novelist; but, as it is, it is as ridiculous to be angry with any generalizations of his on American institutions and politics, as it would be to inveigh against him for any heresies he might blunder into about innate ideas, the freedom of the will, or original sin. Besides, as Americans, we have a decided advantage over our transatlantic friends, even in the matter of being caricatured by the novelist whom both are rivals in admiring; for certainly, if there be any character in which Dickens has seized on a national trait, that character is Pecksniff, and that national trait is English.

The whole originality and power of Dickens lies in this instinctive insight into individual character, to which we have already referred. He has gleaned all his facts from observation and sympathy, in a diligent scrutiny of actual life, and no contemporary author is less indebted to books. His style is all his own, its quaint texture of fancy and humor being spun altogether from his own mind, with hardly a verbal felicity which bears the mark of being stolen. In painting character he is troubled by no uneasy sense of himself. When he is busy with Sam Weller or Mrs. Nickleby, he forgets Charles Dickens. Not taking his own character as the test of character, but entering with genial warmth into the peculiarities of others, and making their joys and sorrows his own, his perceptions are not bounded by his personality, but continually apprehend and interpret new forms of individual being; and thus his mind, by the readiness with which it genially assimilates other minds, and the constancy with which it is fixed on objects external to itself, grows with every exercise of its powers. By this felicity of nature, the man who began his literary life with a condemned farce, a mediocre opera, and some slight sketches of character, written in a style which but feebly indicated the germs of genius, produced before the expiration of eight years, *The Pickwick Papers, Oliver Twist, Nicholas Nickleby, The Old Curiosity Shop,* and *Martin Chuzzlewit,* in a continually ascending scale of intellectual excellence, and achieved a fame not only gladly recognized wherever the English tongue was spoken, but which extended into France, Germany, Italy, and Holland, and caused the translation of his works into languages of which he hardly understood a word. Had he been an egotist, devoured by a ravenous vanity for personal display, and eager to print the image of himself on the popular imagination, his talents would hardly have made him known beyond the street in which he lived, and his mind by self-admiration would soon have been self-consumed. His fellow-feeling with his race is his genius.

—Edwin P. Whipple, "Novels and Novelists: Charles Dickens" (1844), *Literature and Life,* 1849, pp. 58–63

Leigh Hunt "To Charles Dickens" (1849)

Leigh Hunt was a poet and literary critic. Harold Skimpole, a character in *Bleak House*, was supposedly based on Hunt, though Dickens would disavow the satire as accidental.

As when a friend (himself in music's list)
Stands by some rare, full-handed organist,
And glorying as he sees the master roll
The surging sweets through all their depths of soul,
Cannot, encouraged by his smile, forbear
With his own hand to join them here and there;
And so, if little, yet add something more
To the sound's volume and the golden roar;
So I, dear friend, Charles Dickens, though thy hand
Needs but itself, to charm from land to land,
Make bold to join in summoning men's ears
To this thy new-found music of our spheres,
In hopes that by thy Household Words and thee
The world may haste to days of harmony.

—Leigh Hunt, "To Charles Dickens," 1849

MARY RUSSELL MITFORD (1853)

Mary Russell Mitford was a fiction writer, a playwright, and a prolific letter writer. Her most enduring play was *Rienzi* (1828). Mitford was a close friend of Elizabeth Barrett's. Famously, Mitford gave Barrett her dog, Flush, later immortalized by Virginia Woolf.

The English novels of these days seem to me the more detestable the one than the other—Dickens all cant (Liberal cant, the worst sort) and caricature.

—Mary Russell Mitford, Letter to Mr. Starkey (January 31, 1853)

GEORGE ELIOT (1856)

Born Mary Ann Evans, George Eliot would go on to become, in the 1860s, Dickens's most important novelistic rival, praised as a psychological realist and moral sage. Eliot and Dickens make a powerful contrast: the former scrupulously registering shades of psychological or emotional nuance, and the latter focused as attentively on manner, speech, and action.

We have one great novelist who is gifted with the utmost power of rendering the external traits of our town population; and if he could give us their psychological character—their conceptions of life, and their emotions—with the same truth as their idiom and manners, his books would be the greatest contribution Art has ever made to the awakening of social sympathies. But while he can copy Mrs. Plornish's colloquial style with the delicate accuracy of a sun-picture, while there is the same startling inspiration in his description of the gestures and phrases of "Boots," as in the speeches of Shakespeare's mobs or numskulls, he scarcely ever passes from the humorous and external to the emotional and tragic, without becoming as transcendent in his unreality as he was a moment before in his artistic truthfulness. But for the precious salt of his humour, which compels him to reproduce external traits that serve, in some degree, as a corrective to his frequently false psychology, his preternaturally virtuous poor children and artisans, his melodramatic boatmen and courtesans, would be as noxious as Eugene Sue's idealized proletaires in encouraging the miserable fallacy that high morality and refined sentiment can grow out of harsh social relations, ignorance, and want; or that the working classes are in a condition to enter at once into a millennial state of *altruism,* wherein every one is caring for every one else, and no one for himself.

—George Eliot, "Natural History of
German Life: Riehl," 1856

Ralph Waldo Emerson "Literature" (1856)

Essayist, philosopher, and poet, Ralph Waldo Emerson was the founder of American transcendentalism, a cultural and philosophical movement emphasizing human intellectual and spiritual intuition over mere materialism. Whether a proponent (such as Henry David Thoreau), a fellow traveler (such as Thomas Carlyle), or an opponent (such as Nathaniel Hawthorne) of the movement, many nineteenth-century writers in England and the United States were influenced by Emersonian transcendentalism.

Dickens, with preternatural apprehension of the language of manners and the varieties of street life; with pathos and laughter, with patriotic and still enlarging generosity, writes London tracts. He is a painter of English details, like Hogarth; local and temporary in his tints and style, and local in his aims.

—Ralph Waldo Emerson, "Literature," English Traits, 1856

John Ruskin (1856)

John Ruskin was the most important Victorian art critic, and, more broadly, a moral critic to rival Carlyle. Ruskin extolled modern painters such as J.M.W. Turner and the Pre-Raphaelite Brotherhood as opposed to the idealism of the Royal Academy and Sir Joshua Reynolds.

If we glance over the wit and satire of the popular writers of the day, we shall find that the *manner* of it, so far as it is distinctive, is always owing to Dickens; and that out of his first exquisite ironies branched innumerable other forms of wit, varying with the disposition of the writers; original in the matter and substance of them, yet never to have been expressed as they now are, but for Dickens.

—John Ruskin, Modern Painters,
1856, Vol. 3, Pt. 4, App. 3

Peter Bayne "The Modern Novel: Dickens—Bulwer—Thackeray" (1857)

Peter Bayne was a Scottish theologian, biographer, and journalist. Like David Masson (but unlike critics such as Whipple), Bayne argues that Dickens's characters are somewhat impersonal—they are not properly individuals, but rather types. Students investigating Dickens's characterization, his humor, or his psychology will find this extract useful.

And his genius is worthy of honor. No writer could be named on whom the indefinable gift has been more manifestly conferred. His early works are all aglow with genius. The supreme potency with which he commands it, is shown in the total absence of effort, in the classic chasteness and limpid flow, of thought, fancy, and diction. You are in a meadow just after dawn; the flowers are fresh as if they had awakened from slumber, and the dew is on them all. A word, an idea, a glimpse of beauty, is always at hand; the writer never tarries a moment; yet there is no display, no profusion, of opulence. You do not see him waving the wand; the tear of the smile is on your cheek before you are aware.

The distinctive power of Dickens lies, we think, in a sympathy of extraordinary range, exquisite delicacy, and marvellous truth. He does not so much look, with steady, unparticipating gaze, until he knows and remembers the exact features of life: he feels. With all human sorrow he could weep; with all human mirth he could laugh; and when he came to write, every emotion he aimed at exciting was made sure, by being first experienced in his own breast. It was not with the individual man, in the wholeness of his life, in the depths of his identity, that he naturally concerned himself. It was kindness, rather than the one kind man, that he saw. It was mirth, rather than the whole character which is modified by humor. Qualities, capacities, characteristics, rather than complete men, glassed themselves in the mirror of his clear and open soul. With all his accuracy in detailed portraiture, it is a superficial perception of the order of his genius, which does not see that its power rested naturally less on realism, than on a peculiar, delicate and most captivating idealization. Pickwick, at least in the whole earlier part of his history, is an impossible personage. He belongs to broad farce. But we laugh at his impossible conversation with the cabman. We laugh at his impossible credulity as he listens to Jingle. We laugh at his impossible simplicity at the review. The far-famed Sam Weller, too, corresponds to no reality. The Londoner born and bred is apt to be the driest and most uninteresting of beings. All things lost for him the gloss of novelty when he was fifteen years old. He would suit the museum of a *nil admirari* philosopher, as a specimen, shrivelled and adust, of the ultimate result of his principle. But Dickens collected more jokes than all the cabmen in London would utter in a year, and bestowed the whole treasure upon Sam. His eye was far too acute for the comical to let it rest on any one funny man. In the case of those of his characters whom we are simply to admire and love, the same distinctive mode of treatment is exhibited. Rose Maylie and Esther Summerson are breathing epitomes of the tendernesses, the sweetnesses, the beauties, of life. Oliver Twist concentrates the single good qualities of a hundred children. The kind-hearted man, Dickens's stock character, be his name Pickwick, Jarndyce, or Clennam, seems always radically the same, and corresponds well enough with our theory. Perhaps it is essential deficiency in the highest power of individualization, which drives Mr. Dickens, it may be unconsciously, to affix by way of labels, to the personages of his story, those insignificant peculiarities which all can perceive. Amid the tumult and distracting blaze of his fame, one is by no means safe from the blunder of overlooking the kernel of genuine and precious humanity, of honest kindliness, of tender yet expansive benignity, which is in the centre of Dickens's being. His nature must originally have been most sweetly tuned. He must from the first have abounded in those qualities, which are so beautiful and winning when combined with manly character and vigorous powers; a cheerful gentleness, a loving hopefulness, a willingness to take all things and men for the best, an eye for the loveable; such a disposition as one finds in Goldsmith, a passionate admiration of happy human faces, a delight in the sports and laughter of children.

—Peter Bayne, "The Modern Novel: Dickens—Bulwer—Thackeray," *Essays in Biography and Criticism: First Series*, 1857, pp. 384–86

WALTER BAGEHOT "CHARLES DICKENS" (1858)

Walter Bagehot was an influential editor of the *National Review* and the *Economist*, as well as a political essayist and critic. His *The English Constitution* anatomizes, from a pragmatic and witty perspective, the governance of England during the nineteenth century. However appealing as an approach to public affairs, though, Bagehot's pragmatism conflicted with Dickens's gifts for satire and exaggeration. In this excerpt, the novelist abuses his platform by ceaselessly satirizing the workings of government, without ever offering a constructive alternative. Further, Bagehot claims that Dickens could see only the strain of middle-class life and not its compensations or intellectual accomplishments. Bagehot's essay is an important resource for any student writing on Dickens's political and social views, on his humor, or on his characterization.

Bagehot argues that Dickens's humor, great as it is, is fundamentally less interesting than that of other artists. It arises most directly from his ability to personify a trait—the humbleness of Uriah Heep, or the grandiose financial destitution of Micawber. No living person would behave in exactly these ways, but all of us have some of these traits to some extent. As a result, his characters do not resemble people; rather, they embody traits and qualities of personality made manifest in the world—that is why they are funny. Bagehot admits that Dickens's fictive creations are frequently funny, even uproariously so, but he also insists that true greatness in art depends on representing people as they really are. A viable contrast to Bagehot's views might be those of Santayana, who claims that Dickens's humor is in fact more realistic than "reality."

In his criticism of Dickens's political views, Bagehot coins a phrase that many critics have found useful: the novelist is a "sentimental radical." On one hand, Bagehot concedes that sentiment, in particular the hatred of needless oppression and poverty, animates much of Dickens's best work, citing in particular the workhouse scenes of *Oliver Twist*. (Though, for a different view of these scenes, see Harriet Martineau.) Bagehot notes that Dickens reacts to the apparent indifference of utilitarians and other reformers to the real, if unintended, suffering of those affected adversely by poor law reform. Dickensian outrage, then, is capable of shocking his readers into action.

Dickens's impulse for caricature, however, inevitably mars his treatment of politics, Bagehot argues. He notes that all governments, of whatever type or benevolence, are capable of being caricatured, and, as a result, caricature tends to flatten all governments into various species of the absurd. For Bagehot, that point of view slanders those in government who genuinely seek to do public good, and who have devoted their careers to doing so. He thus asserts that sentimental radicalism has perverse consequences, inasmuch as it leads naturally to a withdrawal from public life. For contrasting arguments, students might consult George Bernard Shaw's contention that Dickens's later fiction goads readers into action, or Chesterton's pervasive argument that the truest reform is self-reform.

There is a near universal tendency to identify Dickens as a profoundly middle-class novelist. What emerges in Bagehot is, in effect, middle-class dissent of Dickens's vision. Bagehot wants to show the good intentions and the capabilities of the middle class, while Dickens focuses chiefly, in Bagehot's view, on the absurdities of this group.

His genius is essentially irregular and unsymmetrical. Hardly any English writer perhaps is much more so. His style is an example of it. It is descriptive, racy, and flowing; it is instinct with new imagery and singular illustration; but it does not indicate that due proportion of the faculties to one another which is a beauty in itself, and which cannot help diffusing beauty over every happy word and moulded clause.

The truth is that Mr. Dickens wholly wants the two elements which we have spoken of as one or other requisite for a symmetrical genius. He is utterly deficient in the faculty of reasoning. 'Mamma, what shall I think about?' said the small girl. 'My dear, don't think,' was the old-fashioned reply. We do not allege that in the strict theory of education this was a correct reply; modern writers think otherwise; but we wish someone would say it to Mr. Dickens. He is often troubled with the idea that he must reflect, and his reflections are perhaps the worst reading in the world. There is a sentimental confusion about them; we never find the consecutive precision of mature theory, or the cold distinctness of clear thought. Vivid facts stand out in his imagination, and a fresh illustrative style brings them home to the imagination of his readers; but his continuous philosophy utterly fails in the attempt to harmonise them,—to educe a theory or elaborate a precept from them. Of his social thinking we shall have a few words to say in detail; his didactic humour is very unfortunate: no writer is less fitted for an excursion to the imperative mood. At present we only say what is so obvious as scarcely to need saying, that his abstract understanding is so far inferior to his picturesque imagination as to give even to his best works the sense of jar and incompleteness, and to deprive them altogether of the crystalline finish which is characteristic of the clear and cultured understanding.

Nor has Mr. Dickens the easy and various sagacity which, as has been said, gives a unity to all which it touches. He has, indeed, a quality which is near allied to it in appearance. His shrewdness in some things, especially in traits and small things, is wonderful. His works are full of acute remarks on petty doings, and well exemplify the telling power of minute circumstantiality. But the minor species of perceptive sharpness is so different from diffused sagacity, that the two scarcely ever are to be found in the same mind. There is nothing less like the great lawyer, acquainted with broad principles and applying them with distinct deduction, than the attorney's clerk who catches at small points like a dog biting at flies. 'Over-sharpness' in the student is the most unpromising symptom of the logical jurist. You must not ask a horse in blinkers for a large view of a landscape. In the same way, a detective ingenuity in microscopic detail is of all mental qualities most unlike the broad sagacity by which the great painters of human affairs have unintentionally stamped the mark of unity on their productions. They show by their treatment of each case that they understand the whole of life; the special delineator of fragments and points shows that he understands them only. In one respect the defect is more striking in Mr. Dickens than in any other novelist of the present day. The most remarkable deficiency in modern fiction is its omission of the business of life, of all those countless occupations, pursuits, and callings in which most men live and move, and by which they have their being. In most novels money *grows*. You have no idea of the toil, the patience, and the wearing anxiety by which men of action provide for the day, and lay up for the future, and support those that are given into their care. Mr. Dickens is not chargeable with this omission. He perpetually deals with the pecuniary part of life. Almost all his characters have determined occupations, of which he is apt to talk even at too much length. When he rises from the toiling to the luxurious classes, his genius in most cases deserts him. The delicate refinement and discriminating taste of the idling orders are not in his way; he knows the dry arches of London Bridge better than Belgravia. He excels in inventories of poor furniture, and is learned in pawnbrokers' tickets. But, although his creative power lives and works among the middle class and industrial section of English society, he has never painted the highest part of their daily intellectual life. He made, indeed, an attempt to paint specimens of the apt and able man of business in *Nicholas Nickleby;* but the Messrs. Cheeryble are among the stupidest of his characters. He forgot that breadth of platitude is rather different from breadth of sagacity. His delineations of middle-class life have in consequence a harshness and meanness which do not belong to that life in reality. He omits the relieving element. He describes the figs which are sold, but not the talent which sells figs well. And it is the same want of the diffused sagacity in his own nature which has made his pictures of life so odd and disjointed, and which has deprived them of symmetry and unity. . . .

Mr. Dickens's humour is indeed very much a result of . . . two peculiarities . . . His power of detailed observation and his power of idealising individual traits of character—sometimes of one or other of them, sometimes of both of them together. His similes on matters of external observation are so admirable that everybody appreciates them, and it would be absurd to quote specimens of them; nor is it the sort of excellence which best bears to be paraded for the purposes of critical example. Its off-hand air and natural connection with the adjacent circumstances are inherent parts of its peculiar merit. Every reader of Mr. Dickens's works knows well what we mean. And who is not a reader of them?

But his peculiar humour is even more indebted to his habit of vivifying external traits, than to his power of external observation. He, as we have explained, expands traits into people; and it is a source of true humour to place these, when so expanded, in circumstances in which only people—that is, complete human beings—can appropriately act. The humour of Mr. Pickwick's character is entirely of this kind. He is a kind of incarnation of simple-mindedness and what we may call obvious-mindedness. The conclusion which each occurrence or position in life most immediately presents to the unsophisticated mind is that which Mr. Pickwick is sure to accept. The proper accompaniments are given to him. He is a stout gentleman in easy circumstances, who is irritated into originality by no impulse from within, and by no stimulus from without. He is stated to have 'retired from business.' But no one can fancy what he was in business. Such guileless simplicity of heart and easy impressibility of disposition would soon have induced a painful failure amid the harsh struggles and the tempting speculations of pecuniary life. As he is represented in the narrative, however, nobody dreams of such antecedents. Mr. Pickwick moves easily over all the surface of English life from Goswell Street to Dingley Dell, from Dingley Dell to the Ipswich elections, from drinking milk-punch in a wheelbarrow to sleeping in the approximate pound, and no one ever thinks of applying to him the ordinary maxims which we should apply to any common person in life, or to any common personage in a fiction. Nobody thinks it is wrong in Mr. Pickwick to drink too much milk-punch in a wheelbarrow, to introduce worthless people of whom he knows nothing to the families of people for whom he really cares; nobody holds him responsible for the consequences; nobody thinks there is anything wrong in his taking Mr. Bob Sawyer and Mr. Benjamin Allen to visit Mr. Winkle senior, and thereby almost irretrievably offending him with his son's marriage. We do not reject moral remarks such as these, but they never occur to us. Indeed, the indistinct consciousness that such observations are possible, and that they are hovering about our minds, enhances the humour of the narrative. We are in a conventional world, where the mere maxims of common life do not apply, and yet which has all the amusing detail, and picturesque elements, and singular eccentricities of common life. Mr. Pickwick is a personified ideal; a kind of amateur in life, whose course we watch through all the circumstances of ordinary existence, and at whose follies we are amused just as really skilled people are at the mistakes of an amateur in their art. His being in the pound is not wrong; his being the victim of Messrs. Dodson is not foolish. 'Always shout with the mob,' said Mr. Pickwick. 'But suppose there are two mobs,' said Mr. Snodgrass. 'Then shout with the loudest,' said Mr. Pickwick. This is not in him weakness or time-serving or want of principle, as in most even of fictitious people it would be. It is his way. Mr. Pickwick was expected to say something, so he said 'Ah!' in a grave voice. This is not pompous as we might fancy, or clever as it might be if intentionally devised; it is simply his way. Mr. Pickwick gets late at night over the wall behind the back-door of a young-ladies' school, is found in that sequestered place by the schoolmistress and the boarders and the cook, and there is a dialogue between them. There is nothing out of possibility in this; it is his way. The humour essentially consists in treating as a moral agent a being who really is not a moral agent. We treat a vivified accident as a man, and we are surprised at the absurd results. We are reading about an acting thing, and we wonder at its scrapes, and laugh at them as if they were those of the man. There is something of this humour in every sort of farce. Everybody knows these are not real beings acting in real life, though they talk as if they were, and want us to believe that they are. Here, as in Mr. Dickens's books, we have exaggerations pretending to comport themselves as ordinary beings, caricatures acting as if they were characters.

At the same time it is essential to remember, that however great may be and is the charm of such exaggerated personifications, the best specimens of them are immensely less excellent, belong to an altogether lower range of intellectual achievements, than the real depiction of actual living men. It is amusing to read of beings *out* of the laws of morality, but it is more profoundly interesting, as well as more instructive, to read of those whose life in its moral conditions resembles our own. We see this most distinctly when both the representations are given by the genius of the same writer. Falstaff is a sort of sack-holding paunch, an exaggerated over-development which no one thinks of holding down to the commonplace rules of the ten commandments and the statute-law. We do not think of them in connection with him. They belong to a world apart. Accordingly, we are vexed when the king discards him and reproves him. Such a fate was a necessary adherence on Shakespeare's part to the historical tradition; he never probably thought of departing from it, nor would his audience have perhaps endured his doing so. But to those who look at the historical plays as pure works of imaginative art, it seems certainly an artistic misconception to have developed so marvellous an unmoral impersonation, and then to have subjected it to an ethical and punitive judgment. Still, notwithstanding this error, which was very likely inevitable, Falstaff is probably the most remarkable specimen of caricature-representation to be found in literature. And its very excellence of execution only shows how inferior is the kind of art which creates only such representations. Who could compare the genius, marvellous as must be its fertility, which was needful to create a Falstaff, with that shown in the higher productions of the same mind in Hamlet, Ophelia, and Lear? We feel instantaneously the difference between the aggregating accident which rakes up from the externalities of life other accidents analogous to itself, and the central ideal of a real character which cannot show itself wholly in any accidents, but which exemplifies itself partially in many, which unfolds itself gradually in wide spheres of action, and yet, as with those we know best in life, leaves something hardly to be understood, and after years of familiarity is a problem and a difficulty to the last. In the same way, the embodied characteristics and grotesque exaggerations of Mr. Dickens, notwithstanding all their humour and all their marvellous abundance, can never be for a moment compared with the great works of the real painters of essential human nature.

There is one class of Mr. Dickens's pictures which may seem to form an exception to this criticism. It is the delineation of the outlaw, we might say the anti-law, world in *Oliver Twist*. In one or two instances Mr. Dickens has been so fortunate as to hit on characteristics which, by his system of idealisation and continual repetition, might really be brought to look like a character. A man's trade or profession in regular life can only exhaust a very small portion of his nature; no approach is made to the essence of humanity by the exaggeration of the traits which typify a beadle or an undertaker. With the outlaw world it is somewhat different. The bare fact of a man belonging to that world is so important to his nature, that if it is artistically developed with coherent accessories, some approximation to a distinctly natural character will be almost inevitably made. In the characters of Bill Sykes and Nancy this is so. The former is the skulking ruffian who may be seen any day at the police-courts, and whom any one may fancy he sees by walking through St. Giles's. You cannot attempt to figure to your imagination the existence of such a person without being thrown into the region of the passions, the will, and the conscience; the mere fact of his maintaining, as a condition of life and by settled profession, a struggle with regular society, necessarily brings these deep parts of his nature into prominence; great crime usually proceeds from abnormal impulses or strange effort. Accordingly, Mr. Sykes is the character most approaching to a coherent man who is to be found in Mr. Dickens's works. We do not say that even here there is not some undue heightening admixture of caricature; but this defect is scarcely thought of amid the general coherence of the picture, the painful subject, and the wonderful command of strange accessories. Miss Nancy is a still more delicate artistic effort. She is an idealisation of the girl who may also be seen at the police-courts and St. Giles's; as bad, according to occupation and common character, as a woman can be, yet retaining a tinge of womanhood, and a certain compassion for interesting suffering, which under favouring circumstances might be the germ of a regenerating influence. We need not stay to prove how much the imaginative development of such a personage must concern itself with our deeper humanity; how strongly, if excellent, it must be contrasted with everything conventional or casual or superficial. Mr. Dickens's delineation is in the highest degree excellent. It possesses not only the more obvious merits belonging to the subject, but also that of a singular delicacy of expression and idea. Nobody fancies for a moment that they are reading about anything beyond the pale of ordinary propriety. We read the account of the life which Miss Nancy leads with Bill Sykes without such an idea occurring to us: yet when we reflect upon it, few things in literary painting are more wonderful than the depiction of a professional life of sin and sorrow, so as not even to startle those to whom the deeper forms of either are but names and shadows. Other writers would have given as vivid a picture: Defoe would have poured out even a more copious measure of telling circumstantiality, but he would have narrated his story with an inhuman distinctness which, if not impure is unpure; French writers, whom we need not name, would have enhanced the interest of their narrative by trading on the excitement of stimulating scenes. It would be injustice to Mr. Dickens to say that he has surmounted these temptations; the unconscious evidence of innumerable details proves that, from a certain delicacy of imagination and purity of spirit, he has not even experienced them. Criticism is the more bound to dwell at length on the merits of these delineations, because no artistic merit can make *Oliver Twist* a pleasing work. The squalid detail of crime and misery oppresses us too much. If it is to be read at all, it should be read in the first hardness of the youthful imagination, which no touch can move too deeply, and which is never stirred with tremulous suffering at the 'still sad music of humanity.' The coldest critic in later life may never hope to have again the apathy of his boyhood.

It perhaps follows from what has been said of the characteristics of Mr. Dickens's genius, that he would be little skilled in planning plots for his novels. He certainly is not so skilled. He says in his preface to the *Pickwick Papers,* 'that they were designed for the introduction of diverting characters and incidents; that no ingenuity of plot was attempted, or even at that time considered very feasible by the author in connection with the desultory plan of publication adopted;' and he adds an expression of regret that 'these chapters had not been strung together on a stronger thread of more general interest.' It is extremely fortunate that no such attempt was made. In the cases in which Mr. Dickens has attempted to make a long connected story, or to develop into scenes or incidents a plan in any degree elaborate, the result has been a complete failure. A certain consistency of genius seems necessary for the construction of a consecutive plot. An irregular mind naturally shows itself in incoherency of incident and aberration of character. The method in which Mr. Dickens's mind works, if we are correct in our criticism upon it, tends naturally to these blemishes. Caricatures are necessarily isolated; they are produced by the exaggeration of certain conspicuous traits and features; each being is enlarged on its greatest side; and we laugh at the grotesque grouping and the startling contrast. But the connection between human beings on which a plot depends is rather severed than elucidated by the enhancement of their diversities. Interesting stories are founded on the intimate relations of men and women. These intimate relations are based not on their superficial traits, or common occupations, or most visible externalities, but on the inner life of heart and feeling. You simply divert attention from that secret life by enhancing the perceptible diversities of common human nature, and the strange anomalies into which it may be distorted. The original germ of *Pickwick* was a 'Club of Oddities.' The idea was professedly abandoned; but traces of it are to be found in all Mr. Dickens's books. It illustrates the professed grotesqueness of the characters as well as their slender connection. The defect of plot is heightened by Mr. Dickens's great, we might say complete, inability to make a love-story. A pair of lovers is by custom a necessity of narrative fiction, and writers who possess a great general range of mundane knowledge, and but little knowledge of the special sentimental subject, are often in amusing difficulties. The watchful reader observes the transition from the hearty description of well-known scenes, of prosaic streets, or journeys by wood and river, to the pale colours of ill-attempted poetry, to such sights as the novelist wishes he need not try to see. But few writers exhibit the difficulty in so aggravated a form as Mr. Dickens. Most men by taking thought can make a lay figure to look not so very unlike a young gentleman, and can compose a telling schedule of ladylike charms. Mr. Dickens has no power of doing either. The heroic character—we do not mean the form of character so-called in life and action, but that which is hereditary in the heroes of novels—is not suited to his style of art. Hazlitt wrote an essay to inquire 'Why the heroes of romances are insipid;' and without going that length, it may safely be said that the character of the agreeable young gentleman who loves and is loved should not be of the most marked sort. Flirtation ought not to be an exaggerated pursuit. Young ladies and their admirers should not express themselves in the heightened and imaginative phraseology suited to Charley Bates and the Dodger. Humour is of no use, for no one makes love in jokes: a tinge of insidious satire may perhaps be permitted as a rare and occasional relief, but it will not be thought 'a pretty book' if so malicious an element be at all habitually perceptible. The broad farce in which Mr. Dickens indulges is thoroughly out of place. If you caricature a pair of lovers ever so little, by the necessity of their calling you make them ridiculous. One of Sheridan's best comedies is remarkable for having no scene in which the hero and heroine are on the stage together; and Mr. Moore suggests that the shrewd wit distrusted his skill in the light dropping love-talk which would have been necessary. Mr. Dickens would have done well to imitate so astute a policy; but he has none of the managing shrewdness which those who look at Sheridan's career attentively will probably think not the least remarkable feature in his singular character. Mr. Dickens, on the contrary, pours out painful sentiments as if he wished the abundance should make up for the inferior quality. The excruciating writing which is expended on Miss Ruth Pinch passes belief. Mr. Dickens is not only unable to make lovers talk, but to describe heroines in mere narrative. As has been said, most men can make a jumble of blue eyes and fair hair and pearly teeth, that does very well for a young lady, at least for a good while; but Mr. Dickens will not, probably cannot, attain even to this humble measure of descriptive art. He vitiates the repose by broad humour, or disenchants the delicacy by an unctuous admiration.

This deficiency is probably nearly connected with one of Mr. Dickens's most remarkable excellencies. No one can read Mr. Thackeray's writings without feeling that he is perpetually treading as close as he dare to the border-line that separates the world which may be described in books from the world which it is prohibited so to describe. No one knows better than this accomplished artist where that line is, and how curious are its windings and turns. The charge against him is that he knows it but too well; that with an anxious care and a wistful eye he is ever approximating to its edge, and hinting with subtle art how thoroughly he is familiar with, and how interesting he could make the interdicted region on the other side. He never violates a single conventional rule; but at the same time the shadow of the immorality that is not seen is scarcely ever wanting to his delineation of the society that is seen. Everyone may perceive what is passing in his fancy. Mr. Dickens is chargeable with no such defect: he does not seem to feel the temptation. By what we may fairly call an instinctive purity of genius, he not only observes the conventional rules, but makes excursions into topics which no other novelist could safely handle, and, by a felicitous instinct, deprives them of all impropriety. No other writer could have managed the humour of Mrs. Gamp without becoming unendurable. At the same time it is difficult not to believe that this singular insensibility to the temptations to which many of the greatest novelists have succumbed is in some measure connected with his utter inaptitude for delineating the portion of life to which their art is specially inclined. He delineates neither the love-affairs which ought to be, nor those which ought not to be.

Mr. Dickens's indisposition to 'make capital' out of the most commonly tempting part of human sentiment is the more remarkable because he certainly does not show the same indisposition in other cases. He has naturally great powers of pathos; his imagination is familiar with the common sorts of human suffering; and his marvellous conversancy with the detail of existence enables him to describe sick-beds and death-beds with an excellence very rarely seen in literature. A nature far more sympathetic than that of most authors has familiarised him with such subjects. In general, a certain apathy is characteristic of book-writers, and dulls the efficacy of their pathos. Mr. Dickens is quite exempt from this defect; but, on the other hand, is exceedingly prone to a very ostentatious exhibition of the opposite excellence. He dwells on dismal scenes with a kind of fawning fondness; and he seems unwilling to leave them, long after his readers have had more than enough of them. He describes Mr. Dennis the hangman as having a professional fondness for his occupation: he has the same sort of fondness apparently for the profession of death painter. The painful details he accumulates are a very serious drawback from the agreeableness of his writings. Dismal 'light literature' is the dismallest of reading. The reality of the police-reports is sufficiently bad, but a fictitious police-report would be the most disagreeable of conceivable compositions. Some portions of Mr. Dickens's books are liable to a good many of the same objections. They are squalid from noisome trivialities, and horrid with terrifying crime. In his earlier books this is commonly relieved at frequent intervals by a graphic and original mirth. As—we will not say age, but maturity, has passed over his powers, this counteractive element has been lessened; the humour is not so happy as it was, but the wonderful fertility in painful *minutiae* still remains.

Mr. Dickens's political opinions have subjected him to a good deal of criticism, and to some ridicule. He has shown, on many occasions, the desire,—which we see so frequent among able and influential men,—to start as a political reformer. Mr. Spurgeon said, with an application to himself, 'If you've got the ear of the public, *of course* you must begin to tell it its faults.' Mr. Dickens has been quite disposed to make this use of his popular influence. Even in *Pickwick* there are many traces of this tendency; and the way in which it shows itself in that book and in others is very characteristic of the time at which they appeared. The most instructive political characteristic of the years from 1825 to 1845 is the growth and influence of the scheme of opinion which we call radicalism. There are several species of creeds which are comprehended under this generic name, but they all evince a marked reaction against the worship of the English constitution and the affection for the English *status quo,* which were then the established creed and sentiment. All radicals are anti-Eldonites. This is equally true of the Benthamite or philosophical radicalism of the early period, and the Manchester or 'definite-grievance' radicalism, among the last vestiges of which we are now living. Mr. Dickens represents a species different from either. His is what we may call the 'sentimental radicalism;' and if we recur to the history of the time, we shall find that there would not originally have been any opprobrium attaching to such a name. The whole course of the legislation, and still more of the administration, of the first twenty years of the nineteenth century were marked by a harsh unfeelingness which is of all faults the most contrary to any with which we are chargeable now. The world of the 'Six Acts,' of the frequent executions, of the Draconic criminal law, is so far removed from us that we cannot comprehend its having ever existed. It is more easy to understand the recoil which has followed. All the social speculation, and much of the social action of the few years succeeding the Reform Bill bear the most marked traces of the reaction. The spirit which animates Mr. Dickens's political reasonings and observations expresses it exactly. The vice of the then existing social authorities and of the then existing public had been the forgetfulness of the pain which their own acts evidently produced,—an unrealising habit which adhered to official rules and established maxims, and which would not be shocked by the evident consequences, by proximate human suffering. The sure result of this habit was the excitement of the habit precisely opposed to it. Mr. Carlyle, in his *Chartism,* we think, observes of the poor-law reform: 'It was then, above all things, necessary that outdoor relief should cease. But how? What means did great Nature take for accomplishing that most desirable end? She created a race of men who believed the cessation of outdoor relief to be the one thing needful.' In the same way, and by the same propensity to exaggerated opposition which is inherent in human nature, the unfeeling obtuse-ness of the early part of this century was to be corrected by an extreme, perhaps an excessive, sensibility to human suffering in the years which have followed. There was most adequate reason for the sentiment in its origin, and it had a great task to perform in ameliorating harsh customs and repealing dreadful penalties; but it has continued to repine at such evils long after they ceased to exist, and when the only facts that at all resemble them are the necessary painfulness of due punishment and the necessary rigidity of established law.

Mr. Dickens is an example both of the proper use and of the abuse of the sentiment. His earlier works have many excellent descriptions of the abuses which had descended to the present generation from others whose sympathy with pain was less tender. Nothing can be better than the description of the poor debtor's gaol in *Pickwick,* or of the old parochial authorities in *Oliver Twist.* No doubt these descriptions are caricatures, all his delineations are so; but the beneficial use of such art can hardly be better exemplified. Human nature endures the aggravation of vices and foibles in written description better than that of excellencies. We cannot bear to hear even the hero of a book for ever called 'just;' we detest the recurring praise even of beauty, much more of virtue. The moment you begin to exaggerate a character of true excellence, you spoil it; the traits are too delicate not to be injured by heightening or marred by over-emphasis. But a beadle is made for caricature. The slight measure of pomposity that humanises his unfeelingness introduces the requisite comic element; even the turnkeys of a debtors' prison may by skilful hands be similarly used. The contrast between the destitute condition of Job Trotter and Mr. Jingle and their former swindling triumph, is made comic by a rarer touch of unconscious art. Mr. Pickwick's warm heart takes so eager an interest in the misery of his old enemies, that our colder nature is tempted to smile. We endure the over-intensity, at any rate the unnecessary aggravation, of the surrounding misery; and we endure it willingly, because it brings out better than anything else could have done the half-comic intensity of a sympathetic nature.

It is painful to pass from these happy instances of well-used power to the glaring abuses of the same faculty in Mr. Dickens's later books. He began by describing really removable evils in a style which would induce all persons, however insensible, to remove them if they could; he has ended by describing the natural evils and inevitable pains of the present state of being in such a manner as must tend to excite discontent and repining. The result is aggravated, because Mr. Dickens never ceases to hint that these evils are removable, though he does not say by what means. Nothing is easier than to show the evils of anything. Mr. Dickens has not unfrequently spoken, and what is worse, he has taught a great number of parrot-like imitators to speak, in what really is, if they knew it, a tone of objection to the necessary constitution of human society. If you will only write a description of it, any form of government will seem ridiculous. What is more absurd than a despotism, even at its best? A king of ability or an able minister sits in an orderly room filled with memorials, and returns, and documents, and memoranda. These are his world; among these he of necessity lives and moves. Yet how little of the real life of the nation he governs can be represented in an official form! How much of real suffering is there that statistics can never tell! how much of obvious good is there that no memorandum to a minister will ever mention! how much deception is there in what such documents contain! how monstrous must be the ignorance of the closet statesman, after all his life of labour, of much that a ploughman could tell him of! A free government is almost worse, as it must read in a written delineation. Instead of the real attention of a laborious and anxious statesman, we have now the shifting caprices of a popular assembly—elected for one object, deciding on another; changing with the turn of debate; shifting in its very composition; one set of men coming down to vote to-day, to-morrow another and often unlike set, most of them eager for the dinner-hour, actuated by unseen influences,—by a respect for their constituents, by the dread of an attorney in a far-off borough. What people are these to control a nation's destinies, and wield the power of an empire, and regulate the happiness of millions! Either way we are at fault. Free government seems an absurdity, and despotism is so too. Again, every form of law has a distinct expression, a rigid procedure, customary rules and forms. It is administered by human beings liable to mistake, confusion, and forgetfulness, and in the long run, and on the average, is sure to be tainted with vice and fraud. Nothing can be easier than to make a case, as we may say, against any particular system, by pointing out with emphatic caricature its inevitable miscarriages, and by pointing out nothing else. Those who so address us may assume a tone of philanthropy, and for ever exult that they are not so unfeeling as other men are; but the real tendency of their exhortations is to make men dissatisfied with their inevitable condition, and what is worse, to make them fancy that its irremediable evils can be remedied, and indulge in a succession of vague strivings and restless changes. Such, however,—though in a style of expression somewhat different,—is very much the tone with which Mr. Dickens and his followers have in later years made us familiar.

To the second-hand repeaters of a cry so feeble, we can have nothing to say; if silly people cry because they think the world is silly, let them cry; but the founder of the school cannot, we are persuaded, peruse without mirth the lachrymose eloquence which his disciples have perpetrated. The soft moisture of irrelevant sentiment cannot have entirely entered into his soul. A truthful genius must have forbidden it. Let us hope that this pernicious example may incite someone of equal genius to preach with equal efficiency a sterner and a wiser gospel; but there is no need just now for us to preach it without genius.

There has been much controversy about Mr. Dickens's taste. A great many cultivated people will scarcely concede that he has any taste at all; a still larger number of fervent admirers point, on the other hand, to a hundred felicitous descriptions and delineations which abound in apt expressions and skilful turns and happy images,—in which it would be impossible to alter a single word without altering for the worse; and naturally inquire whether such excellences in what is written do not indicate good taste in the writer. The truth is that Mr. Dickens has what we may call creative taste; that is to say, the habit or faculty, whichever we may choose to call it, which at the critical instant of artistic production offers to the mind the right word, and the right word only. If he is engaged on a good subject for caricature, there will be no defect of taste to preclude the caricature from being excellent. But it is only in moments of imaginative production that he has any taste at all. His works nowhere indicate that he possesses in any degree the passive taste which decides what is good in the writings of other people and what is not, and which performs the same critical duty upon a writer's own efforts when the confusing mists of productive imagination have passed away. Nor has Mr. Dickens the gentlemanly instinct which in many minds supplies the place of purely critical discernment, and which, by constant association with those who know what is best, acquires a second-hand perception of that which is best. He has no tendency to conventionalism for good or for evil; his merits are far removed from the ordinary path of writers, and it was not probably so much effort to him as to other men to step so far out of that path: he scarcely knew how far it was. For the same reason he cannot tell how faulty his writing will often be thought, for he cannot tell what people will think.

A few pedantic critics have regretted that Mr. Dickens had not received what they call a regular education. And if we understand their meaning, we believe they mean to regret that he had not received a course of discipline which would probably have impaired his powers. A regular education should mean that ordinary system of regulation and instruction which experience has shown to fit men best for the ordinary pursuits of life. It applies the requisite discipline to each faculty in the exact proportion in which that faculty is wanted in the pursuits of life; it develops understanding, and memory, and imagination, each in accordance with the scale prescribed. To men of ordinary faculties this is nearly essential; it is the only mode in which they can be fitted for the inevitable competition of existence. To men of regular and symmetrical genius also, such a training will often be beneficial. The world knows pretty well what are the great tasks of the human mind, and has learnt in the course of ages with some accuracy what is the kind of culture likely to promote their exact performance. A man of abilities, extraordinary in degree but harmonious in proportion, will be the better for having submitted to the kind of discipline which has been ascertained to fit a man for the work to which powers in that proportion are best fitted; he will do what he has to do better and more gracefully; culture will add a touch to the finish of nature. But the case is very different with men of irregular and anomalous genius, whose excellences consist in the *aggravation* of some special faculty, or at the most of one or two. The discipline which will fit him for the production of great literary works is that which will most develop the peculiar powers in which he excels; the rest of the mind will be far less important; it will not be likely that the culture which is adapted to promote this special development will also be that which is most fitted for expanding the powers of common men in common directions. The precise problem is to develop the powers of a strange man in a strange direction. In the case of Mr. Dickens, it would have been absurd to have shut up his observant youth within the walls of a college. They would have taught him nothing about Mrs. Gamp there; Sam Weller took no degree. The kind of early life fitted to develop the power of apprehensive observation is a brooding life in stirring scenes; the idler in the streets of life knows the streets; the bystander knows the picturesque effect of life better than the player; and the meditative idler amid the hum of existence is much more likely to know its sound and to take in and comprehend its depths and meanings than the scholastic student intent on books, which if they represent any world, represent one which has long passed away, which commonly try rather to develop the reasoning understanding than the seeing observation, which are written in languages that have long been dead. You will not train by such discipline a caricaturist of obvious manners.

Perhaps, too, a regular instruction and daily experience of the searching ridicule of critical associates would have detracted from the *pluck* which Mr. Dickens shows in all his writings. It requires a great deal of courage to be a humorous writer; you are always afraid that people will laugh at you instead of with you: undoubtedly there is a certain eccentricity about it. You take up the esteemed writers, Thucydides and the *Saturday Review;* after all, they do not make you laugh. It is not the function of really artistic productions to contribute to the mirth of human beings. All sensible men are afraid of it, and it is only with an extreme effort that a printed joke attains to the perusal of the public: the chances are many to one that the anxious producer loses heart in the correction of the press, and that the world never laughs at all. Mr. Dickens is quite exempt from this weakness. He has what a Frenchman might call the courage of his faculty. The real daring which is shown in the *Pickwick Papers,* in the whole character of Mr. Weller senior, as well as in that of his son, is immense, far surpassing any which has been shown by any other contemporary writer. The brooding irregular mind is in its first stage prone to this sort of courage. It perhaps knows that its ideas are 'out of the way;' but with the infantine simplicity of youth it supposes that originality is an advantage. Persons more familiar with the ridicule of their equals in station (and this is to most men the great instructress of the college time) well know that of all qualities this one most requires to be clipped and pared and measured. Posterity, we doubt not, will be entirely perfect in every conceivable element of judgment; but the existing generation like what they have heard before—it is much easier. It required great courage in Mr. Dickens to write what his genius has compelled them to appreciate.

We have throughout spoken of Mr. Dickens as he was, rather than as he is; or, to use a less discourteous phrase, and we hope a truer, of his early works rather than of those which are more recent. We could not do otherwise consistently with the true code of criticism. A man of great genius, who has written great and enduring works, must be judged mainly by them; and not by the inferior productions which, from the necessities of personal position, a fatal facility of composition, or other cause, he may pour forth at moments less favourable to his powers. Those who are called on to review these inferior productions themselves, must speak of them in the terms they may deserve; but those who have the more pleasant task of estimating as a whole the genius of the writer, may confine their attention almost wholly to those happier efforts which illustrate that genius. We should not like to have to speak in detail of Mr. Dickens's later works, and we have not done so. There are, indeed, peculiar reasons why a genius constituted as his is (at least if we are correct in the view which we have taken of it) would not endure without injury during a long life the applause of the many, the temptations of composition, and the general excitement of existence. Even in his earlier works it was impossible not to fancy that there was a weakness of fibre unfavourable to the longevity of excellence. This was the effect of his deficiency in those masculine faculties of which we have said so much,—the reasoning understanding and firm farseeing sagacity. It is these two component elements which stiffen the mind, and give a consistency to the creed and a coherence to its effects,—which enable it to protect itself from the rush of circumstances. If to a deficiency in these we add an extreme sensibility to circumstances,—a mobility, as Lord Byron used to call it, of emotion, which is easily impressed, and still more easily carried away by impression,—we have the idea of a character peculiarly unfitted to bear the flux of time and chance. A man of very great determination could hardly bear up against them with such slight aids from within and with such peculiar sensibility to temptation. A man of merely ordinary determination would succumb to it; and Mr. Dickens has succumbed. His position was certainly unfavourable. He has told us that the works of his later years, inferior as all good critics have deemed them, have yet been more read than those of his earlier and healthier years. The most characteristic part of his audience, the lower middle-class, were ready to receive with delight the least favourable productions of his genius. Human nature cannot endure this; it is too much to have to endure a coincident temptation both from within and from without. Mr. Dickens was too much inclined by natural disposition to lachrymose eloquence and exaggerated caricature. Such was the kind of writing which he wrote most easily. He found likewise that such was the kind of writing that was read most readily; and of course he wrote that kind. Who would have done otherwise? No critic is entitled to speak very harshly of such degeneracy, if he is not sure that he could have coped with difficulties so peculiar. If that rule is to be observed, who is there that will not be silent? No other Englishman has attained such a hold on the vast populace; it is little, therefore, to say that no other has surmounted its attendant temptations.

—Walter Bagehot, "Charles Dickens" (1858),
Collected Works, ed. Norman St. John-Stevas,
1965, Vol. 2, pp. 81–107

David Masson (1859)

David Masson was a historian, critic, and biographer perhaps best known for his life of John Milton. Masson concedes to Dickens's critics that the novelist is given to caricature, but argues further that this mode allows him to make visible that which is everywhere concealed. Masson's entry is worth considering in any essay that focuses on Dickens's characterization or use of satire, caricature, or humor.

The true objection to Dickens is, that his idealism tends too much to extravagance and caricature. It would be possible for an ill-natured critic to go through all his works, and to draw out in one long column a list of their chief characters, annexing in a parallel column the phrases or labels by which these characters are distinguished, and of which they are generalizations— the "There's some credit in being jolly here" of Mark Tapley; the "It isn't of the slightest consequence" of Toots; the "Something will turn up" of Mr. Micawber, &c, &c. Even this, however, is a mode of art legitimate, I believe, in principle, as it is certainly most effective in fact. There never was a Mr. Micawber in nature, exactly as he appears in the pages of Dickens; but Micawberism pervades nature through and through; and to have extracted this quality from nature, embodying the full essence of a thousand instances of it in one ideal monstrosity, is a feat of invention. From the incessant repetition by Mr. Dickens of this inventive process openly and without variation, except in the results, the public have caught what is called his mannerism or trick; and hence a certain recoil from his later writings among the cultivated and fastidious. But let any one observe our current table-talk or our current literature, and, despite this profession of dissatisfaction, and in the very circles where it most abounds, let him note how gladly Dickens is used, and how frequently his phrases, his fancies, and the names of his characters come in, as illustration, embellishment, proverb, and seasoning. Take any periodical in which there is a severe criticism of Dickens's last publication; and, ten to one, in the same periodical, and perhaps by the same hand, there will be a leading article, setting out with a quotation from Dickens that flashes on the mind of the reader the thought which the whole article is meant to convey, or containing some allusion to one of Dickens's characters which enriches the text in the middle and floods it an inch round with colour and humour.

—David Masson, British Novelists and Their Styles, 1859, pp. 251–52

Walter Savage Landor "Dickens" (1863)

Walter Savage Landor (1775–1864) was a poet and prose writer known for his idylls and epigrams, as well as for his devotion to classical poetics. *Bleak House*'s Lawrence Boythorn is based on him, and in 1853 Landor dedicated *Imaginary Conversations of Greeks and Romans* to Dickens.

You ask me what I see in Dickens.
A game-cock among bantam chickens.

—Walter Savage Landor, "Dickens," 1863

Alexander Smith
"On Vagabonds" (1863)

Alexander Smith was an influential essayist and a poet associated with the "Spasmodic" school. This excerpt is characteristic of his emphasis on mood or tone rather than on argument. Students exploring Dickens's cityscapes in greater depth might note the way Smith appropriates the novelist's fondness for imagining buildings in human terms.

If Mr. Dickens's characters were gathered together, they would constitute a town populous enough to send a representative to Parliament. Let us enter. The style of architecture is unparalleled. There is an individuality about the buildings. In some obscure way they remind one of human faces. There are houses sly-looking, houses wicked-looking, houses pompous-looking. Heaven bless us! what a rakish pump! what a self-important town-hall! what a hard-hearted prison! The dead walls are covered with advertisements of Mr. Sleary's circus. Newman Noggs comes shambling along. Mr. and the Misses Pecksniff come sailing down the sunny side of the street. Miss Mercy's parasol is gay; papa's neckcloth is white, and terribly starched. Dick Swiveller leans against a wall, his hands in his pockets, a primrose held between his teeth, contemplating the opera of Punch and Judy, which is being conducted under the management of Messrs. Codlings and Short. You turn a corner and you meet the coffin of little Paul Dombey borne along. Who would have thought of encountering a funeral in this place? In the afternoon you hear the rich tones of the organ from Miss La Creevy's first floor, for Tom Pinch has gone to live there now; and as you know all the people as you know your own brothers and sisters, and consequently require no letters of introduction, you go up and talk with the dear old fellow about all his friends and your friends, and towards evening he takes your arm, and you walk out to see poor Nelly's grave—a place which he visits often, and which he dresses with flowers with his own hands.

—Alexander Smith, "On Vagabonds,"
Dreamthorp, 1863, pp. 287–88

Henry James (1865)

The brother of the philosopher William James, Henry James was an American expatriate fiction writer, travel writer, critic, and theorist. Best known today for such novels as *The Portrait of a Lady* and *The Wings of the Dove*, James was a master of psychological nuance and a practitioner of a subtle, densely layered prose style capable of registering that nuance. His prose, indeed his whole vision of the world, is thus arguably antithetical to Dickens's boisterous style. "The Limitations of Dickens" challenges not just Dickens's later work but the whole premise of Dickensian characterization and psychology, ultimately arguing, perhaps hyperbolically, that it demeans humanity to consider Dickens a great writer. Students will find this essay well suited to any consideration of psychology, style, or humor in Dickens, and a helpful foil to such writers as Meynell, Chesterton, and Santayana in their defense of his craft and psychology. Another fruitful comparison might be with George Bernard Shaw's claim that Dickens's later works shift toward a conception of society as corrupt. What James sees as "exhaustion," Shaw extols as the sign of a greater art.

James begins the essay by arguing that Dickens has lapsed into a kind of grim self-parody. Dickens's basic approach in his best novels had been to turn some characteristic gesture or verbal tic into a grotesque, but now, that trick is driven by "a movement lifeless, forced, mechanical." Dickens no longer practices writing, James argues, but rather merely "the manufacture of fiction." As a result, Dickens has lost the sense of proportion that allows his grotesques to find a home in society. In *Our Mutual Friend*, James finds the characters are all exaggerated in some way, but Dickens fails to realize that "a community of eccentrics is impossible." This is the point of comparison with Shaw, who might grant that this is true, but respond that it is capitalism, and not Dickens, that reduces society to such an impossible community.

What frustrates James about Dickens is that the latter has conceived a novel about passion without being able to convey that passion in a realistic way. As a consequence, the main expression of that passion—Bradley Headstone and Eugene Wrayburn's antagonism over the love of Lizzie Hexam—is much paler and indistinct than it deserves to be. James is driven to identify Dickens as "the greatest of superficial novelists," a writer who "has created nothing but figure. He has added nothing to our understanding of human character." The figures might be amusing, they might resemble life in some way, but they cannot show us the meaning of, or offer us consolation for, our lives.

For James, this means that—unlike the views of Chesterton and Santayana—it is foolish to speak of Dickens as a moral writer. Dickens merely observes what he sees, but he does not understand it. What Santayana admires most in Dickens, his ability to reconcile us to the happiness of others, is just what James finds of "questionable" value. The "commonplace" lives of everyday humanity, and the acceptance of those lives, is not, in James's view, the proper aim of art.

Our Mutual Friend is, to our perception, the poorest of Mr Dickens's works. And it is poor with the poverty not of momentary embarrassment, but of permanent exhaustion. It is wanting in inspiration. For the last ten years it has seemed to us that Mr Dickens has been unmistakably forcing himself. *Bleak House* was forced; *Little Dorrit* was labored; the present work is dug out as with a spade and pickaxe.

Of course—to anticipate the usual argument—who but Dickens could have written it? Who, indeed? Who else would have established a lady in business in a novel on the admirably solid basis of her always putting on gloves and tying a handkerchief round her head in moments of grief, and of her habitually addressing her family with "Peace! hold!" It is needless to say that Mrs Reginald Wilfer is first and last the occasion of considerable true humor. When, after conducting her daughter to Mrs Boffin's carriage, in sight of all the envious neighbors, she is described as enjoying her triumph during the next quarter of an hour by airing herself on the door-step "in a kind of splendidly serene trance," we laugh with as uncritical a laugh as could be desired of us. We pay the same tribute to her assertions, as she narrates the glories of the society she enjoyed at her father's table, that she has known as many as three copper-plate engravers exchanging the most exquisite sallies and retorts there at one time. But when to these we have added a dozen more happy examples of the humor which was exhaled from every line of Mr Dickens's earlier writings, we shall have closed the list of the merits of the work before us.

To say that the conduct of the story, with all its complications, betrays a long-practised hand, is to pay no compliment worthy the author. If this were, indeed, a compliment, we should be inclined to carry it further, and congratulate him on his success in what we should call the manufacture of fiction; for in so doing we should express a feeling that has attended us throughout the book. Seldom, we reflected, had we read a book so intensely *written*, so little seen, known, or felt.

In all Mr Dickens's works the fantastic has been his great resource; and while his fancy was lively and vigorous it accomplished great things. But the fantastic, when the fancy is dead, is a very poor business. The movement of Mr Dickens's fancy in Mrs Wilfer and Mr Boffin and Lady Tippins, and the Lammles and Miss Wren, and even in Eugene Wrayburn, is, to our mind, a movement lifeless, forced, mechanical. It is the letter of his old humor without the spirit. It is hardly too much to say that every character here put before us is a mere bundle of eccentricities, animated by no principle of nature whatever.

In former days there reigned in Mr Dickens's extravagances a comparative consistency; they were exaggerated statements of types that really existed. We had, perhaps, never known a Newman Noggs, nor a Pecksniff, nor a Micawber; but we had known persons of whom these figures were but the strictly logical consummation. But among the grotesque creatures who occupy the pages before us, there is not one whom we can refer to as an existing type. In all Mr Dickens's stories, indeed, the reader has been called upon, and has willingly consented, to accept a certain number of figures or creatures of pure fancy, for this was the author's poetry. He was, moreover, always repaid for his concession by a peculiar beauty or power in these exceptional characters. But he is now expected to make the same concession with a very inadequate reward.

What do we get in return for accepting Miss Jenny Wren as a possible person? This young lady is the type of a certain class of characters of which Mr Dickens has made a speciality, and with which he has been accustomed to draw alternate smiles and tears, according as he pressed one spring or another. But this is very cheap merriment and very cheap pathos. Miss Jenny Wren is a poor little dwarf, afflicted, as she constantly reiterates, with a "bad back" and "queer legs," who makes dolls' dresses, and is for ever pricking at those with whom she converses, in the air, with her needle, and assuring them that she knows their "tricks and their manners." Like all Mr Dickens's pathetic characters, she is a little monster; she is deformed, unhealthy, unnatural; she belongs to the troop of hunchbacks, imbeciles, and precocious children who have carried on the sentimental business in all Mr Dickens's novels; the little Nells, the Smikes, the Paul Dombeys.

Mr Dickens goes as far out of the way for his wicked people as he does for his good ones. Rogue Riderhood, indeed, in the present story, is villainous with a sufficiently natural villainy; he belongs to that quarter of society in which the author is most at his ease. But was there ever such wickedness as that of the Lammles and Mr Fledgeby? Not that people have not been as mischievous as they; but was any one ever mischievous in that singular fashion? Did a couple of elegant swindlers ever take such particular pains to be aggressively inhuman?—for we can find no other word for the gratuitous distortions to which they are subjected. The word *humanity* strikes us as strangely discordant, in the midst of these pages; for, let us boldly declare it, there is no humanity here.

Humanity is nearer home than the Boffins, and the Lammles, and the Wilfers, and the Veneerings. It is in what men have in common with each other, and not in what they have in distinction. The people just named have nothing in common with each other, except the fact that they have nothing in common with mankind at large. What a world were this world if the world of *Our Mutual Friend* were an honest reflection of it! But a community of eccentrics is impossible. Rules alone are consistent with each other; exceptions are inconsistent. Society is maintained by natural sense and natural feeling. We cannot conceive a society in which these principles are not in some manner represented. Where in these pages are the depositaries of that intelligence without which the movement of life would cease? Who represents nature?

Accepting half of Mr Dickens's persons as intentionally grotesque, where are those exemplars of sound humanity who should afford us the proper measure of their companions' variations? We ought not, in justice to the author, to seek them among his weaker—that is, his mere conventional—characters; in John Harmon, Lizzie Hexam, or Mortimer Lightwood; but we assuredly cannot find them among his stronger—that is, his artificial creations.

Suppose we take Eugene Wrayburn and Bradley Headstone. They occupy a half-way position between the habitual probable of nature and the habitual impossible of Mr Dickens. A large portion of the story rests upon the enmity borne by Headstone to Wrayburn, both being in love with the same woman. Wrayburn is a gentleman, and Headstone is one of the people. Wrayburn is well-bred, careless, elegant, sceptical, and idle: Headstone is a high-tempered, hard-working, ambitious young schoolmaster. There lay in the opposition of these two characters a very good story. But the prime requisite was that they should *be* characters: Mr Dickens, according to his usual plan, has made them simply figures, and between them the story that was to be, the story that should have been, has evaporated. Wrayburn lounges about with his hands in his pockets, smoking a cigar, and talking nonsense. Headstone strides about, clenching his fists and biting his lips and grasping his stick.

There is one scene in which Wrayburn chaffs the schoolmaster with easy insolence, while the latter writhes impotently under his well-bred sarcasm. This scene is very clever, but it is very insufficient. If the majority of readers were not so very timid in the use of words we should call it vulgar. By this we do not mean to indicate the conventional impropriety of two gentlemen exchanging lively personalities; we mean to emphasize the essentially small character of these personalities. In other words, the moment, dramatically, is great, while the author's conception is weak. The friction of two *men*, of two characters, of two passions, produces stronger sparks than Wrayburn's boyish repartees and Headstone's melodramatic commonplaces.

Such scenes as this are useful in fixing the limits of Mr Dickens's insight. Insight is, perhaps, too strong a word; for we are convinced that it is one of the chief conditions of his genius not to see beneath the surface of things. If we might hazard a definition of his literary character, we should, accordingly, call him the greatest of superficial novelists. We are aware that this definition confines him to an inferior rank in the department of letters which he adorns; but we accept this consequence of our proposition. It were, in our opinion, an offence against humanity to place Mr Dickens among the greatest novelists. For, to repeat what we have already intimated, he has created nothing but figure. He has added nothing to our understanding of human character. He is master of but two alternatives: he reconciles us to what is commonplace, and he reconciles us to what is odd. The value of the former service is questionable; and the manner in which Mr Dickens performs it sometimes conveys a certain impression of charlatanism. The value of the latter service is incontestable, and here Mr Dickens is an honest, an admirable artist.

But what is the condition of the truly great novelist? For him there are no alternatives, for him there are no oddities, for him there is nothing outside of humanity. He cannot shirk it; it imposes itself upon him. For him alone, therefore, there is a true and a false; for him alone it is possible to be right, because it is possible to be wrong. Mr Dickens is a great observer and a great humorist, but he is nothing of a philosopher.

Some people may hereupon say, so much the better; we say, so much the worse. For a novelist very soon has need of a little philosophy. In treating of Micawber, and Boffin, and Pickwick, *et hoc genus omne*, he can, indeed, dispense with it, for this—we say it with all deference—is not serious writing. But when he comes to tell the story of a passion, a story like that of Headstone and Wrayburn, he becomes a moralist as well as an artist. He must know *man* as well as *men*, and to know man is to be a philosopher.

The writer who knows men alone, if he have Mr Dickens's humor and fancy, will give us figures and pictures for which we cannot be too grateful, for he will enlarge our knowledge of the world. But when he introduces men and women whose interest is preconceived to lie not in the poverty, the weakness, the drollery of their natures, but in their complete and unconscious subjection to ordinary and healthy human emotions, all his humor, all his fancy, will avail him nothing, if, out of the fulness of his sympathy, he is unable to prosecute those generalizations in which alone consists the real greatness of a work of art.

This may sound like very subtle talk about a very simple matter; it is rather very simple talk about a very subtle matter. A story based upon those elementary passions in which alone we seek the true and final manifestation of character must be told in a spirit of intellectual superiority to those passions. That is, the author must understand what he is talking about. The perusal of a story so told is one of the most elevating experiences within the reach of the human mind. The perusal of a story which is not so told is infinitely depressing and unprofitable.

—Henry James, "The Limitations of Dickens," (1865)

Charles Eliot Norton "Charles Dickens" (1868)

Charles Eliot Norton was a prolific and influential critic, as well as a professor of fine arts at Harvard. The editor of works by Carlyle, Emerson, Ruskin, and others, and the mentor of poets such as James Russell Lowell and Henry Wadsworth Longfellow, Norton was a pivotal transatlantic literary figure in the second half of the nineteenth century. Here he makes clear to modern students how personally Dickens's readers felt their connection to the author.

To give so much pleasure, to add so much to the happiness of the world, by his writings, as Mr. Dickens has succeeded in doing, is a felicity that has never been attained in such full measure by any other author. For the space of a generation he has done his beneficent work, and there are few English-speaking men or women who do not feel themselves under peculiar obligation to the great novelist, and bound to him, not by any mere cold literary tie, but by the warm and vital cords of personal sympathy. The critic gladly lays down his pen in presence of a genius which has won for itself such a recognition, and willingly adopts the words of Ben Jonson in addressing one of his great contemporaries:—

> I yield, I yield. The matter of your praise
> Flows in upon me, and I cannot raise
> A bank against it: nothing but the round,
> Large clasp of Nature such a wit can bound.

If we reflect what contemporary literature would be without Dickens's works,—how much enjoyment would be taken out of our lives,—how much knowledge of human nature and feeling for it, how much genial humor, how much quickening of sympathy, how much heartiness, would be lost, had this long series of books never appeared, we can better appreciate what we owe to their writer....

No one thinks first of Mr. Dickens as a writer. He is at once, through his books, a friend. He belongs among the intimates of every pleasant-tempered and large-hearted person. He is not so much the guest as the inmate of our homes. He keeps holidays with us, he helps us to celebrate Christmas with heartier cheer, he shares at every New Year in our good wishes: for, indeed, it is not in his purely literary character that he has done most for us, it is as a man of the largest humanity, who has simply used literature as the means by which to bring himself into relation with his fellow-men, and to inspire them with something of his own sweetness, kindness, charity, and good-will.

He is the great magician of our time. His wand is a book, but his power is in his own heart. It is a rare piece of good fortune for us that we are the contemporaries of this benevolent genius, and that he comes among us in bodily presence, bringing in his company such old and valued friends as Mr. Pickwick, and Sam Weller, and Nicholas Nickleby, and David Copperfield, and Boots at the Swan, and Dr. Marigold.

—Charles Eliot Norton, "Charles Dickens,"
North American Review, April 1868, pp. 671–72

F.B. Perkins (1870)

Frederic Beecher Perkins was the father of Charlotte Perkins Gilman, a feminist activist and the influential writer of "The Yellow Wallpaper" and other works. He was a prominent librarian, bibliographer, editor, and biographer. This brief extract introduces a key question for Dickens students: How does the novelist represent the past?

But Mr. Dickens's peculiar gift, and his best gift, was not the accumulation and delineation of such items as paint a past period—costume, antiquarian lexicography, archaeology generally. These are transitory, and are already dead. There have been great masters in the art of grouping and painting them, no doubt. But the art of this master was in painting the qualities of humanity, not of its costume—the feelings, sentiments, and passions that are everlasting as man. It might therefore have been expected that this part of the work would usurp upon the other in the composition of historical fiction; and so it was accordingly.

—F.B. Perkins, *Charles Dickens: A Sketch of His Life and Works*, 1870, p. 63

George Henry Lewes "Dickens in Relation to Criticism" (1872)

The longtime companion of George Eliot, George Henry Lewes was an important Victorian writer in his own right, who addressed a broad range of topics including science, philosophy, drama, and literary criticism. His biography of Goethe was considered the standard of the time. Like Eliot, Lewes generally faulted Dickens's handling of psychology as unrealistic. In this extract, however, Lewes defends Dickens's psychology as a product of his method, which is akin to hallucination. The essay is thus valuable as a reflection on the psychology of artistic creation and of reading.

Lewes does not claim that Dickens was mentally ill; rather, he argues that Dickens's great gift is to perceive his own creations as if they were real. As a result, he is able to describe his characters' external mannerisms with far more vivid detail than is customary. As a result, Lewes claims, "universal experiences became individualized in these types": Dickens's ability to conjure the gestures and speech associated with certain traits causes the traits to coalesce in his readers' minds. As readers, we attribute to characters such as Mark Tapley or Sam Weller any stray perception of the good-humored, capable servant. In turn, the force with which Dickens presents the character causes us to view such servants as Wellers or Tapleys. In effect, Dickens's power is such that he can fuse unconnected details into a wholly new creation, and yet make us believe that we have always known such a thing. The best example here is the Christmas books, wherein Dickens almost singlehandedly reinvents Christmas, but does so by imbuing it with nostalgia. As Lewes suggests, it is more or less beside the point to suggest that the recollection is false, or that the characters are "masks," rather than proper characters. The human mind is given, he suggests, to such simplifications, making Dickens's characters unchallengeable.

Lewes acknowledges that this approach to character portrayal drives some critics to distraction. It is an almost galvanic approach to character, whereby actions are "as uniform and calculable as the movements of a machine." Lewes attributes this quality to Dickens's hallucinatory method. Men such as Micawber may not exist in the world, but every time Dickens thinks of Micawber, he hears the embarrassed man waxing confident that something will turn up.

There probably never was a writer of so vast a popularity whose genius was so little *appreciated* by the critics. The very splendour of his successes so deepened the shadow of his failures that to many eyes the shadows supplanted the splendour. Fastidious readers were loath to admit that a writer could be justly called great whose defects were so glaring. They admitted, because it was indisputable, that Dickens delighted thousands, that his admirers were found in all classes, and in all countries; that he stirred the sympathy of masses not easily reached through Literature, and always stirred healthy, generous emotions; that he impressed a new direction on popular writing, and modified the Literature of his age, in its spirit no less than in its form; but they nevertheless insisted on his defects as if these outweighed all positive qualities; and spoke of him either with condescending patronage, or with sneering irritation. Surely this is a fact worthy of investigation? Were the critics wrong, and if so, in what consisted their error? How are we to reconcile this immense popularity with this critical contempt? The private readers and the public critics who were eager to take up each successive number of his works as it appeared, whose very talk was seasoned with quotations from and allusions to these works, who, to my knowledge, were wont to lay aside books of which they could only speak in terms of eulogy, in order to bury themselves in the "new number" when the well-known green cover made its appearance—were nevertheless at this very time niggard in their praise, and lavish in their scorn of the popular humorist. It is not long since I heard a very distinguished man express measureless contempt for Dickens, and a few minutes afterwards, in reply to some representations on the other side, admit that Dickens had "entered into his life."

Dickens has proved his power by a popularity almost unexampled, embracing all classes. Surely it is a task for criticism to exhibit the sources of that power? If everything that has ever been alleged against the works be admitted, there still remains an immense success to be accounted for. It was not by their defects that these works were carried over Europe and America. It was not their defects which made them the delight of grey heads on the bench, and the study of youngsters in the counting-house and school-room. Other writers have been exaggerated, untrue, fantastic, and melodramatic; but they have gained so little notice that no one thinks of pointing out their defects. It is clear, therefore, that Dickens had powers which enabled him to triumph in spite of the weaknesses which clogged them; and it is worth inquiring what those powers were, and their relation to his undeniable defects.

I am not about to attempt such an inquiry, but simply to indicate two or three general points of view. It will be enough merely to mention in passing the primary cause of his success, his overflowing fun, because even uncompromising opponents admit it. They may be ashamed of their laughter, but they laugh. A revulsion of feeling at the preposterousness or extravagance of the image may follow the burst of laughter, but the laughter is irresistible, whether rational or not, and there is no arguing away such a fact.

Great as Dickens is in fun, so great that Fielding and Smollett are small in comparison, he would have been only a passing amusement for the world had he not been gifted with an imagination of marvellous vividness, and an emotional, sympathetic nature capable of furnishing that imagination with elements of universal power. Of him it may be said with less exaggeration than of most poets, that he was of "imagination all compact;" if the other higher faculties were singularly deficient in him, this faculty was imperial. He was a seer of visions; and his visions were of objects at once familiar and potent. Psychologists will understand both the extent and the limitation of the remark, when I say that in no other perfectly sane mind (Blake, I believe, was not perfectly sane) have I observed vividness of imagination approaching so closely to hallucination. Many who are not psychologists may have had some experience in themselves, or in others, of that abnormal condition in which a man hears voices, and sees objects, with the distinctness of direct perception, although silence and darkness are without him; these *revived* impressions, revived by an internal cause, have precisely the same force and clearness which the impressions originally had when produced by an external cause. In the same degree of vividness are the images *constructed* by his mind in explanation of the voices heard or objects seen: when he imagines that the voice proceeds from a personal friend, or from Satan tempting him, the friend or Satan stands before him with the distinctness of objective reality;

when he imagines that he himself has been transformed into a bear, his hands are seen by him as paws. In vain you represent to him that the voices he hears have no external existence; he will answer, as a patient pertinently answered Lelut: "You believe that I am speaking to you because you hear me, is it not so? Very well, I believe that voices are speaking to me because I hear them." There is no power of effacing such conviction by argument. You may get the patient to assent to any premises you please, he will not swerve from his conclusions. I once argued with a patient who believed he had been transformed into a bear; he was quite willing to admit that the idea of such a transformation was utterly at variance with all experience; but he always returned to his position that God being omnipotent there was no reason to doubt his power of transforming men into bears: what remained fixed in his mind was the image of himself under a bear's form.

The characteristic point in the hallucinations of the insane, that which distinguishes them from hallucinations equally vivid in the sane, is the coercion of the image in *suppressing comparison* and all control of experience. Belief always accompanies a vivid image, for a time; but in the sane this belief will not persist against rational control. If I see a stick partly under water, it is impossible for me not to have the same reeling which would be produced by a bent stick out of the water—if I see two plane images in the stereoscope, it is impossible not to have the feeling of seeing one solid object. But these beliefs are rapidly displaced by reference to experience. I know the stick is not bent, and that it will not appear bent when removed from the water. I know the seeming solid is not an object in relief, but two plane pictures. It is by similar focal adjustment of the mind that sane people know that their hallucinations are unreal. The images may have the vividness of real objects, but they have not the properties of real objects, they do not preserve consistent relations with other facts, they appear in contradiction to other beliefs. Thus if I see a black cat on the chair opposite, yet on my approaching the chair feel no soft object, and if my terrier on the hearthrug looking in the direction of the chair shows none of the well-known agitation which the sight of a cat produces, I conclude, in spite of its distinctness, that the image is an hallucination.

Returning from this digression, let me say that I am very far indeed from wishing to imply any agreement in the common notion that "great wits to madness nearly are allied;" on the contrary, my studies have led to the conviction that nothing is less like genius than insanity, although some men of genius have had occasional attacks; and further, that I have never observed any trace of the insane temperament in Dickens's works, or life, they being indeed singularly free even from the eccentricities which often accompany exceptional powers; nevertheless, with all due limitations, it is true that there is considerable light shed upon his works by the action of the imagination in hallucination. To him also *revived* images have the vividness of sensations; to him also *created* images have the coercive force of realities, excluding all control, all contradiction. What seems preposterous, impossible to us, seemed to him simple fact of observation. When he imagined a street, a house, a room, a figure, he saw it not in the vague schematic way of ordinary imagination, but in the sharp definition of actual perception, all the salient details obtruding themselves on his attention. He, seeing it thus vividly, made us also see it; and believing in its reality however fantastic, he communicated something of his belief to us. He presented it in such relief that we ceased to think of it as a picture. So definite and insistent was the image, that even while knowing it was false we could not help, for a moment, being affected, as it were, by his hallucination.

This glorious energy of imagination is that which Dickens had in common with all great writers. It was this which made him a creator, and made his creations universally intelligible, no matter how fantastic and unreal. His types established themselves in the public mind like personal experiences. Their falsity was unnoticed in the blaze of their illumination. Every humbug seemed a Pecksniff, every nurse a Gamp, every jovial improvident a Micawber, every stinted serving-wench a Marchioness. Universal experiences became individualised in these types; an image and a name were given, and the image was so suggestive that it seemed to *express* all that it was found to *recall,* and Dickens was held to have depicted what his readers supplied. Against such power criticism was almost idle. In vain critical reflection showed these figures to be merely masks,—not characters, but personified characteristics, caricatures and distortions of human nature,—the vividness of their presentation triumphed over reflection: their creator managed to communicate to the public his own unhesitating belief. Unreal and impossible as these types were, speaking a language never heard in life, moving like pieces of simple mechanism always in one way (instead of moving with the infinite fluctuations of organisms, incalculable yet intelligible, surprising yet familiar), these unreal figures affected the uncritical reader with the force of reality; and they did so in virtue of their embodiment of some real characteristic vividly presented. The imagination of the author laid hold of some well-marked physical trait, some peculiarity of aspect, speech, or manner which every one recognised at once; and the force with which this was presented made it occupy the mind to the exclusion of all critical doubts: only reflection could detect the incongruity. Think of what this implies!

Think how little the mass of men are given to reflect on their impressions, and how their minds are for the most part occupied with sensations rather than ideas, and you will see why Dickens held an undisputed sway. Give a child a wooden horse, with hair for mane and tail, and wafer spots for colouring, he will never be disturbed by the fact that this horse does not move its legs, but runs on wheels—the general suggestion suffices for his belief; and this wooden horse, which he can handle and draw, is believed in more than a pictured horse by a Wouvermanns or an Ansdell. It may be said of Dickens's human figures that they too are wooden, and run on wheels; but these are details which scarcely disturb the belief of admirers. Just as the wooden horse is brought within the range of the child's emotions, and dramatizing tendencies, when he can handle and draw it, so Dickens's figures are brought within the range of the reader's interests, and receive from these interests a sudden illumination, when they are the puppets of a drama every incident of which appeals to the sympathies. With a fine felicity of instinct he seized upon situations having an irresistible hold over the domestic affections and ordinary sympathies. He spoke in the mother-tongue of the heart, and was always sure of ready listeners. He painted the life he knew, the life every one knew; for if the scenes and manners were unlike those we were familiar with, the feelings and motives, the joys and griefs, the mistakes and efforts of the actors were universal, and therefore universally intelligible; so that even critical spectators who complained that these broadly painted pictures were artistic daubs, could not wholly resist their effective suggestiveness. He set in motion the secret springs of sympathy by touching the domestic affections. He painted nothing ideal, heroic; but all the resources of the bourgeois epic were in his grasp. The world of thought and passion lay beyond his horizon. But the joys and pains of childhood, the petty tyrannies of ignoble natures, the genial pleasantries of happy natures, the life of the poor, the struggles of the street and back parlour, the insolence of office, the sharp social contrasts, east-wind and Christmas jollity, hunger, misery, and hot punch—these he could deal with, so that we laughed and cried, were startled at the revelation of familiar facts hitherto unnoted, and felt our pulses quicken as we were hurried along with him in his fanciful flight.

Such were the sources of his power. To understand how it is that critics quite competent to recognise such power, and even so far amenable to it as to be moved and interested by the works in spite of all their drawbacks, should have forgotten this undenied power, and written or spoken of Dickens with mingled irritation and contempt, we must take into account two natural tendencies—the bias of opposition, and the bias of technical estimate.

The bias of opposition may be illustrated in a parallel case. Let us suppose a scientific book to be attracting the attention of Europe by the boldness, suggestiveness, and theoretic plausibility of its hypotheses; this work falls into the hands of a critic sufficiently grounded in the science treated to be aware that its writer, although gifted with great theoretic power and occasional insight into unexplored relations, is nevertheless pitiably ignorant of the elementary facts and principles of the science; the critic noticing the power, and the talent of lucid exposition, is yet perplexed and irritated at ignorance which is inexcusable, and a reckless twisting of known facts into impossible relations, which seems wilful; will he not pass from marvelling at this inextricable web of sense and nonsense, suggestive insight and mischievous error, so jumbled together that the combination of this sagacity with this glaring inefficiency is a paradox, and be driven by the anger of opposition into an emphatic assertion that the belauded philosopher is a charlatan and an ignoramus? A chorus of admirers proclaims the author to be a great teacher, before whom all contemporaries must bow; and the critic observes this teacher on one page throwing out a striking hypothesis of some geometric relations in the planetary movements, and on another assuming that the hypothenuse is equal to its perpendicular and base, because the square of the hypothenuse is equal to the squares of its sides—in one chapter ridiculing the atomic theory, and in another arguing that carbonic acid is obtained from carbon and nitrogen—can this critic be expected to join in the chorus of admirers? and will he not rather be exasperated into an opposition which will lead him to undervalue the undeniable qualities in his insistance on the undeniable defects?

Something like this is the feeling produced by Dickens's works in many cultivated and critical readers. They see there human character and ordinary events pourtrayed with a mingled verisimilitude and falsity altogether unexampled. The drawing is so vivid yet so incorrect, or else is so blurred and formless, with such excess of *effort* (as of a showman beating on the drum) that the doubt arises how an observer so remarkably keen could make observations so remarkably false, and miss such very obvious facts; how the rapid glance which could swoop down on a peculiarity with hawk-like precision, could overlook all that accompanied and was organically related to that peculiarity; how the eye for characteristics could be so blind to character, and the ear for dramatic idiom be so deaf to dramatic language; finally, how the writer's exquisite susceptibility to the grotesque could be insensible to the occasional grotesqueness of his own attitude. Michael Angelo is intelligible, and Giotto is intelligible; but a critic is nonplussed at finding the invention of Angelo with the drawing of Giotto. It is indeed surprising that Dickens should have observed man, and not been impressed with the fact that man is, in the words of Montaigne, *un etre ondoyant et diverse*. And the critic is distressed to observe the substitution of mechanisms for minds, puppets for characters. It is needless to dwell on such monstrous failures as Mantalini, Rosa Dartle, Lady Dedlock, Esther Summerson, Mr. Dick, Arthur Gride, Edith Dombey, Mr. Carker—needless, because if one studies the successful figures one finds even in them only touches of verisimilitude. When one thinks of Micawber always presenting himself in the same situation, moved with the same springs, and uttering the same sounds, always confident on something turning up, always crushed and rebounding, always making punch—and his wife always declaring she will never part from him, always referring to his talents and her family—when one thinks of the "catchwords" personified as characters, one is reminded of the frogs whose brains have been taken out for physiological purposes, and whose actions henceforth want the distinctive peculiarity of organic action, that of fluctuating spontaneity. Place one of these brainless frogs on his back and he will at once recover the sitting posture; draw a leg from under him, and he will draw it back again; tickle or prick him and he will push away the object, or take *one* hop out of the way; stroke his back, and he will utter *one* croak. All these things resemble the actions of the unmutilated frog, but they differ in being *isolated* actions, and *always the same:* they are as uniform and calculable as the movements of a machine. The uninjured frog may or may not croak, may or may not hop away; the result is never calculable, and is rarely a single croak or a single hop. It is this complexity of the organism which Dickens wholly fails to conceive; his characters have nothing fluctuating and incalculable in them, even when they embody true observations; and very often they are creations so fantastic that one is at a loss to understand how he could, without hallucination, believe them to be like reality. There are dialogues bearing the traces of straining effort at effect, which in their incongruity painfully resemble the absurd and eager expositions which insane patients pour into the listener's ear when detailing their wrongs, or their schemes. Dickens once declared to me that every word said by his characters was distinctly *heard* by him; I was at first not a little puzzled to account for the fact that he could hear language so utterly unlike the language of real feeling, and not be aware of its preposterousness; but the surprise vanished when I thought of the phenomena of hallucination. And here it may be needful to remark in passing that it is not because the characters are badly drawn and their language unreal, that they are to be classed among the excesses of imagination; otherwise all the bad novelists and dramatists would be credited with that which they especially want—powerful imagination. His peculiarity is not the incorrectness of the drawing, but the vividness of the imagination which while rendering that incorrectness insensible to him, also renders it potent with multitudes of his fellowmen. For although his weakness comes from excess in one direction, the force which is in excess must not be overlooked; and it is overlooked or undervalued by critics who, with what I have called the bias of opposition, insist only on the weakness.

—George Henry Lewes, "Dickens in Relation to Criticism,"
Fortnightly Review, February 1872, pp. 143–49

Edward FitzGerald (1874)

I have been sunning myself in Dickens—even in his later and very inferior *Mutual Friend*, and *Great Expectations*—Very inferior to his best: but with things better than any one else's best, caricature as they may be. I really must go and worship at Gadshill, as I have worshipped at Abbotsford, though with less Reverence, to be sure. But I must look on Dickens as a mighty Benefactor to Mankind.

—Edward FitzGerald, Letter to Fanny Kemble
(August 24, 1874)

Harriet Martineau (1877)

Philosopher, journalist, and novelist, Harriet Martineau (1802–76) was an influential Utilitarian, arguing for reform in British politics. She published frequently in Dickens's *Household Words*, until their relationship ended over disagreements about Catholicism and over legislation aimed at factory conditions. Students approaching Dickens as a social reformer or critic will find this excerpt fascinating, as it presents the Utilitarian critique of Dickens: his overwhelming sympathy and outrage floods his political judgment.

Of Mr. Dickens I have seen but little in face-to-face intercourse; but I am glad to have enjoyed that little. There may be, and I believe there are, many who go beyond me in admiration of his works,—high and strong as is my delight in some of them. Many can more keenly enjoy his peculiar humour,—delightful as it is to me; and few seem to miss as I do the pure plain daylight in the atmosphere of his scenery. So many fine painters have been mannerists as to atmosphere and colour that it may be unreasonable to object to one more: but the very excellence and diversity of Mr. Dickens's powers makes one long that they should exercise their full force under the broad open sky of nature, instead of in the most brilliant palace of art. While he tells us a world of things that are natural and even true, his personages are generally, as I suppose is undeniable, profoundly unreal. It is a curious speculation what effect his universally read works will have on the foreign conception of English character. Washington Irving came here expecting to find the English life of Queen Anne's days, as his *Sketch-Book* shows: and very unlike his preconception was the England he found. And thus it must be with Germans, Americans and French who take Mr. Dickens's books to be pictures of our real life.—Another vexation is his vigorous erroneousness about matters of science, as shown in *Oliver Twist* about the new poor-law (which he confounds with the abrogated old one) and in *Hard Times,* about the controversies of employers. Nobody wants to make Mr. Dickens a Political Economist; but there are many who wish that he would abstain from a set of difficult subjects, on which all true sentiment must be underlain by a sort of knowledge which he has not. The more fervent and inexhaustible his kindliness, (and it is fervent and inexhaustible,) the more important it is that it should be well-informed and well-directed, that no errors of his may mislead his readers on the one hand, nor lessen his own genial influence on the other.

The finest thing in Mr. Dickens's case is that he, from time to time, proves himself capable of progress,—however vast his preceding achievements had been. In humour, he will hardly surpass *Pickwick,* simply because *Pickwick* is scarcely surpassable in humour: but in several crises, as it were, of his fame, when every body was disappointed, and his faults seemed running his graces down, there has appeared something so prodigiously fine as to make us all joyfully exclaim that Dickens can never permanently fail. It was so with *Copperfield:* and I hope it may be so again with the new work which my survivors will soon have in their hands.—Meantime, every indication seems to show that the man himself is rising. He is a virtuous and happy family man, in the first place. His glowing and generous heart is kept steady by the best domestic influences: and we may fairly hope now that he will fulfil the natural purpose of his life, and stand by literature to the last; and again, that he will be an honour to the high vocation by prudence as well as by power: so that the graces of genius and generosity may rest on the finest basis of probity and prudence; and that his old age may be honoured as heartily as his youth and manhood have been admired.—Nothing could exceed the frank kindness and consideration shown by him in the correspondence and personal intercourse we have had; and my cordial regard has grown with my knowledge of him.

—Harriet Martineau, *Autobiography*,
ed. Maria Weston Chapman, 1877, Vol. 2, pp. 61–63

Justin McCarthy (1879–80)

Justin McCarthy was a novelist, critic, historian, and politician. Students discussing Dickens's realism, characterization, or cityscapes, or those writing on his treatment of children's literature, especially fairy tales, will find this brief excerpt useful. McCarthy's insight, arguably supported by Dickens's "Frauds on the Fairies," is that the writer's hyperrealistic descriptions distract us from the fact that his plots are, in effect, mere fairy tales.

Dickens had little or no knowledge of human character, and evidently cared very little about the study. His stories are fairy tales made credible by the masterly realism with which he described all the surroundings and accessories, the costumes and the ways of his men and women. While we are reading of a man whose odd peculiarities strike us with a sense of reality as if we had observed them for ourselves many a time, while we see him surrounded by streets and houses which seem to us rather more real and a hundred times more interesting than those through which we pass every day, we are not likely to observe very quickly, or to take much heed of the fact when we do observe it, that the man acts on various important occasions of his life as only people in fairy stories ever do act.

—Justin McCarthy, *A History of Our Own Times*,
1879–80, Ch. 29

Algernon Charles Swinburne "Dickens" (1882)

Algernon Charles Swinburne was a poet, translator, dramatist, and critic. Although Swinburne's sexual vices and his admiration of French decadence outraged his Victorian readers, he was also recognized as an innovative lyricist. Loosely associated with the Pre-Raphaelite Brotherhood, Swinburne's classicism and ardent republican fervor leavened late-Victorian humanism.

Chief in thy generation born of men
  Whom English praise acclaimed as English-born,
  With eyes that matched the worldwide eyes of morn
For gleam of tears or laughter, tenderest then
When thoughts of children warmed their light, or when
Reverence of age with love and labour worn,
Or godlike pity fired with godlike scorn,
Shot through them flame that winged thy swift live pen:
Where stars and suns that we behold not burn,
Higher even than here, though highest was here thy place,
    Love sees thy spirit laugh and speak and shine
    With Shakespeare and the soft bright soul of Sterne
And Fielding's kindliest might and Goldsmith's grace;
Scarce one more loved or worthier love than thine.

—Algernon Charles Swinburne, "Dickens," 1882

Adolphus William Ward (1882)

Adolphus William Ward was an influential historian and critic. This brief excerpt will be useful to readers researching influences on Dickens, particularly Henry Fielding and Tobias Smollett. Ward helpfully recasts Dickens as more of a canny and sensitive reader than popular accounts usually allow.

Dickens was not—and to whom in these latter ages of literature could such a term be applied?—a self-made writer, in the sense that he owed nothing to those who had gone before him. He was most assuredly no classical scholar,—how could he have been? But I should hesitate to call him an ill-read man, though he certainly was neither a great nor a catholic reader, and though he could not help thinking about *Nicholas Nickleby* while he was reading the *Curse of Kehama*. In his own branch of literature his judgment was sound and sure-footed. It was of course a happy accident, that as a boy he imbibed that taste for good fiction which is a thing inconceivable to the illiterate. Sneers have been directed against the poverty of his bookshelves in his earlier days of authorship; but I fancy there were not many popular novelists in 1839 who would have taken down with them into the country for a summer sojourn, as Dickens did to Petersham, not only a couple of Scott's novels, but Goldsmith, Swift, Fielding, Smollett, and the British Essayists; nor is there one of these national classics—unless it be Swift—with whom Dickens' books or letters fail to show him to have been familiar. Of Goldsmith's books, he told Forster, in a letter which the biographer of Goldsmith modestly suppressed, he "had no indifferent perception—to the best of his remembrance—when little more than a child." He discusses with understanding the relative literary merits of the serious and humorous papers in *The Spectator*; and, with regard to another work of unique significance in the history of English fiction, *Robinson Crusoe*, he acutely observed that "one of the most popular books on earth has nothing in it to make anyone laugh or cry." "It is a book," he added, which he "read very much." It may be noted, by the way, that he was an attentive and judicious student of Hogarth; and that thus his criticisms of humorous pictorial art rested upon as broad a basis of comparison as did his judgment of his great predecessors in English humorous fiction.

Among these predecessors it has become usual to assert that Smollett exercised the greatest influence upon Dickens. It is no doubt true that in David Copperfield's library Smollett's books are mentioned first, and in the greatest number, that a vision of Roderick Random and Strap haunted the very wicket-gate at Blunderstone, that the poor little hero's first thought on entering the King's Bench prison was the strange company whom Roderick met in the Marshalsea; and that the references to Smollett and his books are frequent in Dickens' other books and in his letters. Leghorn seemed to him "made illustrious" by Smollett's grave, and in a late period of his life he criticises his chief fictions with admirable justice. *"Humphry Clinker,"* he writes, "is certainly Smollett's best. I am rather divided between *Peregrine Pickle* and *Roderick Random,* both extraordinarily good in their way, which is a way without tenderness; but you will have to read them both, and I send the first volume of *Peregrine* as the richer of the two." An odd volume of *Peregrine* was one of the books with which the waiter at the *Holly Tree Inn* endeavoured to beguile the lonely Christmas of the snowed-up traveller, but the latter "knew every word of it already." In the *Lazy Tour,* "Thomas, now just able to grope his way along, in a doubled-up condition, was no bad embodiment of Commodore Trunnion." I have noted, moreover, coincidences of detail which bear witness to Dickens' familiarity with Smollett's works. To Lieutenant Bowling and Commodore Trunnion, as to Captain Cuttle, every man was a "brother," and to the Commodore, as to Mr. Smallweed, the most abusive substantive addressed to a woman admitted of intensification by the epithet "brimstone." I think Dickens had not forgotten the opening of the *Adventures of an Atom* when he wrote a passage in the opening of his own *Christmas Carol;* and that the characters of Tom Pinch and Tommy Traddles—the former more especially—were not conceived without some thought of honest Strap. Furthermore, it was Smollett's example that probably suggested to Dickens the attractive jingle in the title of his *Nicholas Nickleby*. But these are for the most part mere details. The manner of Dickens as a whole resembles Fielding's more strikingly than Smollett's, as it was only natural that it should. The irony of Smollett is drier than was reconcileable with Dickens' nature; it is only in the occasional extravagances of his humour that the former anticipates anything in the latter, and it is only the coarsest scenes of Dickens earlier books—such as that between Noah, Charlotte, and Mrs. Sowerberry in *Oliver Twist*—which recall the whole manner of his predecessor. They resemble one another in their descriptive accuracy, and in the accumulation of detail by which they produce instead of obscuring vividness of impression; but it was impossible that Dickens should prefer the general method of the novel of adventure pure and simple, such as Smollett produced after the example of *Gil Bias*, to the less crude form adopted by Fielding, who adhered to earlier and nobler models. With Fielding's, moreover, Dickens' whole nature was congenial; they both had that tenderness which Smollett lacked; and the circumstance that of all English writers of the past, Fielding's name alone was given by Dickens to one of his sons, shows how, like so many of Fielding's readers, he had learnt to love him with an almost personal affection. The very spirit of the author of *Tom Jones*—that gaiety which, to borrow the saying of a recent historian concerning Cervantes, renders even brutality agreeable, and that charm of sympathetic feeling which makes us love those of his characters which he loves himself—seem astir in some of the most delightful passages of Dickens' most delightful books.

—Adolphus William Ward, *Dickens*, 1882, pp. 197–200

Anthony Trollope (1883)

The prolific Trollope wrote nearly fifty novels and innumerable other works of short fiction, travel writing, and criticism in his lifetime. Trollope's best-known works, the Barchester and Palliser series, are wry, nuanced expositions of the self-perceptions and self-delusions of the gentry. Students writing on Dickens's humor or his use of emotion, as well as his style, will want to consult Trollope's excerpt. Trollope recoils slightly from the broadness of Dickens's approach to emotion and comedy, while nearly averting his eyes from Dickens's prose.

There can be no doubt that the most popular novelist of my time—probably the most popular English novelist of any time—has been Charles Dickens. He has now been dead nearly six years, and the sale of his books goes on as it did during his life. The certainty with which his novels are found in every house—the familiarity of his name in all English-speaking countries—the popularity of such characters as Mrs. Gamp, Micawber, and Pecksniff, and many others whose names have entered into the English language and become well-known words—the grief of the country at his death, and the honours paid to him at his funeral,—all testify to his popularity. Since the last book he wrote himself, I doubt whether any book has been so popular as his biography by John Forster. There is no withstanding such testimony as this. Such evidence of popular appreciation should go for very much, almost for everything, in criticism on the work of a novelist. The primary object of a novelist is to please; and this man's novels have been found more pleasant than those of any other writer. It might of course be objected to this, that though the books have pleased they have been injurious, that their tendency has been immoral and their teaching vicious; but it is almost needless to say that no such charge has ever been made against Dickens. His teaching has ever been good. From all which, there arises to the critic a question whether, with such evidence against him as to the excellence of this writer, he should not subordinate his own opinion to the collected opinion of the world of readers. To me it almost seems that I must be wrong to place Dickens after Thackeray and George Eliot, knowing as I do that so great a majority put him above those authors.

My own peculiar idiosyncrasy in the matter forbids me to do so: I do acknowledge that Mrs. Gamp, Micawber, Pecksniff, and others have become household words in every house, as though they were human beings; but to my judgment they are not human beings, nor are any of the characters human which Dickens has portrayed. It has been the peculiarity and the marvel of this man's power, that he has invested his puppets with a charm that has enabled him to dispense with human nature. There is a drollery about them, in my estimation, very much below the humour of Thackeray, but which has reached the intellect of all; while Thackeray's humour has escaped the intellect of many. Nor is the pathos of Dickens human. It is stagey and melodramatic. But it is so expressed that it touches every heart a little. There is no real life in Smike. His misery, his idiotcy, his devotion for Nicholas, his love for Kate, are all overdone and incompatible with each other. But still the reader sheds a tear. Every reader can find a tear for Smike. Dickens's novels are like Boucicault's plays. He has known how to draw his lines broadly, so that all should see the colour.

He, too, in his best days, always lived with his characters;—and he, too, as he gradually ceased to have the power of doing so, ceased to charm. Though they are not human beings, we all remember Mrs. Gamp and Pickwick. The Boffins and Veneerings do not, I think, dwell in the minds of so many.

Of Dickens's style it is impossible to speak in praise. It is jerky, ungrammatical, and created by himself in defiance of rules—almost as completely as that created by Carlyle. To readers who have taught themselves to regard language, it must therefore be unpleasant. But the critic is driven to feel the weakness of his criticism, when he acknowledges to himself—as he is compelled in all honesty to do—that with the language, such as it is, the writer has satisfied the great mass of the readers of his country. Both these great writers have satisfied the readers of their own pages; but both have done infinite harm by creating a school of imitators. No young novelist should ever dare to imitate the style of Dickens. If such a one wants a model for his language, let him take Thackeray.

—Anthony Trollope, *An Autobiography*, 1883, Ch. 13

Edwin P. Whipple "In Dickens-Land" (1887)

Edwin Percy Whipple was a notable American literary critic, arguing for the moral relevance of Romantic literary ideals. This remarkable excerpt stands in contrast to the previous Whipple excerpt, in which he argued for Dickens's particularizing genius. Here, the emphasis changes to a contemplation of Dickens's grotesques, and to the process by which a reader becomes "Dickensized."

Dickens must not only have had exceptional powers of observation and imagination, but extra-ordinary intensity of sympathy with *ordinary* feelings and beliefs. His genius in characterization tends to the grotesque and extravagant; his personages, in their names as in their qualities, produce on us the effect of strangeness; the plots of the novels in which they appear would with any other characters seem grossly improbable, and yet his mind is unmistakably rooted in common sense and common humanity. He thus succeeds in giving his readers all the pleasure which comes from contemplating what is strange, odd, and eccentric, without disquieting them by any paradoxes in morals or shocking them by any perversions of homely natural sentiment. The *Christmas Carol*, for example, is as wild in grotesque fancy as a dream of Hoffmann, yet in feeling as solid and sweet and humane as a sermon of Channing. It impresses us somewhat as we are impressed by the sight of the Bible as illustrated by Gustave Dore. Thus held fast to common, homely truths and feelings by his sentiments, he can safely give reins to his imagination in his creations. The keenest of observers, both of things and persons, all that he observes is still taken up and transformed by his imagination—becomes *Dickensized,* in fact—so that, whether he describes a landscape, or a boot-jack, or a building, or a man, we see the object, not as it is in itself, but as it is deliciously bewitched by his method of looking at it. Everything is suggested by his outward experience, but modified by his inward experience. The result is that we do not have in him an exact transcript of life, but an individualized ideal of life from his point of view. He has, in short, discovered and colonized one of the waste districts of Imagination, which we may call Dickens-land or Dickens-ville; from his own brain he has peopled it with some fourteen hundred persons, and it agrees with the settlements made there by Shakespeare and Scott in being better known than such geographical countries as Canada and Australia, and it agrees with them equally in confirming us in the belief of the *reality* of a population which has no *actual* existence. It is distinguished from all other colonies in Brainland by the ineffaceable peculiarities of its colonizer; its inhabitants don't die like other people, but, alas! they also now can't increase; but whithersoever any of them may wander they are recognized at once, by an unmistakable birthmark, as belonging to the race of Dickens. A man who has done this is not merely one of a thousand, but one of a thousand millions; for he has created an ideal population which is more interesting to human beings than the great body of their own actual friends and neighbors.

—Edwin P. Whipple, "In Dickens-Land,"
Scribner's Magazine, December 1887, pp. 744–45

Robert Louis Stevenson (1888)

Essayist, fiction writer, and children's author, Robert Louis Stevenson's major works include *Treasure Island, Kidnapped,* and *The Strange Case of Dr. Jekyll and Mr. Hyde.* In his view, Dickens's passionate search for something "more definite ... than nature" makes him unsuited to portray the Victorian gentleman, by nature "inconspicuous." Students investigating Dickens's portrayal of the gentleman might also consult the entry by W.H. Mallock.

Here was a man and an artist, the most strenuous, one of the most endowed; and for how many years he laboured in vain to create a gentleman! With all his watchfulness of men and manners, with all his fiery industry, with his exquisite native gift of characterisation, with his clear knowledge of what he meant to do, there was yet something lacking. In part after part, novel after novel, a whole menagerie of characters, the good, the bad, the droll, and the tragic, came at his beck like slaves about an Oriental despot; there was only one who stayed away: the gentleman. If this ill fortune had persisted it might have shaken man's belief in art and industry. But years were given and courage was continued to the indefatigable artist; and at length, after so many and such lamentable failures, success began to attend upon his arms. David Copperfield scrambled through on hands and knees; it was at least a negative success; and Dickens, keenly alive to all he did, must have heaved a sigh of infinite relief. Then came the evil days, the days of *Dombey* and *Dorrit,* from which the lover of Dickens willingly averts his eyes; and when that temporary blight had passed away, and the artist began with a more resolute arm to reap the aftermath of his genius, we find him able to create a Carton, a Wrayburn, a Twemlow. No mistake about these three; they are all gentlemen: the sottish Carton, the effete Twemlow, the insolent Wrayburn, all have doubled the cape.

There were never in any book three perfect sentences on end; there was never a character in any volume but it somewhere tripped. We are like dancing dogs and preaching women: the wonder is not that we should do it well, but that we should do it at all. And Wrayburn, I am free to admit, comes on one occasion to the dust. I mean, of course, the scene with the old Jew. I will make you a present of the Jew for a card-board figure; but that is neither here nor there: the ineffectuality of the one presentment does not mitigate the grossness, the baseness, the inhumanity of the other. In this scene, and in one other (if I remember aright) where it is echoed, Wrayburn combines the wit of the omnibus-cad with the good feeling of the Andaman Islander: in all the remainder of the book, throughout a thousand perils, playing (you would say) with difficulty, the author swimmingly steers his hero on the true course. The error stands by itself, and it is striking to observe the moment of its introduction. It follows immediately upon one of the most dramatic passages in fiction, that in which Bradley Headstone barks his knuckles on the churchyard wall. To handle Bradley (one of Dickens's superlative achievements) were a thing impossible to almost any man but his creator; and even to him, we may be sure, the effort was exhausting. Dickens was a weary man when he had barked the schoolmaster's knuckles, a weary man and an excited; but the tale of bricks had to be finished, the monthly number waited; and under the false inspiration of irritated nerves, the scene of Wrayburn and the Jew was written and sent forth; and there it is, a blot upon the book and a buffet to the reader.

I make no more account of his passage than of that other in *Hamlet*: a scene that has broken down, the judicious reader cancels for himself. And the general tenor of Wrayburn, and the whole of Carton and Twemlow, are beyond exception. Here, then, we have a man who found it for years an enterprise beyond his art to draw a gentleman, and who in the end succeeded. Is it because Dickens was not a gentleman himself that he so often failed? and if so, then how did he succeed at last? Is it because he was a gentleman that he succeeded? and if so, what made him fail? I feel inclined to stop this paper here, after the manner of conundrums, and offer a moderate reward for a solution. But the true answer lies probably deeper than did ever plummet sound. And mine (such as it is) will hardly appear to the reader to disturb the surface.

These verbal puppets (so to call them once again) are things of a divided parentage: the breath of life may be an emanation from their maker, but they themselves are only strings of words and parts of books; they dwell in, they belong to, literature; convention, technical artifice, technical gusto, the mechanical necessities of the art, these are the flesh and blood with which they are invested. If we look only at Carton and Wrayburn, both leading parts, it must strike us at once that both are most ambitiously attempted; that Dickens was not content to draw a hero and a gentleman plainly and quietly; that after all his ill-success, he must still handicap himself upon these fresh adventures, and make Carton a sot, and sometimes a cantankerous sot, and Wrayburn insolent to the verge, and sometimes beyond the verge, of what is pardonable. A moment's thought will show us this was in the nature of his genius, and a part of his literary method. His fierce intensity of design was not to be slaked with any academic portraiture; not all the arts of individualisation could perfectly content him; he must still seek something more definite and more express than nature. All artists, it may be properly argued, do the like; it is their method to discard the middling and the insignificant, to disengage the charactered and the precise. But it is only a class of artists that pursue so singly the note of personality; and is it not possible that such a preoccupation may disable men from representing gentlefolk? The gentleman passes in the stream of the day's manners, inconspicuous. The lover of the individual may find him scarce worth drawing. And even if he draw him, on what will his attention centre but just upon those points in which his model exceeds or falls short of his subdued ideal—but just upon those points in which the gentleman is not genteel? Dickens, in an hour of irritated nerves, and under the pressure of the monthly number, defaced his Wrayburn. Observe what he sacrifices. The ruling passion strong in his hour of weakness, he sacrifices dignity, decency, the essential human beauties of his hero; he still preserves the dialect, the shrill note of personality, the mark of identification. Thackeray, under the strain of the same villainous system, would have fallen upon the other side; his gentleman would still have been a gentleman, he would have only ceased to be an individual figure.

There are incompatible ambitions. You cannot paint a Vandyke and keep it a Franz Hals.

—Robert Louis Stevenson,
"Some Gentlemen in Fiction," 1888

W.E. Henley "Dickens" (1890)

William Earnest Henley was an influential editor—most notably of the *Scots Observer/National Observer* and of the *New Review*—and an advocate of realism in fiction and of French symbolism in poetry as opposed to what he saw as lifeless, dandified aestheticism. Henley famously identifies *The Pickwick Papers* as a "comic middle-class epic," as he defends Dickens's movement away from such quasi-improvisational art. Henley sees Dickens as a committed, if somewhat self-taught, artist and argues that there is a progressive increase in plan and execution over the course of his career. Students should note, however, that the list of characters cited to demonstrate this point is not chronological.

Dickens's imagination was diligent from the outset; with him conception was not less deliberate and careful than development; and so much he confesses when he describes himself as 'in the first stage of a new book, which consists in going round and round the idea, as you see a bird in his cage go about and about his sugar before he touches it.' 'I have no means,' he writes to a person wanting advice, 'of knowing whether you are patient in the pursuit of this art; but I am inclined to think that you are not, and that you do not discipline yourself enough. When one is impelled to write this or that, one has still to consider: "How much of this will tell for what I mean? How much of it is my own wild emotion and superfluous energy—how much remains that is truly belonging to this ideal character and these ideal circumstances?" It is in the laborious struggle to make this distinction, and in the determination to try for it, that the road to the correction of faults lies. [Perhaps I may remark, in support of the sincerity with which I write this, that I am an impatient and impulsive person myself, but that it has been for many years the constant effort of my life to practise at my desk what I preach to you.]' Such golden words could only have come from one enamoured of his art, and holding the utmost endeavour in its behalf of which his heart and mind were capable for a matter of simple duty. They are a proof that Dickens—in intention at least, and if in intention then surely, the fact of his genius being admitted, to some extent in fact as well—was an artist in the best sense of the term.

In the beginning he often wrote exceeding ill, especially when he was doing his best to write seriously. He developed into an artist in words as he developed into an artist in the construction and the evolution of a story. But his development was his own work, and it is a fact that should redound eternally to his honour that he began in newspaper English, and by the production of an imitation of the *novela picaresca*—a string of adventures as broken and disconnected as the adventures of Lazarillo de Tormes or Peregrine Pickle, and went on to become an exemplar. A man self-made and self-taught, if he knew anything at all about the 'art for art' theory—which is doubtful—he may well have held it cheap enough. But he practised Millet's dogma—*Dans l'art il faut sa peau*—as resolutely as Millet himself, and that, too, under conditions that might have proved utterly demoralising had he been less robust and less sincere. He began as a serious novelist with Ralph Nickleby and Lord Frederick Verisopht; he went on to produce such masterpieces as Jonas Chuzzlewit and Doubledick, and Eugene Wrayburn and the immortal Mrs. Gamp, and Fagin and Sikes and Sydney Carton, and many another. The advance is one from positive weakness to positive strength, from ignorance to knowledge, from incapacity to mastery, from the manufacture of lay figures to the creation of human beings.

His faults were many and grave. He wrote some nonsense; he sinned repeatedly against taste; he could be both noisy and vulgar; he was apt to be a caricaturist where he should have been a painter; he was often mawkish and often extravagant; and he was sometimes more inept than a great writer has ever been. But his work, whether bad or good, has in full measure the quality of sincerity. He meant what he did; and he meant it with his whole heart. He looked upon himself as representative and national—as indeed he was; he regarded his work as a universal possession; and he determined to do nothing that for lack of pains should prove unworthy of his function. If he sinned it was unadvisedly and unconsciously; if he failed it was because he knew no better.

You feel that as you read. The freshness and fun *of Pickwick*—a comic middle-class epic, so to speak—seem mainly due to high spirits; and perhaps that immortal book should be described as a first improvisation by a young man of genius not yet sure of either expression or ambition and with only vague and momentary ideas about the duties and necessities of art. But from *Pickwick* onwards to *Edwin Drood* the effort after improvement is manifest. What are *Dombey* and *Dorrit* themselves but the failures of a great and serious artist? In truth the man's genius did but ripen with years and labour; he spent his life in developing from a popular writer into an artist. He extemporised *Pickwick*, it may be, but into *Copperfield* and *Chuzzlewit* and the *Tale of Two Cities* and *Our Mutual Friend* he put his whole might, working at them with a passion of determination not exceeded by Balzac himself. He had enchanted the public without an effort; he was the best-beloved of modern writers almost from the outset of his career. But he had in him at least as much of the French artist as of the middle-class Englishman; and if all his life he never ceased from self-education but went unswervingly in pursuit of culture, it was out of love for his art and because his conscience as an artist would not let him do otherwise. We have been told so often to train ourselves by studying the practice of workmen like Gautier and Hugo and imitating the virtues of work like *Hernani* and *Quatre-Vingt-Treize* and *L'Education sentimentale*—we have heard so much of the aesthetic impeccability of Young France and the section of Young England that affects its qualities and reproduces its fashions—that it is hard to refrain from asking if, when all is said, we should not do well to look for models nearer home? if in place of such moulds of form as *Mademoiselle de Maupin* we might not take to considering stuff like *Rizpah* and *Our Mutual Friend*?

Yes, he had many and grave faults. But so had Sir Walter and the good Dumas; so, to be candid, had Shakespeare himself—Shakespeare the king of poets. To myself he is always the man of his unrivalled and enchanting letters—is always an incarnation of generous and abounding gaiety, a type of beneficent earnestness, a great expression of intellectual vigour and emotional vivacity. I love to remember that I came into the world contemporaneously with some of his bravest work, and to reflect that even as he was the inspiration of my boyhood so is he a delight of my middle age. I love to think that while English literature endures he will be remembered as one that loved his fellow-men, and did more to make them happy and amiable than any other writer of his time.

—W.E. Henley, "Dickens," *Views and Reviews*, 1890, pp. 3–9

WILLIAM DEAN HOWELLS (1891)

William Dean Howells was an important American novelist, author of *The Rise of Silas Lapham* and *A Hazard of New Fortunes* and editor of *The Atlantic Monthly* and *Harper's Weekly*. Here Howells displays his characteristic inability to make up his mind about Dickens's contribution—he "rescued Christmas," "humanized it and consecrated it," yet as a result of his "erring force." Likewise, Howells's mesmeric simile for Dickens's creative process is appropriate.

The might of that great talent no one can gainsay, though in the light of the truer work which has since been done his literary principles seem almost as grotesque as his theories of political economy. In no one direction was his erring force more felt than in the creation of holiday literature as we have known it for the last half-century. Creation, of course, is the wrong word; it says too much; but in default of a better word, it may stand. He did not make something out of nothing; the material was there before him; the mood and even the need of his time contributed immensely to his success, as the volition of the subject helps on the mesmerist; but it is within bounds to say that he was the chief agency in the development of holiday literature as we have known it, as he was the chief agency in universalizing the great Christian holiday as we now have it. Other agencies wrought with him and after him; but it was he who rescued Christmas from Puritan distrust, and humanized it and consecrated it to the hearts and homes of all.

—William Dean Howells, *Criticism and Fiction*,
1891, pp. 174–75

W.H. MALLOCK "ARE SCOTT, DICKENS, AND THACKERAY OBSOLETE?" (1892)

William Hurrell Mallock was a novelist, philosopher, and economist who defended traditional religious views against the secularizing force of science and traditional economic views against the radical claims of socialism. Here Mallock makes three interrelated claims about Dickens: first, that "for him everything was alive with the life of his own day"—that is, every gesture, every detail of street life or of architecture expresses the London of the day. His second claim is that Dickens is, for this reason, a "national" writer, the one who represents the national mood accurately (perhaps except for the aristocracy). Finally, Mallock argues that Dickens's prose, despite its manifold faults, nonetheless conjures the associative, evocative atmosphere of life and rises above mere description.

He accepted the past; it was the present by which he was consciously fascinated; and the past had no meaning for him except as connected with it. An old building for him was not like a dead man, but like an old man—an old man making faces either grotesque or sinister. For him everything was alive with the life of his own day. Houses, crooked courts, four-post bedsteads, cabs, portmanteaus, chimney-pots, and all inanimate objects winked at him, laughed with him, and spoke to him in the vernacular of the streets, and were forever saying to him something fresh and pungent. He had all the familiarity with the life around him that could be produced by the most close acquaintance with it; and yet he was always watching it with the surprise and expectant freshness which, as a rule, belong only to those to whom it is still a novelty. And this vision of his he communicated to his readers. He made them see not what they had not seen before, but what they had not noticed before. He made them conscious of their own unconscious observations. His genius acted on the surface of English life as spilt water acts on the surface of unpolished marble. It suddenly made visible all its colors and veinings; and in this way he may be said to have revealed England to itself: and he still does so.

It is true that this general statement must be made with one reservation. One part of English life was entirely beyond his grasp. He knew nothing of the highest class. He had no true knowledge even of the upper ranks of the middle class. His lords, his baronets, his majors, his ladies and gentlemen generally are not even like enough to reality to be called caricatures. But if we accept these classes and speak only of the bulk of the nation, no writer ever knew the English nation and represented the English nation so thoroughly and comprehensively as Dickens. His style is full of the faults of a man imperfectly educated. Errors of taste abound in it, and much of his sentiment is mawkish, or constrained, or false; and yet, in spite of this, not only do his writings embody the shrewdest, the truest, the widest, and the most various observations of the life around him, but they show him to be, in a certain sense, one of the greatest of English poets. In saying this I am making no allusion to any passages which sentimental admirers of him may consider poetical, or which he probably thought poetical himself. I am alluding to the manner in which, throughout his works, he not only presents what are commonly called the facts of life, but actually gives us that elusive atmosphere which in life surrounds these facts and imparts to them those changing aspects by which in life we know them; an atmosphere impregnated with wandering thoughts and sentiments and volatile associations—an element which would seem to defy description. This Dickens has described. It penetrates his works and permeates them.

One example may be given, a single touch. He is describing some lawyer's office with dim, dusty windows, and among other details he notes this: that there was on the floor an enormous faded stain, "as if some by-gone clerk had cut his throat there and had bled ink." The whole past and present of the place is suggested in these few words, and what he felt and described in a lawyer's office he felt and described in nearly every scene he dealt with. He felt and he seized its human and, above all, its national meaning. He did this even in cases where it might be thought he would have failed to do so. I said he knew nothing of the highest upper classes; but in a certain way he understood their life as a factor in the life of the country, through certain of their surroundings. He knew the meaning and the sentiment of old English parks, of lodges, and gray gate-posts, damp and mottled with lichens. He knew the spirit which haunted the whispering avenue and hung above the twisted chimney-stacks and mullioned window of the hall; but his comprehension stopped at the front door. It was never at home inside. With this reservation, Dickens is England; and if he could not describe what the upper class see among themselves, he describes what they see whenever they go out of doors. To move out of the seclusion of polite life in England is to walk with Dickens. It is so still, as it was in his own days; and if any proof is needed in addition to those I have already mentioned, it may be found in the English language as spoken at this moment. Dickens' characters exist not in his books only. They have walked out of his books and taken their places among living people. Their looks and manners are social and not literary facts; their jokes and phrases are the common property of the nation. Of one other novelist only can this be said, and that novelist is Scott.

—W.H. Mallock, "Are Scott, Dickens, and Thackeray Obsolete?," *Forum*, December 1892, pp. 511–12

Frederic Harrison "Charles Dickens" (1895)

Frederic Harrison was a lawyer, historian, and the author of biographies of John Ruskin, Oliver Cromwell, and others. He is best remembered, however, as a Positivist and a popularizer in England of Auguste Comte. Comte's sociological views, which called for integrating scientific principles into discussions of public policy, appealed to Harrison's radicalism. This essay is characteristic of a strain in late Victorian radical criticism. Some writers admired Dickens for "having closely observed the lowest strata of city life," but faulted his insufficiently advanced politics.

Students writing about Dickens's humor, characterization, interest in social reform, or his use of realism will find much to mull over here. For Harrison these are all the same problem: Dickens's is a distorting imagination, bent toward caricature and the grotesque, presented with "incessant repetition and unwearied energy." Unwearied, at least, until the "rollicking fun begins to pall." Those students examining conventions and notions of genre might note Harrison's insistence that Dickensian humor remains mere farce, never rising to genuine satire. Dickens pursues his jokes and the comic strain so mercilessly that his novels lose all reforming force. For a point-by-point rebuttal, students can read Chesterton's "On the Alleged Optimism of Dickens," in which the critic asserts that Dickens's distorted vision corrects our own blindness.

Students discussing Dickens's handling of plot may be perplexed by Harrison's inability to find an intelligible plot after *Bleak House*. (Not even in *Great Expectations*!) In Harrison's view, Dickens is less a novelist than an editorial cartoonist, unable to embed his characters into an "epical narration."

Here lies the secret of his power over such countless millions of readers. He not only paints a vast range of ordinary humanity and suffering or wearied humanity, but he speaks for it and lives in it himself, and throws a halo of imagination over it, and brings home to the great mass of average readers a new sense of sympathy and gaiety. This humane kinship with the vulgar and the common, this magic which strikes poetry out of the dust of the streets, and discovers traces of beauty and joy in the most monotonous of lives, is, in the true and best sense of the term, Christ-like, with a message and gospel of hope. Thackeray must have had Charles Dickens in his mind when he wrote: "The humourous writer professes to awaken and direct your love, your pity, your kindness,—your scorn for untruth, pretension, imposture,—your tenderness for the weak, the poor, the oppressed, the unhappy." Charles Dickens, of all writers of our age, assuredly did this in every work of his pen, for thirty-three years of incessant production. It is his great title to honour; and a novelist can desire no higher title than this.

There is another quality in which Charles Dickens is supreme,—in purity. Here is a writer who is realistic, if ever any writer was, in the sense of having closely observed the lowest strata of city life, who has drawn the most miserable outcasts, the most abandoned men and women in the dregs of society, who has invented many dreadful scenes of passion, lust, seduction, and debauchery; and yet in forty works and more you will not find a page which a mother need withhold from her grown daughter. As Thackeray wrote of his friend: "I am grateful for the innocent laughter and the sweet and unsullied page which the author of *David Copperfield* gives to my children." We need not formulate any dogma or rule on such a topic, nor is it essential that all books should be written *virginibus puerisque*; but it is certain that every word of Charles Dickens was so written, even when he set himself (as he sometimes did) to describe animal natures and the vilest of their sex. Dickens is a realist in that he probes the gloomiest recesses and faces the most disheartening problems of life: he is an idealist in that he never presents us the common or the vile with mere commonplace or repulsiveness, and without some ray of humane and genial charm to which ordinary eyes are blind. Dickens, then, was above all things a humourist, an inexhaustible humourist, to whom the humblest forms of daily life wore a certain sunny air of genial mirth; but the question remains if he was a humourist of the highest order: was he a poet, a creator of abiding imaginative types? Old Johnson's definition of humour as "grotesque imagery," and "grotesque" as meaning some distortion in figure, may not be adequate as a description of humour, but it well describes the essential feature of Charles Dickens. His infallible instrument is caricature,—which strictly means an "overload," as Johnson says, "an exaggerated resemblance." Caricature is a likeness having some comical exaggeration or distortion. Now, caricature is a legitimate and potent instrument of humour, which great masters have used with consummate effect. Leonardo da Vinci, Michael Angelo, Rembrandt, Hogarth, use it; but only at times, and in a subsidiary way. Rabelais, Swift, Fielding, use this weapon not unfrequently; Shakespeare very sparingly; Goldsmith and Scott, I think, almost never. Caricature, the essence of which is exaggeration of some selected feature, distortion of figure, disproportion of some part, is a potent resource, but one to which the greater masters resort rarely and with much moderation.

Now, with Charles Dickens caricature—that comical exaggeration of a particular feature, distortion of some part beyond nature—is not only the essence of his humour, but it is the universal and ever-present source of his mirth. It would not be true to say that exaggeration is the sole form of humour that he uses, but there is hardly a character of his to which it is not applied, nor a scene of which it is not the pervading "motive." Some feature, some oddity, some temperament is seized, dwelt upon, played with, and turned inside out, with incessant repetition and unwearied energy. Every character, except the walking gentleman and the walking lady, the insipid lover, or the colourless friend, have some feature thrust out of proportion, magnified beyond nature. Sam Weller never speaks without his anecdote, Uriah is always "'umble," Barkis is always "willin'," Mark Tapley is always "jolly," Dombey is always solemn, and Toots is invariably idiotic. It is no doubt natural that Barnaby's Raven should always want tea, whatever happens, for the poor bird has but a limited vocabulary. But one does not see why articulate and sane persons like Captain Cuttle, Pecksniff, and Micawber should repeat the same phrases under every condition and to all persons. This, no doubt, is the essence of farce: it may be irresistibly droll as farce, but it does not rise beyond farce. And at last even the most enthusiastic Pickwickian wearies of such monotony of iteration.

Now, the keynote of caricature being the distortion of nature, it inevitably follows that humourous exaggeration is unnatural, however droll; and, where it is the main source of the drollery, the picture as a whole ceases to be within the bounds of nature. But the great masters of the human heart invariably remain true to nature; not merely true to a selected feature, but to the natural form as a whole. Falstaff, in his wildest humour, speaks and acts as such a man really might speak and act. He has no catchphrase on which he harps, as if he were a talking-machine wound up to emit a dozen sounds. Parson Adams speaks and acts as such a being might do in nature. The comic characters of Goldsmith, Scott, or Thackeray do not outrun and defy nature, nor does their drollery depend on any special and abnormal feature, much less on any stock phrase which they use as a label. The illustrations of Cruikshank and Phiz are delightfully droll, and often caricatures of a high order. But being caricatures they overload and exaggerate nature, and indeed are always, in one sense, impossible in nature. The grins, the grimaces, the contortions, the dwarfs, the idiots, the monstrosities of these wonderful sketches could not be found in human beings constructed on any known anatomy. And Dickens's own characters have the same element of unnatural distortion. It is possible that these familiar caricatures have even done harm to his reputation. His creations are of a higher order of art and are more distinctly spontaneous and original. But the grotesque sketches with which he almost uniformly presented his books accentuate the element of caricature on which he relied; and often add an unnatural extravagance beyond that extravagance which was the essence of his own method.

The consequence is that everything in Dickens is "in the excess," as Aristotle would say, and not "in the mean." Whether it is Tony Weller, or "the Shepherd," or the Fat Boy, Hugh or the Raven, Toots or Traddles, Micawber or Skimpole, Gamp or Mantalini,—all are overloaded in the sense that they exceed nature, and are more or less extravagant. They are wonderful and delightful caricatures, but they are impossible in fact. The similes are hyperbolic; the names are grotesque; the incidents partake of harlequinade, and the speeches of roaring farce. It is often wildly droll, but it is rather the drollery of the stage than of the book. The characters are never possible in fact; they are not, and are not meant to be, nature; they are always and everywhere comic distortions of nature. Goldsmith's Dr. Primrose tells us that he chose his wife for the same qualities for which she chose her wedding gown. That is humour, but it is also pure, literal, exact truth to nature. David Copperfield's little wife is called a lap-dog, acts like a lap-dog, and dies like a lap-dog; the lap-dog simile is so much overdone that we are glad to get rid of her, and instead of weeping with Copperfield, we feel disposed to call him a ninny.

Nothing is more wonderful in Dickens than his exuberance of animal spirits, that inexhaustible fountain of life and gaiety, in which he equals Scott and far surpasses any other modern. The intensity of the man, his electric activity, his spasmodic nervous power, quite dazzle and stun us. But this restless gaiety too often grows fatiguing, as the rollicking fun begins to pall upon us, as the jokes ring hollow, and the wit gets stale by incessant reiteration. We know how much in real life we get to hate the joker who does not know when to stop, who repeats his jests, and forces the laugh when it does not flow freely. Something of the kind the most devoted of Dickens's readers feel when they take in too much at one time. None but the very greatest can maintain for long one incessant outpour of drollery, much less of extravagance. Aristophanes could do it; Shakespeare could do it; so could Cervantes; and so, too, Rabelais. But then, the wildest extravagance of these men is so rich, so varied, so charged with insight and thought, and in the case of Rabelais, so resplendent with learning and suggestion, that we never feel satiety and the cruel sense that the painted mask on the stage is grinning at us, whilst the actor behind it is weary and sad. When one who is not amongst the very greatest pours forth the same inextinguishable laughter in the same key, repeating the same tricks, and multiplying kindred oddities, people of cultivation enjoy it heartily once, twice, it may be a dozen times, but at last they make way for the young bloods who can go thirty-seven times to see "Charley's Aunt."

A good deal has been said about Dickens's want of reading; and his enthusiastic biographer very fairly answers that Charles Dickens's book was the great book of life, of which he was an indefatigable student. When other men were at school and at college, he was gathering up a vast experience of the hard world, and when his brother writers were poring over big volumes in their libraries, he was pacing up and down London and its suburbs with inexhaustible energy, drinking in oddities, idiosyncrasies, and wayside incidents at every pore. It is quite true: London is a microcosm, an endless and bottomless Babylon; which, perhaps, no man has ever known so well as did Charles Dickens. This was his library: here he gathered that vast encyclopaedia of human nature, which some are inclined to call "cockney," but if it be, "Cockayne" must be a very large country indeed. Still, the fact remains, that of book-learning of any kind Dickens remained, to the end of his days, perhaps more utterly innocent than any other famous English writer since Shakespeare. His biographer labours to prove that he had read Fielding and Smollett, *Don Quixote* and *Gil Bias, The Spectator,* and *Robinson Crusoe*. Perhaps he had, like most men who have learned to read. But, no doubt, this utter severance from books, which we feel in his tales, will ultimately tell against their immortality.

This rigid abstinence from books, which Dickens practised on system, had another reaction that we notice in his style. Not only do we feel in reading his novels that we have no reason to assume that he had ever read anything except a few popular romances, but we note that he can hardly be said to have a formed literary style of his own. Dickens had mannerisms, but hardly a style. In some ways, this is a good thing: much less can he be said to have a bad style. It is simply no style. He knows nothing of the crisp, modulated, balanced, and reserved mastery of phrase and sentence which marks Thackeray. Nor is it the easy simplicity of *Robinson Crusoe* and the *Vicar of Wakefield.* The tale spins along, and the incidents rattle on with the volubility of a good story-teller who warms up as he goes, but who never stops to think of his sentences and phrases. He often gets verbose, rings the changes on a point which he sees to have caught his hearers; he plays with a fancy out of measure, and turns his jest inside out and over and over, like a fine comic actor when the house is in a roar. His language is free, perfectly clear, often redundant, sometimes grandiloquent, and usually addressed more to the pit than to the boxes. And he is a little prone to slide, even in his own proper person, into those formal courtesies and obsolete compliments which forty years ago survived amongst the superior orders of bagmen and managing clerks.

There is an old topic of discussion whether Dickens could invent an organic and powerful plot, and carry out an elaborate scheme with perfect skill. It is certain that he has never done so, and it can hardly be said that he has ever essayed it. The serial form in parts, wherein almost all his stories were cast, requiring each number of three chapters to be "assorted," like sugar-plums, with grave and gay, so as to tell just enough but not too much, made a highly wrought scheme almost impossible. It is plain that Charles Dickens had nothing of that epical gift which gave us *Tom Jones* and *Ivanhoe*. Perhaps the persistent use of the serial form shows that he felt no interest in that supreme art of an immense drama duly unfolded to a prepared end. In *Pickwick* there neither was, nor could there be, any organic plot. In *Oliver Twist*, in *Barnaby Rudge*, in *Dombey*, in *Bleak House*, in the *Tale of Two Cities*, there are indications of his possessing this power, and in certain parts of these tales we seem to be in the presence of a great master of epical narration. But the power is not sustained; and it must be confessed that in none of these tales is there a complete and equal scheme. In most of the other books, especially in those after *Bleak House*, the plot is so artless, so *decousu*, so confused, that even practised readers of Dickens fail to keep it clear in their mind. The serial form, where a leading character wanders about to various places, and meets a succession of quaint parties, seems to be that which suited his genius and which he himself most entirely enjoyed.

In contrast with the Pickwickian method of comic rambles in search of human "curios," Dickens introduced some darker effects and persons of a more or less sensational kind. Some of these are as powerful as anything in modern fiction; and Fagin and Bill Sikes, Smike and poor Jo, the Gordon riots and the storms at sea, may stand beside some tableaux of Victor Hugo for lurid power and intense realism. But it was only at times and during the first half of his career that Dickens could keep clear of melodrama and somewhat stagey blue fire. And at times his blue fire was of a very cheap kind. Rosa Dartle and Carker, Steerforth and Blandois, Quilp and Uriah Heep, have a melancholy glitter of the footlights over them. We cannot see what the villains want, except to look villainous, and we fail to make out where is the danger to the innocent victims. We find the villain of the piece frantically struggling to get some paper, or to get hold of some boy or girl. But as the scene is in London in the nineteenth century, and not in Naples in the fifteenth century, we cannot see who is in real danger, or why, or of what. And with all this, Dickens was not incapable of bathos, or tragedy suddenly exploding in farce.

The end of Krook by spontaneous combustion is such a case: but a worse case is the death of Dora, Copperfield's baby wife, along with that of the lapdog, Jip. This is one of those unforgotten, unpardonable, egregious blunders in art, in feeling, even in decency, which must finally exclude Charles Dickens from the rank of the true immortals.

But his books will long be read for his wonderful successes, and his weaker pieces will entirely be laid aside, as are the failures of so many great men, the rubbish of Fielding, of Goldsmith, of Defoe; which do nothing now to dim the glory of *Tom Jones, The Vicar of Wakefield,* and *Robinson Crusoe.* The glory of Charles Dickens will always be in his *Pickwick,* his first, his best, his inimitable triumph. It is true that it is a novel without a plot, without beginning, middle, or end, with much more of caricature than of character, with some extravagant tom-foolery, and plenty of vulgarity. But its originality, its irrepressible drolleries, its substantial human nature, and its intense vitality, place it quite in a class by itself. We can no more group it, or test it by any canon of criticism, than we could group or define *Pantagruel* or *Faust.* There are some works of genius which seem to transcend all criticism, of which the very extravagances and incoherences increase the charm. And *Pickwick* ought to live with *Gil Bias* and *Tristram Shandy.* In a deeper vein, the tragic scenes in *Oliver Twist* and in *Barnaby Rudge* must long hold their ground, for they can be read and reread in youth, in manhood, in old age. The story of Dotheboys Hall, the Yarmouth memories of Copperfield, little Nell, Mrs. Gamp, Micawber, Toots, Captain Cuttle, Pecksniff, and many more will long continue to delight the youth of the English-speaking races. But few writers are remembered so keenly by certain characters, certain scenes, incidental whimsies, and so little for entire novels treated strictly as works of art. There is no reason whatever for pretending that all these scores of tales are at all to be compared with the best of them, or that the invention of some inimitable scenes and characters is enough to make a supreme and faultless artist. The young and the uncritical make too much of Charles Dickens, when they fail to distinguish between his best and his worst. Their fastidious seniors make too little of him, when they note his many shortcomings and fail to see that in certain elements of humour he has no equal and no rival. If we mean Charles Dickens to live we must fix our eye on these supreme gifts alone.

—Frederic Harrison, "Charles Dickens,"
Studies in Early Victorian Literature, 1895, pp. 133–44

WILLIAM SAMUEL LILLY "DICKENS" (1895)

Writer, civil servant in India, and Catholic convert William Samuel Lilly (1840–1919) shares the late Victorian prejudice against Dickens's later works. Of most interest here is Lilly's argument that Dickens could not competently handle sexual passion, especially when compared to such female contemporaries as George Sand or George Eliot.

He is at his best in his earlier works, where he makes small pretence to art. In my opinion his masterpiece is *Pickwick*—"a comic middle-class epic" it has been called, perhaps not unhappily. It is irresistibly funny; inimitably fresh; incomparably fantastic; a farce, but a farce of a very high order. Dickens himself always thought slightingly of it. He was ambitious, laudably ambitious, to do greater things. And during the whole of his literary life he toiled earnestly, passionately, to attain a higher standard. I think he came nearest to that standard in *David Copperfield*. There is much—very much—there which we could wish away. In fact I, if I take the book up, give effect to my wish, and practically put aside a great deal of it. And no doubt many other readers do the same. But it is informed by a simple power, a sober veracity, a sustained interest, peculiarly its own among its author's works. Dickens's young men are, as a rule, impossible. They are well-nigh all of the same inane type. He seems to have got them out of an Adelphi melodrama. But David Copperfield, who is a transcript from his own troublous and distressed childhood and youth, is, at all events, human. His young women are as inane as his young men. His amatory scenes—good heavens let us not speak of them and their mawkish sentimentalities! What a theme for a poet had he in Steerforth and Little Em'ly! How George Sand would have treated it! How George Eliot has treated a similar theme in *Adam Bede*! But Dickens possessed no words to tell forth that idyll. And if he had possessed them he dared not to have uttered them. He stood in too much awe of Mr. Podsnap's "young person." The history of the love of Steerforth and Little Em'ly was impossible to him. He could not have narrated it if he would; and he would not if he could.

I think he never again wrote so felicitously as in *David Copperfield*. No doubt he did many fine things afterwards in the way of genre painting. We may regard him as a literary Teniers. But as years went on his manner seems to me to grow more unnatural, more stilted, more intolerable. The higher art which he tried to grasp, ever eluded him. There is an absence of composition in his work; there is no play of light and shade; there is no proportion, no perspective. His books cannot be said to be composed, they are improvised.

> —William Samuel Lilly, "Dickens," *Four English Humourists of the Nineteenth Century,* 1895, pp. 14–15

DAVID CHRISTIE MURRAY (1897)

Novelist David Christie Murray focused, in many of his thirty novels, on life in the West Midlands. Here he observes that late Victorian distaste for Dickens is simultaneously a filial prejudice against the prior generation, and also a perverse indicator of his success. "The famous Dickens pie," he suggests, is only unpalatable because it is so often and slavishly copied.

Now, with the solitary exception of Sir Walter Scott, it is probable that no man ever inspired such a host of imitators as Charles Dickens. There is not a writer of fiction at this hour, in any land where fiction is a recognised trade or art, who is not, whether he knows it and owns it, or no, largely influenced by Dickens. His method has got into the atmosphere of fiction, as that of all really great writers must do, and we might as well swear to unmix our oxygen and hydrogen as to stand clear of his influences. To stand clear of those influences you must stand apart from all modern thought and sentiment. You must have read nothing that has been written in the last sixty years, and you must have been bred on a desert island. Dickens has a living part in the life of the whole wide world. He is on a hundred thousand magisterial benches every day. There is not a hospital patient in any country who has not at this minute a right to thank God that Dickens lived. What his blessed and bountiful hand has done for the poor and oppressed, and them that had no helper, no man knows. He made charity and good feeling a religion. Millions and millions of money have flowed from the coffers of the rich for the benefit of the poor because of his books. A great part of our daily life, and a good deal of the best of it, is of his making.

No single man ever made such opportunities for himself. No single man was ever so widely and permanently useful. No single man ever sowed gentleness and mercy with so broad a sweep. . . .

The chief fault the superficial modern critic has to find with Dickens is a sort of rumbustious boisterousness in the expression of emotion. But let one thing be pointed out, and let me point it out in my own fashion. Tom Hood, who was a true poet, and the best of our English wits, and probably as good a judge of good work as any person now alive, went home after meeting with Dickens, and in a playful enthusiasm told his wife to cut off his hand and bottle it, because it had shaken hands with Boz. Lord Jeffrey, who was cold as a critic, cried over little Nell. So did Sydney Smith, who was very far from being a blubbering sentimentalist. To judge rightly of any kind of dish you must bring an appetite to it. Here is the famous Dickens pie, when first served, pronounced inimitable, not by a class or a clique, but by all men in all lands. But you get it served hot, and you get it served cold, it is rehashed in every literary restaurant, you detect its flavour in your morning leader and your weekly review. The pie gravy finds its way into the prose and the verse of a whole young generation. It has a striking flavour, an individual flavour. It gets into everything. We are weary of the ceaseless resurrections of that once so toothsome dish. Take it away.

The original pie is no worse and no better, but thousands of cooks have had the recipe for it, and have tried to make it. Appetite may have vanished, but the pie was a good pie.

No simile runs on all fours, and this parable in a pie-dish is a poor traveller.

But this principle of judgment applies of necessity to all great work in art. It does not apply to merely good work, for that is nearly always imitative, and therefore not much provocative of imitation. It happens sometimes that an imitator, to the undiscerning reader, may even seem better than the man he mimics, because he has a modern touch. But remember, in his time the master also was a modern.

The new man says of Dickens that his sentiment rings false. This is a mistake. It rings old-fashioned. No false note ever moved a world, and the world combined to love his very name. There were tears in thousands of households when he died, and they were as sincere and as real as if they had arisen at the loss of a personal friend.

We, who in spite of fashion remain true to our allegiance to the magician of our youth, who can never worship or love another as we loved and worshipped him, are quite contented in the slight inevitable dimming of his fame.

—David Christie Murray, *My Contemporaries in Fiction*, 1897, pp. 9–14

Herbert Paul "The Apotheosis of the Novel" (1897)

Dickens has been called the favourite novelist of the middle classes. If the statement be true, it is creditable to their good taste and freedom from prejudice. He certainly did not flatter them. He disliked Dissenters quite as much as Matthew Arnold, whereas Thackeray gave them the Clapham Sect, to which they are not entitled. But the popularity of Dickens in his lifetime was in fact universal. Everybody read his books, because nobody could help reading them. They required no education except a knowledge of the alphabet, and they amused scholars as much as crossing-sweepers. No man ever made a more thorough conquest of his generation. Indeed he was only too successful. Imitation may be the sincerest form of flattery. It is the most dangerous form of admiration. And if ever there was an *exemplar vitiis imitabile*, it was Dickens. His influence upon literature, apart from his contributions to it, has been disastrous. The school of Dickens, for which he cannot be held responsible, is happily at last dying out. Their dreary mechanical jokes, their hideous unmeaning caricatures, their descriptions that describe nothing, their spasms of false sentiment, their tears of gin and water, have ceased to excite even amusement, and provoke only unmitigated disgust. With their disappearance from the stage, and consignment to oblivion, the reputation of the great man they injured is relieved from a temporary strain. The position of Dickens himself is unassailed and unassailable. In this or that generation he may be less read or more. He must always remain an acknowledged master of fiction and a prince of English humorists.

—Herbert Paul, "The Apotheosis of the Novel,"
Nineteenth Century, May 1897, p. 773

George Gissing "Humour and Pathos" (1898)

The British novelist George Gissing was known for his realistic portrayals in such works as *The Odd Women* (1893) and *New Grub Street* (1904). He is also the author of a study of Dickens (1898), from which this excerpt is taken. Gissing is interested here in three interrelated tones: farce, humor, and pathos (feeling or sentiment). Dickens's strength as a humorist is, on Gissing's account, to leaven farce with pathos, thereby making bitter or otherwise objectionable realities endurable, both for those who suffer them and those who read about them.

Gissing wants to solve a genuine puzzle: Why is it that Dickens is able to write about scenes of poverty and degradation without offending the sensibilities of his readers? The answer, he suggests, is in a surprisingly delicate infusion of pathos with farce. Without the comedy, readers would find such scenes intolerable or preachy. Without the sentiment, readers might well blame the poor for their own degradation. When sentiment and farce are fused in true humor, however, the result suggests something resembling wisdom. Gissing's views on the topic might be compared with any writer—Harrison, Bagehot, and Lewes are possible examples—who focuses on Dickens as a rigid caricaturist.

Because Gissing sees pathos as central to Dickens's insight, he also defends the novelist against the charge of excessive, even mawkish, sentimentality. In general, Gissing identifies "the pathos of child-life" as the most authentic form of sentiment in Dickens, especially involving scenes of poverty. At its best, then, the sentiment in a Dickens novel is not manipulative, but rather is the touch of the real man—the biography of the author serving as a guarantor of the novel's sentiment.

To write of Dickens at all, is to presuppose his humour. The plan of my essay has necessitated a separate consideration of the various features of his work, and at moments it may have appeared that I found fault without regard to a vast counterbalance; but it was never possible for me to lose sight of that supreme quality of his genius which must be now dwelt upon with undivided attention. It was as a humorist that Dickens made his name; and in a retrospect of his life's activity one perceives that his most earnest purposes depended for their furtherance upon this genial power, which he shares with nearly all the greatest of English writers. Holding, as he did, that the first duty of an author is to influence his reader for good, Dickens necessarily esteemed as the most precious of his gifts that by virtue of which he commanded so great an audience. Without his humour, he might have been a vigorous advocate of social reform, but as a novelist assuredly he would have failed; and as to the advocacy of far-reaching reforms by men who have only earnestness and eloquence to work with, English history tells its tale. Only because they laughed with him so heartily, did multitudes of people turn to discussing the question his page suggested. As a story-teller pure and simple, the powers that remain to him, if humour be subtracted, would never have ensured popularity. Nor, on the other hand, would they have availed him in the struggle for artistic perfection, which is a better thing. Humour is the soul of his work. Like the soul of man, it permeates a living fabric which, but for its creative breath, could never have existed.

In his earliest writing we discover only the suggestion of this quality. The *Sketches* have a touch of true humour, but (apart from the merits of acute observation and great descriptive power) there is much more of merely youthful high spirits, tending to the farcical. Such a piece as "The Tuggs's at Ramsgate" is distinct farce, and not remarkably good of its kind. This vein Dickens continued to work throughout his career, and often with great success. One must distinguish between the parts of his writing which stir to mere hilarity, and his humour in the strict sense of the word. It is none of my business to define that term, which has long ago been adequately expounded; enough that the humorist has by no means invariably a chuckle in his throat; at moments of his supreme success, he will hardly move us to more of merriment than appears in a thoughtful smile. But there is a perfectly legitimate, and tolerably wide, range for the capers of a laughing spirit, and as a writer of true farce I suppose Dickens has never been surpassed. *Pickwick* abounds in it, now quite distinct from, and now all but blending with, the higher characteristic. One can imagine that the public approval of his *Sketches* had given the author an impetus which carried him of a sudden into regions of extravagant buoyancy and mirthfulness. The first few pages are farce of the frankest. Winkle, Snodgrass, and Tupman remain throughout farcical characters, but not so Mr. Pickwick himself. Farce is the election at Eatanswill, and the quarrel of the rival Editors, and many another well-remembered passage. Only a man of genius has the privilege of being so emphatically young. "Though the merriment was rather boisterous, still it came from the heart and not from the lips; and this is the right sort of merriment after all." How could one better describe, than in these words from the book itself, that overflowing cheeriness which conquered Dickens's first public! Or take the description of old Wardle coming through the early sunshine to bid Mr. Pickwick good morning,—"out of breath with his own anticipations of pleasure." Alas! old gentlemen, however jolly, do not get breathless in this fashion; but the young may, and Dickens, a mere boy himself, was writing for the breathless boyhood of many an age to come.

The farce in his younger work always results from this exuberance of spirits; later, he introduces it deliberately; with conscious art—save perhaps at those moments when the impulse of satire is too much for him. One easily recalls his best efforts in this direction. The wild absurdity of the Muffin Company at the beginning of *Nickleby* shows him still in his boyish mood, and the first chapter of *Chuzzlewit* finds him unluckily reverting to it at the moment when he was about to produce a masterpiece of genuine humour. Mr. Mantalini is capital fun; he never quite loses his hold upon one, and to the end we shall laugh over the "demnition egg" and the "demnition bow-wows". At this stage Dickens was capable of a facetiousness of descriptive phrase which hints the peril involved in a reputation such as he had won. "Madame Mantalini wrung her hands for grief and rung the bell for her husband; which done, she fell into a chair and a fainting fit simultaneously." When he had written that passage, and allowed it to stand, his genius warned him; I remember nothing so dangerous in aftertime. Quilp, at his best, is rich entertainment; in Dick Swiveller we touch higher things. The scene between little David Copperfield and the waiter (chapter v) seems to me farce, though very good; country innkeepers were never in the habit of setting a dish-load of cutlets before a little boy who wanted dinner, and not even the shrewdest of waiters, having devoured them all, could make people believe that it was the little boy's achievement; but the comic vigour of the thing is irresistible. Better still is the forced marriage of Jack Bunsby to the great MacStinger. Here, I think, Dickens reaches his highest point. We cannot call it "screaming" farce; it appeals not only to the groundlings. Laughter holding both his sides was never more delightfully justified; gall and the megrims were never more effectually dispelled. It is the ludicrous in its purest form, tainted by no sort of unkindliness, and leaving behind it nothing but the wholesome aftertaste of self-forgetful mirth.

We may notice how Dickens makes use of farcical extravagance to soften the bitterness of truth. When Sally Brass goes down into the grimy cellar-kitchen to give the little slavey her food, we are told that she cut from the joint "two square inches of cold mutton", and bade her victim never say that she had not had meat in *that* house. This makes one laugh; who can refrain? If he had avoided exaggeration, and shown us the ragged, starving child swallowing the kind of meal which was really set before her, who could have endured it? The point is vastly important for an understanding of Dickens's genius and his popularity. That "two square inches" makes all the difference between painful realism and fiction universally acceptable; it is the secret of Dickens's power for good. Beside it may be set another instance. Judy Smallweed, in *Bleak House,* likewise has her little slavey over whom she tyrannizes; a child, too, who has won our sympathy in a high degree, and whom we could not bear to see brutally used. She is brutally used; but then Judy Smallweed is a comical figure; so comical that no one takes her doings with seriousness. Harsh words and broken meats are again provocative of laughter, when in very truth we should sob. With Dickens's end in view, how wise his method!

After merriment comes the thought: "But what a shame!" And henceforth the reader thinks sympathetically of poor little girls, whether ruled by vicious trollops or working under easier conditions. Omit the jest—and the story becomes too unpleasant to remember.

Between Dickens's farce and his scenes of humour the difference is obvious. In Mantalini or Jack Bunsby we have nothing illuminative; they amuse, and there the matter ends. But true humour always suggests a thought, always throws light on human nature. The humorist may not be fully conscious of his own meaning; he always, indeed, implies more than he can possibly have thought out; and therefore it is that we find the best humour inexhaustible, ever fresh when we return to it, ever, as our knowledge of life increases, more suggestive of wisdom. . . .

Inseparable from the gift of humour is that of pathos. It was Dickens's misfortune that, owing to habits of his mind already sufficiently discussed, he sometimes elaborated pathetic scenes, in the theatrical sense of the word. I do not attribute to him the cold insincerity so common in the work of playwrights; but at times he lost self-restraint and unconsciously responded to the crude ideals of a popular audience. Emphasis and iteration, however necessary for such hearers, were out of place in pathetic narrative. Thus it comes about that he is charged with mawkishness, and we hear of some who greatly enjoy his humour rapidly turning the pages meant to draw a tear. Chiefly, I suppose, it is the death of Paul Dombey that such critics have in mind; they would point also to the death of Jo, the crossing-sweeper, and to that of little Nell. On a re-perusal of these chapters, I feel that nothing can be said in defence of Jo; on his death-bed he is an impossible creature, and here for once moral purpose has been undeniably fatal to every quality of art. Regarding the other narratives, it strikes me that they have been too hastily condemned. The one line which describes the death of Paul's mother is better, no doubt, than the hundreds through which we follow the fading of Paul himself; but these pages I cannot call mawkish, for I do not feel that they are flagrantly untrue. The tear may rise or not—that depends upon how we are constituted—but we are really standing by the bed of a gentle little child, precociously gifted and cruelly overwrought, and, if the situation is to be presented at all, it might be much worse done. Such pathos is called "cheap". I can only repeat that in Dickens's day, the lives, the happiness of children were very cheap indeed, and that he had his purpose in insisting on their claims to attention. As for the heroine of *The Old Curiosity Shop*, distaste for her as a pathetic figure seems to me unintelligent. She is a child of romance; her death is purely symbolical, signifying the premature close of any sweet, innocent, and delicate life. Heaven forbid that I should attribute to Dickens a deliberate allegory; but, having in mind those hapless children who were then being tortured in England's mines and factories, I like to see in Little Nell a type of their sufferings; she, the victim of avarice, dragged with bleeding feet along the hard roads, ever pursued by heartless self-interest, and finding her one safe refuge in the grave. Look back upon the close of that delightful novel, and who can deny its charm? Something I shall have to say presently about the literary style; but as a story of peaceful death it is beautifully imagined and touchingly told.

Of true pathos Dickens has abundance. The earliest instance I can call to mind is the death of the Chancery prisoner in *Pickwick,* described at no great length, but very powerful over the emotions. It worthily holds a place amid the scenes of humour enriching that part of the book. We feel intensely the contrast between the prisoner's life and that which was going on in the free world only a few yards away; we see in his death a pitifulness beyond words. A scene in another book,—*Bleak House,*—this, too, connected with that accursed system of imprisonment for debt, shows Dickens at his best in bringing out the pathos of child-life. The man known to Mr. Skimpole as "Coavinses" has died, and Coavinses' children, viewed askance by neighbours because of their father's calling, are living alone in a garret. They are presented as simply as possible—nothing here of stage emphasis—yet the eyes dazzle as we look. I must quote a line or two. "We were looking at one another," says Esther Summerson, "and at these two children, when there came into the room a very little girl, childish in figure but shrewd and older-looking in the face—pretty faced too—wearing a womanly sort of bonnet much too large for her, and drying her bare arms on a womanly sort of apron. Her fingers were white and wrinkled with washing, and the soapsuds were yet smoking which she wiped off her arms. But for this, she might have been a child playing at washing and imitating a poor working-woman with a quick observation of the truth." It is Charley, of course, who had found a way to support herself and the younger ones. We see how closely the true pathetic and a "quick observation" are allied. Another picture shown us in Esther's narrative, that of the baby's death in the starved labourer's cottage, moves by legitimate art. Still more of it is felt in the story of Doctor Marigold, the Cheap-Jack, whose child is dying in his arms, whilst for daily bread he plays buffoon before the crowd. This is a noble piece of work, and defies criticism. The tale is told by the man himself as simply as possible; he never insists upon the pitifulness of his position. We hear his whispers to the child, between his hoarse professional shoutings and the guffaws in front; then he finds his word of tenderness brings no response—he looks closer—he turns from the platform. A piece of work that might atone for literary sins far worse than Dickens ever committed.

Little Dorrit is strong in pathos, as in humour. Dickens's memories of childhood made his touch very sure whenever he dealt with the squalid prison-world, and life there was for him no less fertile in pathos than death. Very often it is inextricably blended with his humour; in the details of the Marshalsea picture, who shall say which element of his genius prevails? Yet, comparing it with the corresponding scenes in *Pickwick,* we perceive a subdual of tone, which comes not only of advancing years, but of riper art; and as we watch the Dorrits step forth from the prison door, it is another mood than that which accompanied the release of Mr. Pickwick. Pathos of this graver and subtler kind is the distinguishing note of *Great Expectations,* a book which Dickens meant, and rightly meant, to end in the minor key. The old convict, Magwitch, if he cannot be called a tragical personality, has feeling enough to move the reader's deeper interest, and in the very end acquires through suffering a dignity which makes him very impressive. Rightly seen, is there not much pathos in the story of Pip's foolishness? It would be more manifest if we could forget Lytton's imbecile suggestion, and restore the original close of the story.

To the majority of readers it seemed—and perhaps still seems—that Dickens achieved his best pathos in the Christmas books. Two of those stories answered their purpose admirably; the other two showed a flagging spirit; but not even in the *Carol* can we look for anything to be seriously compared with the finer features of his novels. The true value of these little books lies in their deliberate illustration of a theme which occupied Dickens's mind from first to last. Writing for the season of peace, good-will, and jollity, he sets himself to exhibit these virtues in an idealization of the English home. The type of domestic beauty he finds, as a matter of course, beneath a humble roof. And we have but to glance in memory through the many volumes of his life's work to recognize that his gentlest, brightest humour, his simplest pathos, occur in those unexciting pages which depict the everyday life of poor and homely English folk. This is Dickens's most delightful aspect, and I believe it is the most certainly enduring portion of what he has left us.

—George Gissing, "Humour and Pathos,"
Charles Dickens: A Critical Study, 1898, pp. 197–215

Laurence Hutton "Charles Dickens" (1898)

The American writer Laurence Hutton was literary editor at *Harper's Magazine* and one of the organizers of the International Copyright League. Apparently intending to defend Dickens against charges of irrelevance, Hutton nearly concedes that "little children" are his primary readers.

The question, "Will Dickens last?" has been asked a hundred times in print since Dickens died; and many times, and in various ways, has the question been answered. All men admit that Sir Charles Grandison has become a bore, where he is known at all; that G. P. R. James's solitary horseman has ridden on, entirely out of the sight of the present-day reader; that Cooper's Indians and backwoodsmen no longer scalp the imagination of the boy of the period; that Marryat's midshipmen have been left alone and neglected at the mastheads to which he was so fond of sending them; that no one but the antiquary in literature cares now for Waverley or Rob Roy. But it is too soon yet to say how long it will be before Bleak House will become an uninhabitable ruin, or when the firm of Dombey and Son will go out of business altogether. Don Quixote is as vigorous as he was three centuries ago. Robinson Crusoe, born in 1719, still retains all the freshness of youth; who can prophesy how Mr. Samuel Pickwick, the Don Quixote of 1839, will be regarded in 1998? or how Mr. Samuel Weller, his man Friday, will be looked upon by the readers of a hundred years from to-day?

Dickens certainly wrote for his own time, and generally *of* his own time. And during his own time he achieved a popularity without parallel in the history of fiction. But the fashions of all times change; and although Dickens has been in fashion longer than most of his contemporaries, and is still the fashion among old-fashioned folk, there are acute critics who say that his day is over. The booksellers and the officials of circulating libraries tell a different story, however; and when little children, who never heard the name of Dickens, who knew nothing of his great reputation, turn from *Alice in Wonderland* and *Little Lord Fauntleroy* to the *Cricket on the Hearth,* loving the old as much as they love the new, it would seem as if the sun had not yet set upon Dickens; and that the night which is to leave him in total darkness is still far off.

—Laurence Hutton, "Charles Dickens,"
Outlook, October 1898, p. 321

WILBUR L. CROSS (1899)

Wilbur Lucius Cross was a critic, a Yale professor of English, and a governor of Connecticut in the 1930s. Cross identifies Dickens as the savior of English fiction from the mere antiquarianism with which Scott's imitators had saddled it. Dickens makes the novel a fiction "founded upon facts."

Dickens was from the very first a check to mediaevalism. After he began writing, knights and ladies and tournaments became rarer. He awakened the interest of the public in the social condition of England after the Napoleonic wars. The Scott novel had come swollen with prefaces, notes, and appendixes, to show that it was true to the spirit of history; the Dickens novel came considerably enlarged with personal experiences, anecdotes, stories from friends, and statistics, to show that it was founded upon facts. Instead of the pageant of the Middle Age, we now have, in the novels of those who have learned their art from Dickens, strikes and riots, factories and granaries and barns in blaze, employee shooting employer, underground tenements, sewing-garrets, sweating-establishments, workhouses, truck-stores, the ravages of typhus, enthusiastic descriptions of model factories, model prisons, model cottages, discussions of the new poor law, of trade unions, of Chartism, and of the relations of the rich and the poor. The new characters are operatives in factories, agricultural laborers, miners, tailors, seamstresses, and paupers. Patience, longsuffering, gentleness, in stalwart or angelic form, is oppressed by viragoes, tall and bearded and of flashing eyes, or by gentlemen of bloated red faces. Dickens never advocated in his novels any specific means of reform.

—Wilbur L. Cross, *The Development of the English Novel*, 1899, pp. 192–93

RICHARD BURTON
"THE FUNDAMENTALS OF FICTION" (1902)

The American poet and critic Richard Burton sums up Dickens in a slightly patronizing way, defending his "adorable grotesques" against a variety of authorial sins.

Is there any other maker of story in modern English literature—after all allowances have been made, and not forgetting that some current criticism of the man of Gadshill will have it that he is for a more careless age—who has begun to furnish such a portrait-gallery of worthies and adorable grotesques—a motley crowd whom we all know and enjoy and love? I wot not. The fact that Dickens is at times a trifle inchoate or careless in his English, or allows his exuberance to lead him into exaggeration, or fails to blend perfectly the discordant elements of comedy and tragedy, sinks into insignificance when set over against such a faculty as this.

—Richard Burton, "The Fundamentals of Fiction,"
Forces in Fiction and Other Essays, 1902, p. 7

Algernon Charles Swinburne "Charles Dickens" (1902)

Algernon Charles Swinburne was a poet, translator, dramatist, and critic. It came as a surprise to some readers that the notorious Swinburne would admire the allegedly sentimental and even moralistic Dickens so enthusiastically. But Swinburne finds in the novelist a tragic conception of existence, as well as the spasm or pulse of lived reality, and these qualities overshadow all else. Swinburne's essay serves, thus, as an apt comparison to Chesterton's entry "On the Alleged Optimism of Dickens," or to the previous Gissing selection.

To Swinburne, Dickens's humor is Shakespearean—or even classical—because it carries with it a self-justifying energy that answers to no morality. Dickens's "unsurpassable triumph" is to "have made malignity as delightful for an instant as simplicity." Those interested in Dickensian misanthropy or villainy—the malicious joy that seems to animate some of Dickens's most wicked characters—might wish to consult this essay, in particular the discussions of Sarah Gamp and Jonas Chuzzlewit.

Just as Dickens's humor is deemed classical, so too does Swinburne affirm that Dickens possesses a tragic vision of the world, and even sometimes a "classic and poetic symmetry of perfect execution and perfect design." While Dickens's strict contemporaries usually faulted him as deficient, even wholly lacking, in execution and design (see the entry by Bagehot), Swinburne anticipates a turn in twentieth-century reevaluations of Dickens's plots, an evolving perspective that suggests the novels are more carefully structured than his initial readers sometimes gave him credit for.

It is only when such names as Shakespeare's or Hugo's rise and remain as the supreme witnesses of what was highest in any particular country at any particular time that there can be no question among any but irrational and impudent men as to the supremacy of their greatest. England, under the reign of Dickens, had other great names to boast of which may well be allowed to challenge the sovereignty of his genius. But as there certainly was no Shakespeare and no Hugo to rival and eclipse his glory, he will probably and naturally always be accepted and acclaimed as the greatest Englishman of his generation. His first works or attempts at work gave little more promise of such a future than if he had been a Coleridge or a Shelley. No one could have foreseen what all may now foresee in the *Sketches by Boz*—not only a quick and keen-eyed observer, 'a chiel amang us takin' notes' more notable than Captain Grose's, but a great creative genius. Nor could any one have foreseen it in the early chapters of *Pickwick*—which, at their best, do better the sort of thing which had been done fairly well before. Sam Weller and Charles Dickens came to life together, immortal and twin-born. In *Oliver Twist* the quality of a great tragic and comic poet or dramatist in prose fiction was for the first time combined with the already famous qualities of a great humorist and a born master in the arts of narrative and dialogue.

Like the early works of all other great writers whose critical contemporaries have failed to elude the kindly chance of beneficent oblivion, the early works of Dickens have been made use of to depreciate his later, with the same enlightened and impartial candour which on the appearance of *Othello* must doubtless have deplored the steady though gradual decline of its author's genius from the unfulfilled promise of excellence held forth by *Two Gentlemen of Verona*. There may possibly be some faint and flickering shadow of excuse for the dullards, if unmalignant, who prefer *Nicholas Nickleby* to the riper and sounder fruits of the same splendid and inexhaustible genius. Admirable as it is, full of life and sap and savour, the strength and the weakness of youth are so singularly mingled in the story and the style that readers who knew nothing of its date might naturally have assumed that it must have been the writer's first attempt at fiction. There is perhaps no question which would more thoroughly test the scholarship of the student than this:—What do you know of Jane Dibabs and Horatio Peltiogrus? At fourscore and ten it might be thought 'too late a week' for a reader to revel with insuppressible delight in a first reading of the chapters which enrol all worthy readers in the company of Mr Vincent Crummles; but I can bear witness to the fact that this effect was produced on a reader of that age who had earned honour and respect in public life, affection and veneration in private. It is not, on the other hand, less curious and significant that Sydney Smith, who had held out against Sam

Weller, should have been conquered by Miss Squeers; that her letter, which of all Dickens's really good things is perhaps the most obviously imitative and suggestive of its model, should have converted so great an elder humorist to appreciation of a greater than himself; that the echo of familiar fun, an echo from the grave of Smollett, should have done what finer and more original strokes of comic genius had unaccountably failed to do. But in all criticism of such work the merely personal element of the critic, the natural atmosphere in which his mind or his insight works, and uses its faculties of appreciation, is really the first and last thing to be taken into account.

No mortal man or woman, no human boy or girl, can resist the fascination of Mr and Mrs Quilp, of Mr and Miss Brass, of Mr Swiveller and his Marchioness; but even the charm of Mrs Jarley and her surroundings, the magic which enthrals us in the presence of a Codlin and a Short, cannot mesmerise or hypnotise us into belief that the story of *The Old Curiosity Shop* is in any way a good story. But it is the first book in which the background or setting is often as impressive as the figures which can hardly be detached from it in our remembered impression of the whole design. From Quilp's Wharf to Plashwater Weir Mill Lock, the river belongs to Dickens by right of conquest or creation. The part it plays in more than a few of his books is indivisible from the parts played in them by human actors beside it or upon it. Of such actors in this book, the most famous as an example of her creator's power as a master of pathetic tragedy would thoroughly deserve her fame if she were but a thought more human and more credible. 'The child' has never a touch of childhood about her; she is an impeccable and invariable portent of devotion, without a moment's lapse into the humanity of frailty in temper or in conduct. Dickens might as well have fitted her with a pair of wings at once. A woman might possibly be as patient, as resourceful, as indefatigable in well-doing and as faultless in perception of the right thing to do; it would be difficult to make her deeply interesting, but she might be made more or less of an actual creature. But a child whom nothing can ever irritate, whom nothing can ever baffle, whom nothing can ever misguide, whom nothing can ever delude, and whom nothing can ever dismay, is a monster as inhuman as a baby with two heads.

Outside the class which excludes all but the highest masterpieces of poetry it is difficult to find or to imagine a faultless work of creation—in other words, a faultless work of fiction; but the story of *Barnaby Rudge* can hardly, in common justice, be said to fall short of this crowning praise. And in this book, even if not in any of its precursors, an appreciative reader must recognise a quality of humour which will remind him of Shakespeare, and perhaps of Aristophanes. The impetuous and irrepressible volubility of Miss Miggs, when once her eloquence breaks loose and finds vent like raging water or fire, is powerful enough to overbear for the moment any slight objection which a severe morality might suggest with respect to the rectitude and propriety of her conduct. It is impossible to be rigid in our judgment of

> a toiling, moiling, constant-working, always-being-found-fault-with, never-giving-satisfactions, nor-hav-ing-no-time-to-clean-oneself, potter's wessel,' whose 'only becoming occupations is to help young flaunting pagins to brush and comb and titiwate theirselves into whitening and suppulchres, and leave the young men to think that there an't a bit of padding in it nor no pinching-ins nor fillings-out nor pomatums nor deceits nor earthly wanities.

To have made malignity as delightful for an instant as simplicity, and Miss Miggs as enchanting as Mrs Quickly or Mrs Gamp, is an unsurpassable triumph of dramatic humour.

But the advance in tragic power is even more notable and memorable than this. The pathos, indeed, is too cruel; the tortures of the idiot's mother and the murderer's wife are so fearful that interest and sympathy are wellnigh superseded or overbalanced by a sense of horror rather than of pity; magnificent as is the power of dramatic invention which animates every scene in every stage of her martyrdom. Dennis is the first of those consummate and wonderful ruffians, with two vile faces under one frowsy hood, whose captain or commander-in-chief is Rogue Riderhood; more fearful by far, though not (one would hope) more natural, than Henriet Cousin, who could hardly breathe when fastening the rope round Esmeralda's neck, 'tant la chose l'apitoyait'; a divine touch of surviving humanity which would have been impossible to the more horrible hangman whose mortal agony in immediate prospect of the imminent gallows is as terribly memorable as anything in the tragedy of fiction or the poetry of prose. His fellow hangbird is a figure no less admirable throughout all his stormy and fiery career till the last moment; and then he drops into poetry. Nor is it poetry above the reach of Silas Wegg which 'invokes the curse of all its victims on that black tree, of which he is the ripened fruit.' The writer's impulse was noble; but its expression or its effusion is such as indifference may deride and sympathy must deplore. Twice only did the greatest English writer of his day make use of history as a background or a stage for fiction; the use made of it in *Barnaby Rudge* is even more admirable in the lifelike tragedy and the terrible comedy of its presentation than the use made of it in *A Tale of Two Cities*.

Dickens was doubtless right in his preference of 'David Copperfield' to all his other masterpieces; it is only among dunces that it is held improbable or impossible for a great writer to judge aright of his own work at its best, to select and to prefer the finest and the fullest example of his active genius; but, when all deductions have been made from the acknowledgment due to the counter-claim of *Martin Chuzzlewit*, the fact remains that in that unequal and irregular masterpiece his comic and his tragic genius rose now and then to the very highest pitch of all. No son of Adam and no daughter of Eve on this God's earth, as his occasional friend Mr Carlyle might have expressed it, could have imagined it possible—humanly possible—for anything in later comedy to rival the unspeakable perfection of Mrs Quickly's eloquence at its best; at such moments as when her claim to be acknowledged as Lady Falstaff was reinforced, if not by the spiritual authority of Master Dumb, by the correlative evidence of Mrs Keech; but no reader above the level of intelligence which prefers to Shakespeare the Parisian Ibsen and the Norwegian Sardou can dispute the fact that Mrs Gamp has once and again risen even to that unimaginable supremacy of triumph.

At the first interview vouchsafed to us with the adorable Sairey, we feel that no words can express our sense of the divinely altruistic and devoted nature which finds utterance in the sweetly and sublimely simple words—'If I could afford to lay all my feller creeturs out for nothink, I would gladly do it: sich is the love I bear 'em.' We think of little Tommy Harris, and the little red worsted shoe gurgling in his throat; of the previous occasion when his father sought shelter and silence in an empty dog-kennel; of that father's immortally infamous reflection on the advent of his ninth; of religious feelings, of life, and the end of all things; of Mr Gamp, his wooden leg, and their precious boy; of her calculations and her experiences with reference to birth and death; of her views as to the expediency of travel by steam, which anticipated Ruskin's and those of later dissenters from the gospel of hurry and the religion of mechanism; of the contents of Mrs Harris's pocket; of the incredible incredulity of the infidel Mrs Prig; we think of all this, and of more than all this, and acknowledge with infinite thanksgiving of inexhaustible laughter and of rapturous admiration the very greatest comic poet or creator that ever lived to make the life of other men more bright and more glad and more perfect than ever, without his beneficent influence, it possibly or imaginably could have been.

The advance in power of tragic invention, the increased strength in grasp of character and grip of situation, which distinguishes Chuzzlewit from Nickleby, may be tested by comparison of the leading villains. Ralph

Nickleby might almost have walked straight off the boards on which the dramatic genius of his nephew was employed to bring into action two tubs and a pump: Jonas Chuzzlewit has his place of eminence for ever among the most memorable types of living and breathing wickedness that ever were stamped and branded with immortality by the indignant genius of a great and unrelenting master. Neither Vautrin nor Thenardier has more of evil and of deathless life in him.

It is not only by his masterpieces, it is also by his inferior works or even by his comparative failures that the greatness of a great writer may be reasonably judged and tested. We can measure in some degree the genius of Thackeray by the fact that *Pendennis,* with all its marvellous wealth of character and humour and living truth, has never been and never will be rated among his very greatest works. *Dombey and Son* cannot be held nearly so much of a success as *Pendennis.* I have known a man of the very highest genius and the most fervent enthusiasm for that of Dickens who never could get through it. There is nothing of a story, and all that nothing (to borrow a phrase from Martial) is bad. The Roman starveling had nothing to lose, and lost it all: the story of Dombey has no plot, and that a very stupid one. The struttingly offensive father and his gushingly submissive daughter are failures of the first magnitude. Little Paul is a more credible child than little Nell; he sometimes forgets that he is foredoomed by a more than Pauline or Calvinistic law of predestination to die in the odour of sentiment, and says or thinks or does something really and quaintly childlike. But we get, to say the least, a good deal of him; and how much too little do we get of Jack Bunsby! Not so very much more than of old Bill Barley; and yet those two ancient mariners are berthed for ever in the inmost shrine of our affections. Another patch of the very brightest purple sewn into the sometimes rather threadbare stuff or groundwork of the story is the scene in which the dissolution of a ruined household is so tragicomically set before us in the breaking up of the servants' hall. And when we think upon the cherished names of Toots and Nipper, Gills and Cuttle, Rob the Grinder and good Mrs Brown, we are tempted to throw conscience to the winds, and affirm that the book is a good book.

But even if we admit that here was an interlude of comparative failure, we cannot but feel moved to acclaim with all the more ardent gratitude the appearance of the next and perhaps the greatest gift bestowed on us by this magnificent and immortal benefactor. *David Copperfield,* from the first chapter to the last, is unmistakable by any eye above the level and beyond the insight of a beetle's as one of the masterpieces to which time can only add a new charm and an unimaginable value. The narrative is as coherent and harmonious as that of *Tom Jones;* and to say this is to try it by the very highest and apparently the most unattainable standard. But I must venture to reaffirm my conviction that even the glorious masterpiece of Fielding's radiant and beneficent genius, if in some points superior, is by no means superior in all. Tom is a far completer and more living type of gallant boyhood and generous young manhood than David; but even the lustre of Partridge is pallid and lunar beside the noontide glory of Micawber. Blifil is a more poisonously plausible villain than Uriah: Sophia Western remains unequalled except by her sister heroine Amelia as a perfectly credible and adorable type of young English womanhood, naturally 'like one of Shakespeare's women,' socially as fine and true a lady as Congreve's Millamant or Angelica. But even so large-minded and liberal a genius as Fielding's could never have conceived any figure like Miss Trotwood's, any group like that of the Peggottys. As easily could it have imagined and realised the magnificent setting of the story, with its homely foreground of street or wayside and its background of tragic sea.

The perfect excellence of this masterpiece has perhaps done some undeserved injury to the less impeccable works of genius which immediately succeeded it. But in *Bleak House* the daring experiment of combination or alternation which divides a story between narrative in the third person and narrative in the first is justified and vindicated by its singular and fascinating success. 'Esther's narrative' is as good as her creator's; and no enthusiasm of praise could overrate the excellence of them both. For wealth and variety of character none of the master's works can be said to surpass and few can be said to equal it. When all necessary allowance has been made for occasional unlikeliness in detail or questionable methods of exposition, the sustained interest and the terrible pathos of Lady Dedlock's tragedy will remain unaffected and unimpaired. Any reader can object that a lady visiting a slum in the disguise of a servant would not have kept jewelled rings on her fingers for the inspection of a crossing-sweeper, or that a less decorous and plausible way of acquainting her with the fact that a scandalous episode in her early life was no longer a secret for the family lawyer could hardly have been imagined than the public narrative of her story in her own drawing-room by way of an evening's entertainment for her husband and their guests. To these objections, which any Helot of culture whose brain may have been affected by habitual indulgence in the academic delirium of self-complacent superiority may advance or may suggest with the most exquisite infinity of impertinence, it may be impossible to retort an equally obvious and inconsiderable objection.

But to a far more serious charge, which even now appears to survive the confutation of all serious evidence, it is incomprehensible and inexplicable that Dickens should have returned no better an answer than he did. Harold Skimpole was said to be Leigh Hunt; a rascal after the order of Wainewright, without the poisoner's comparatively and diabolically admirable audacity of frank and fiendish self-esteem, was assumed to be meant for a portrait or a caricature of an honest man and a man of unquestionable genius. To this most serious and most disgraceful charge Dickens merely replied that he never anticipated the identification of the rascal Skimpole with the fascinating Harold—the attribution of imaginary villainy to the original model who suggested or supplied a likeness for the externally amiable and ineffectually accomplished lounger and shuffler through life. The simple and final reply should have been that indolence was the essential quality of the character and conduct and philosophy of Skimpole—'a perfectly idle man: a mere amateur,' as he describes himself to the sympathetic and approving Sir Leicester; that Leigh Hunt was one of the hardest and steadiest workers on record, throughout a long and chequered life, at the toilsome trade of letters; and therefore that to represent him as a heartless and shameless idler would have been about as rational an enterprise, as lifelike a design after the life, as it would have been to represent Shelley as a gluttonous and canting hypocrite or Byron as a loyal and unselfish friend. And no one as yet, I believe, has pretended to recognise in Mr Jarndyce a study from Byron, in Mr Chadband a libel on Shelley.

Of the two shorter novels which would suffice to preserve for ever the fame of Dickens, some readers will as probably always prefer *Hard Times* as other will prefer *A Tale of Two Cities*. The later of these is doubtless the most ingeniously and dramatically invented and constructed of all the master's works; the earlier seems to me the greater in moral and pathetic and humorous effect. The martyr workman, beautiful as is the study of his character and terrible as is the record of his tragedy, is almost too spotless a sufferer and a saint; the lifelong lapidation of this unluckier Stephen is somewhat too consistent and insistent and persistent for any record but that of a martyrology; but the obdurate and histrionic affectation which animates the brutality and stimulates the selfishness of Mr Bounderby is only too lamentably truer and nearer to the unlovely side of life. Mr Ruskin—a name never to be mentioned without reverence—thought otherwise; but in knowledge and insight into character and ethics that nobly minded man of genius was no more comparable to Dickens that in sanity of ardour and rationality of aspiration for progressive and practical reform.

As a social satirist Dickens is usually considered to have shown himself at his weakest; the curious and seemingly incorrigible ignorance which imagined that the proper title of Sir John Smith's wife was Lady John Smith, and that the same noble peer could be known to his friends and parasites alternately as Lord Jones and Lord James Jones, may naturally make us regret the absence from their society of our old Parisian friend Sir Brown, Esquire; but though such singular designations as these were never rectified or removed from the text of 'Nicholas Nickleby,' and though a Lady Kew was as far outside the range of his genius as a Madame Marneffe, his satire of social pretension and pretence was by no means always 'a swordstroke in the water' or a flourish in the air. Mrs Sparsit is as typical and immortal as any figure of Moliere's; and the fact that Mr Sparsit was a Powler is one which can never be forgotten.

There is no surer way of testing the greatness of a really great writer than by consideration of his work at its weakest, and comparison of that comparative weakness with the strength of lesser men at their strongest and their best. The romantic and fanciful comedy of *Love's Labour's Lost* is hardly a perceptible jewel in the sovereign crown of Shakespeare; but a single passage in a single scene of it—the last of the fourth act—is more than sufficient to outweigh, to outshine, to eclipse and efface for ever the dramatic lucubrations or prescriptions of Dr Ibsen—Fracastoro of the drama—and his volubly grateful patients. Among the mature works of Dickens and of Thackeray, I suppose most readers would agree in the opinion that the least satisfactory, if considered as representative of the author's incomparable powers, are *Little Dorrit* and *The Virginians;* yet no one above the intellectual level of an Ibsenite or a Zolaist will doubt or will deny that there is enough merit in either of these books for the stable foundation of an enduring fame.

The conception of *Little Dorrit* was far happier and more promising than that of *Dombey and Son;* which indeed is not much to say for it. Mr Dombey is a doll; Mr Dorrit is an everlasting figure of comedy in its most tragic aspect and tragedy in its most comic phase. Little Dorrit herself might be less untruly than unkindly described as Little Nell grown big, or, in Milton's phrase, 'writ large.' But on that very account she is a more credible and therefore a more really and rationally pathetic figure. The incomparable incoherence of the parts which pretend in vain to compose the incomposite story may be gauged by the collapse of some of them and the vehement hurry of cramped and halting invention which huddles up the close of it without an attempt at the rational and natural evolution of others. It is like a child's dissected map with some of the counties or kingdoms missing. Much, though certainly not all, of the humour is of the poorest kind possible to Dickens; and the reiterated repetition of comic catchwords and tragic illustrations of character is such as to affect the nerves no less than the intelligence of the reader with irrepressible irritation. But this, if he be wise, will be got over and kept under by his sense of admiration and of gratitude for the unsurpassable excellence of the finest passages and chapters. The day after the death of Mr Merdle is one of the most memorable dates in all the record of creative history—or, to use one word in place of two, in all the record of fiction. The fusion of humour and horror in the marvellous chapter which describes it is comparable only with the kindred work of such creators as the authors of *Les Miserables* and *King Lear*. And nothing in the work of Balzac is newer and truer and more terrible than the relentless yet not unmerciful evolution of the central figure in the story. The Father of the Marshalsea is so pitiably worthy of pity as well as of scorn that it would have seemed impossible to heighten or to deepen the contempt or the compassion of the reader; but when he falls from adversity to prosperity he succeeds in soaring down and sinking up to a more tragicomic ignominy of more aspiring degradation. And his end is magnificent.

It must always be interesting as well as curious to observe the natural attitude of mind, the inborn instinct of intelligent antipathy or sympathy, discernible or conjecturable in the greatest writer of any nation at any particular date, with regard to the characteristic merits or demerits of foreigners. Dickens was once most unjustly taxed with injustice to the French, by an evidently loyal and cordial French critic, on the ground that the one Frenchman of any mark in all his books was a murderer. The polypseudonymous ruffian who uses and wears out as many stolen names as ever did even the most cowardly and virulent of literary poisoners is doubtless an unlovely figure: but not even Mr Peggotty and his infant niece are painted with more tender and fervent sympathy than the good Corporal and little Bebelle. Hugo could not—even omnipotence has its limits—have given a more perfect and living picture of a hero and a child. I wish I could think he would have given it as the picture of an English hero and an English child. But I do think that Italian readers of *Little Dorrit* ought to appreciate and to enjoy the delightful and admirable personality of Cavalletto. Mr Baptist in Bleeding Heart Yard is as attractively memorable a figure as his excellent friend Signor Panco. And how much more might be said—would the gods annihilate but time and space for a worthier purpose than that of making two lovers happy—of the splendid successes to be noted in the least successful book or books of this great and inexhaustible writer! And if the figure or development of the story in *Little Dorrit,* the shapeliness in parts or the proportions of the whole, may seem to have suffered from tight-lacing in this part and from padding in that, the harmony and unity of the masterpiece which followed it made ample and magnificent amends. In *A Tale of Two Cities* Dickens, for the second and last time, did history the honour to enrol it in the service of fiction. This faultless work of tragic and creative art has nothing of the rich and various exuberance which makes of *Barnaby Rudge* so marvellous an example of youthful genius in all the glowing growth of its bright and fiery April; but it has the classic and poetic symmetry of perfect execution and of perfect design. One or two of the figures in the story which immediately preceded it are unusually liable to the usually fatuous objection which dullness has not yet grown decently ashamed of bringing against the characters of Dickens: to the charge of exaggeration and unreality in the posture or the mechanism of puppets and of daubs, which found its final and supremely offensive expression in the chattering duncery and the impudent malignity of so consummate and pseudosophical a quack as George Henry Lewes. Not even such a past-master in the noble science of defamation could plausibly have dared to cite in support of his insolent and idiotic impeachment either the leading or the supplementary characters in *A Tale of Two Cities*. The pathetic and heroic figure of Sydney Carton seems rather to have cast into the shade of comparative neglect the no less living and admirable figures among and over which it stands and towers in our memory. Miss Pross and Mr Lorry, Madame Defarge and her husband, are equally and indisputably to be recognised by the sign of eternal life.

Among the highest landmarks of success ever reared for immortality by the triumphant genius of Dickens, the story of *Great Expectations* must for ever stand eminent beside that of *David Copperfteld*. These are his great twin masterpieces. Great as they are, there is nothing in them greater than the very best things in some of his other books: there is certainly no person preferable and there is possibly no person comparable to Samuel Weller or to Sarah Gamp. Of the two childish and boyish autobiographers, David is the better little fellow though not the more lifelike little friend; but of all first chapters is there any comparable for impression and for fusion of humour and terror and pity and fancy and truth to that which confronts the child with the convict on the marshes in the twilight? And the story is incomparably the finer story of the two; there can be none superior, if there be any equal to it, in the whole range of English fiction. And except in *Vanity Fair* and *The Newcomes,* if even they may claim exception, there can surely be found no equal or nearly equal number of living and everliving figures. The tragedy and the comedy, the realism and the dreamery of life, are fused or mingled together with little less than Shakesperean strength and skill of hand. To have created Abel Magwitch is to be a god indeed among the creators of deathless men. Pumblechook is actually better and droller and truer to imaginative life than Pecksniff: Joe Gargery is worthy to have been praised and loved at once by Fielding and by Sterne: Mr Jaggers and his clients, Mr Wemmick and his parent and his bride, are such figures as Shakespeare, when dropping out of poetry, might have created, if his lot had been cast in a later century. Can as much be said for the creatures of any other man or god? The ghastly tragedy of Miss Havisham could only have been made at once credible and endurable by Dickens; he alone could have reconciled the strange and sordid horror with the noble and pathetic survival of possible emotion and repentance. And he alone could have eluded condemnation for so gross an oversight as the escape from retribution of so important a criminal as the 'double murderer and monster' whose baffled or inadequate attempts are enough to make Bill Sikes seem comparatively the gentlest and Jonas Chuzzlewit the most amiable of men. I remember no such flaw in any other story I ever read. But in this story it may well have been allowed to pass unrebuked and unobserved; which yet I think it should not.

—Algernon Charles Swinburne, "Charles Dickens" *Quarterly Review*, July 1902, pp. 20–32

ALICE MEYNELL (1903)

Alice Meynell was a well-known poet and essayist at the turn of the century. Like Swinburne, she defends Dickens on account of, rather than despite, his craftsmanship. Unlike those critics who find the essence of Dickens to be improvisation, Meynell argues that in his comedy, "the idea is inseparable from the phrase." Her essay will be indispensable to students writing on Dickens's language or his comedy.

Many critics in this volume discuss Dickens's attention to external detail; Meynell shows how poorly this attention is usually understood. For example, in her view, Micawber's preposterously overinflated language becomes an indictment, not of himself, nor even of Dickens's tin ear (as Lewes would have it), but rather a scathing satire of Victorian business jargon. She also adduces example after example of the sensorial consistency of Dickens's images, wherein descriptive passages contain only things that may be seen, such as the often complex interaction of physical gestures.

Although it is a slight anachronism to say so, Meynell's defense of Dickens reconfigures him as a precursor to modernism, rather than as a tired holdover from the Victorian period. She casts him as a restless inventor, tearing up received conventions of style and construction because they are inadequately precise. If his style is sometimes problematic, it is at least closer to reality than that which it replaces. This position is strikingly like the defense of modernist fiction offered up by Virginia Woolf in such essays as "Modern Fiction" and "Mr. Bennett and Mrs. Brown," and might be a useful starting point for essays on Dickens's legacy.

The purely literary character of a greatly popular writer is apt to be neglected; or at least to remain a matter of lax or irresponsible opinion. His admirers have one reason, his detractors another, for leaving it in abeyance; both classes seem to consider it hardly worth attention. In England there has long been a middle public,—a class still sufficiently large,—lettered readers who do not set Dickens aside, and yet who cannot be said to study him; and their tendency is to make light, without much examination, of his specific power as a writer. Men have the habit of saving their reputation as readers by disavowing his literature even while they confess the amplitude of its effects. There is laughter for his humor, tears for his pathos, praise for his spirit, and contempt for his authorship. The least every man holds himself urged to say is that he need not say he prefers Thackeray.

Dickens, however, was very much a craftsman. He had a love of his *métier*, and the genius for words, which the habitual indifference of his time, of his readers, and of his contemporaries in letters could not quench. To read him after a modern man who had the like preoccupation, displayed it, and was applauded for it phrase by phrase,—Robert Louis Stevenson, for example,—is to undergo a new conviction of his authorship, of the vitality of his diction, of a style that springs, strikes, and makes a way through the burden of custom. Of the great exceptions to that custom the writers who made a conscious choice of a worthy vocabulary—I need not speak. Few of them were read by Dickens in the years when his own literature was taking shape. He had Fielding and Smollett for his authors as a boy, and nothing read thus by one so ardent is without influence. But his contemporaries—all the journalists, all the novelists of the hour—were not men who cared for the spirit, precision, or nobility of a phrase, or gave much time to any other century than that which was then plodding on a foot neither jocund nor majestic. The daily leading article in the *Times* newspaper (little altered) shows us still what was the best effect looked for in that day from the journeymen of literature. The language had to serve a certain purpose of communication; but as to the nobler, or the fuller, or the more delicate sense of words, it meant as little as was possible to any human tongue.

Refuse words, too emphatic, but with a worn, an abused emphasis; strained rhetoric that had lost its elasticity; grave phrases dimmed and dulled—authors worked with these as with the English of their inheritance, sufficiently well content. The phrase filled the mouth, though there were dregs in the mouthful. In the work of Dickens also there are passages of such English, neither gentle nor simple. He wrote thus as a mere matter of use and custom. But his own lively genius proved itself to be a writer's genius, not only here and there, or suddenly, but often. It had its way of revealing the authentic writer as the springs and sources of his work. For the authentic author is an author throughout. His art is lodged so deeply within as to be beforehand with his emotions and his passions, especially the more vehement. He does not clothe his feeling in poetry or prose, for clothing is assumed. It would be better to say that his thought and feeling are incarnated, not dressed, and that in poetry it wears already the spiritual body. According to this theory of language no man can possibly have a true *style* who has not something to write, something for the sake of which he writes. This should not need to be said—it is so simple, and seems so plain. Yet authors are found to aspire to style for its own sake, and to miss it as happiness is missed. The writer who has taken captive the fancy and the cheaper emotions—not the imagination and the graver passions—of modern Italy is surely to be very simply and obviously described as an ambitious and a careful author who has *little* or nothing to say. Against such as he the coming reaction toward blunt and homely writing is as just as a "movement" can ever *be*. And it is only against such as he that the insults "precious" and "preciosity" are justifiably to be used. The style of Dickens is assuredly not great. It has life enough for movement; but not life for peace. That its life, whether restless or "at rest, is the fact which proves its title to the name of style. To write much about style is, unfortunately, to tamper somewhat with that rare quality; if only because such writing has suggested to too many the addition of "style" to all their other literary offenses—the last addition, like that of the "architecture" which was to be added to the rich man's new house as soon as he should get it built. Let us, however, leave this mere fashion out of sight; it will soon pass. Already a reaction is beginning, and those who praised what they called style will soon be scorning it, in chorus. Which way such a weak current of criticism may chance to turn between to-day and to-morrow matters nothing. The style that is the life and value of English literature suffers no lasting injury or change; and all who have written well, whether in the greater manner or the lesser which Dickens practiced, have their share in the laws and the constitution of Letters. It cannot be necessary to insist upon Dickens's sense of words. He had his craft at heart, and made instant appropriations of words that describe and define. This felicity is style in a humble form. It even fulfills that ancient demand for frequent "slight surprise," which, so stated, is in itself an example, as well as a precept, of Greek style. See, for an instance of Dickens's felicity, the brief phrase that gives us Mr. Micawber as he sat by to hear Captain Hopkins read the petition in the prison "from His Most Gracious Majesty's unfortunate subjects." Mr. Micawber listened, Dickens tells us, "with a little of an author's vanity, contemplating (not severely) the spikes upon the opposite wall." The happy parenthesis! And here is another masterly phrase: "It went from me with a shock, like a ball from a rifle," says David Copperfield, after the visit of a delirious impulse; and what other writer has named that blow of departure, the volley of passion as it goes?

In comedy again: "Mr. Micawber" (he was making punch) "resumed his peeling with a desperate air." We had read but a moment before that he had made a "random but expressive flourish with the knife" in reference to his own prospects and to those of his disastrous family. Traddles, in the same book, with his hair standing on end, "looked as though he had seen a cheerful ghost." And if the heart-easing humor of this little phrase, which sets laughter free, should be accused of a lower intelligence than that of wit, has Dickens not wit in a phrase, as well as humor? Is it not witty to say of the man who had held a sinecure office against all protest, "He died with his drawn salary in his hand?"

Is it not witty, too, to banter the worst English of his day by an imitation that shows an author's sense of its literary baseness? The mere words, "gratifying emotions of no common description," do this to admiration. It is Mr. Micawber again (excellent figure of comedy—there are no heights of humorous literature whereon Mr. Micawber has not the right to stand with the greatest of companions)—it is he who writes that portly phrase. "Tinged with the prismatic hues of memory" is another sentence in the same paragraph, but this is something more farcical, whereas "gratifying emotions of no common description" hits the whole language as it were with one sure arrow. The thickness of the words, as when Charlotte Brontë, at her primmest, writes of "establishing an eligible connection," and of "an institution on the Continent," has not escaped the ear of Dickens the writer. Try as one may to describe a certain kind of English, one is easily outdone by him with a single phrase, invented for an example, such as this of Mr. Micawber's—"gratifying emotions of no common description."

Comedy in literature is evidently of three kinds, and the kinds are named respectively, humor, wit, and derision. Humor is in the phrase that describes Traddles with his hair—Traddles who looked as though he had seen a cheerful ghost. Wit is in the phrase about the drawn salary. And derision is in that sentence of Mr. Micawber's composition.

In all this—the humor of authorship, its wit and its derision, cited here successively, in representative phrases that had to be chosen among thousands of their kind—the idea is inseparable from the phrase. Nevertheless, perhaps a student might be willing to find so important a thing as style elsewhere, in deliberate description, such as this: The autumn leaves fall thick, "but never fast, for they come circling down with a dead lightness." Here, again, is a noble piece of writing which a classic English name might well have signed: "I held my mother in my embrace, and she held me in hers; and among the still woods in the silence of the summer day there seemed to be nothing but our two troubled minds that was not at peace."

Again, how simple and fine is this: "Now the woods settle into great masses as if they were one profound tree": not only admirably choice in words, but a lesson in vision, a lesson for a painter. It instructs the sense of sight, so that a master of landscape painting could not put a better lesson into words. And this, also simple, also good, seems to instruct the sense of hearing—the scene is in the Court of Chancery on a London November day: "Leaving this address ringing in the rafters of the roof, the very little counsel drops, and the fog knows him no more." Again: "Mr. Vholes here emerged into the silence he could hardly be said to have broken, so stifled was his tone." Here again are hearing and vision in admirable words: "Within the grill-gate of the chancel, up the steps surmounted loomingly by the fast darkening organ, white robes could be dimly seen, and one feeble voice, rising and falling in a cracked monotonous mutter, could at intervals be faintly heard . . . until the organ and the choir burst forth and drowned it in a sea of music. Then the sea fell, and the dying voice made another feeble effort; and then the sea rose high and beat its life out, and lashed the roof, and surged among the arches, and pierced the heights of the great tower; and then the sea was dry and all was still."

Take another example: This is how a listener overheard men talking in the cathedral hollows: "The word 'confidence,' shattered by the echoes, but still capable of being pieced together, is uttered."

In another passage, moreover, Dickens stops at the mere sense of vision, and confirms that intent impression by instantly using a certain word where a writer of lesser vigilance would have used another; thus: "Mr. Vholes gauntly stalked to the fire, and warmed his funeral gloves." A less simple and less subtle author—a less admirable impressionist—would have surely said "hands" where Dickens, stopping at the sense of vision—as though he did nothing but see—says "gloves." This is the purest and most perfect "impressionism," yet it does not bind Dickens to impressionism as a formula. He uses that manner precisely when he needs it, and only then. There is another similar and excellent passage, where Dickens writes of Mr. Vholes's "sleeve," and writes so with a peculiar appropriateness to the inscrutable person he is describing. "'I thank you,' said Mr. Vholes, putting out his long black sleeve, to check the ringing of the bell, 'not any.'" And here is the expression of a sense that is hardly either sight or hearing: "Beyond was a burial ground in which the night was very slowly stirring." How subtle a phrase for the earliest dawn!

Then there is the description of the gesture of little David Copperfield at the end of his journey, when he first confronts his aunt: "A movement of my hands, intended to show her my ragged state, and to call it to witness that I had suffered something." If the sense of hearing is opened and urged, and struck to greater life by one phrase; and the sense of vision by another; both are quickened by the storm in *David Copperfield*, and the sense of touch is roused by the touches of that tempest. "I dream of it," says the narrator, "sometimes, though at lengthened and uncertain intervals, to this hour." "There had been a wind all day, and it was rising then, with an extraordinary great sound. . . . We found a cluster of people in the market place." That last phrase, in all its simplicity, marks the strange day. "Long before we saw the sea its spray was on our lips. . . . The water was out, over miles and miles of the flat country; and every sheet and puddle lashed its banks, and had its stress of little breakers setting heavily towards us. When we came within sight of the sea, the waves on the horizon, caught at intervals above the rolling abyss, were like glimpses of another shore, with towers and buildings. When at last we got into the town, the people came out to their doors all aslant, and with streaming hair. I went down to look at the sea, staggering along the street, which was strewn with sand and seaweed, and with flying blotches of sea foam." Here, again, is the storm in the morning light: "The wind by this time might have lulled a little, *though* not more sensibly than if the cannonading I had dreamed of had been diminished by the silencing of half a dozen guns out of hundreds." Wonderful here, again, is the perception of things silenced within the stress of sound. Then read all that follows, in the unrelaxed urgency of that great chapter, to the end.

Whoever would try to do Dickens this tardy justice (and I have space for no more than an indication of the way of it) must choose passages that have the quality of dignity. They are not so very few. Elegance he has not, but his dignity is clear to readers who prize this quality too much to be hasty to deny it.

In estimating Charles Dickens's capacity for a prose style of dignity we ought to bear in mind his own singular impatience of antiquity of almost all degrees, and also the sense of fresh life he had—his just conviction of his own new leadership. He had read the eighteenth-century novelists in his boyhood, but when he became a man and a master, he broke with the past, and his *renouveau* was somewhat too stimulating to his own genius. It was in spite of this, in spite of his popularity, and in spite of a public that was modern, excitable, boastful of the age, boastful about steam and trade, eager to frolic with a new humorist, and yet more eager to weep with a new sentimentalist, that Dickens possessed himself, in no infrequent passages, of a worthy and difficult dignity.

His people, his populace, and the first critic of his day at the head of all classes, pushed him further and yet further on the way of abandonment—the way of easy extremes; by praise, by popularity, by acclamation they sent their novelist in search of yet more occasion for laughter and tears, for caricature and intemperate pathos.

Moreover, as has just been said, Dickens was urged by his own modern conviction, and excused by his splendid sense of words. He was tempted everywhere. As you read him, you learn to understand how his vitality was at work, how it carried him through his least worthy as well as his most worthy moments, and justified his confidence where a weaker man had confessed unconsciously the ignominies of false art and luxurious sentiment. Charles Dickens seems to defy us to charge him with these. None the less do we accuse him—at Little Paul's death, for example. Throughout this child's life—admirably told—the art is true, but at the very last few lines the writer seems to yield to applause and to break the strengthening laws of nature down. We may indeed say the strengthening laws; because in what Hamlet calls the modesty of nature there is not only beauty, not only dignity, but an inimitable strength. The limitations of nature, and of natural art, are bracing. A word or two astray in this death scene; a phrase or two put into the mouth of the dying child,—"the light about the head," "shining on me as I go," phrases that no child ever spoke, and that make one shrink as though with pain by their untruthfulness,—and the sincerity of literature is compromised.

But it is not with such things that the work of Dickens is beset; it is rather filled with just felicities—so filled that on our search for passages of composure and dignity we are tempted to linger rather among excellent words that are to be praised merely because they are the words of precision—arms of precision—specific for his purpose. Two proper names are worthy to be placed among these,—that of Vholes, for the predatory yet not fraudulent lawyer in *Bleak House*, and that of Tope, for the cathedral verger in *Edwin Drood*: something dusty and dusky, with wings, is Vholes; something like a church mouse, silent and a little stealthy, is Tope.

Mr. and Mrs. Tope. There is naturally a pair engaged about the cathedral stalls and the hassocks—within the "precincts" generally. It is Christmas; and Mr. and Mrs. Tope, Dickens tells us, "are daintily sticking sprigs of holly into the carvings and sconces of the cathedral stalls, as if they were sticking them into the coat-buttonholes of the Dean and Chapter." From the same book comes this fine description of the young Eurasians: "a certain air upon them of hunter and huntress; yet withal a certain air of being the objects of the chase, rather than the followers." The words may lack elegance, but they are vivid; and these follow: "An indefinable kind of pause coming and going on their whole expression, both of face and form." . . .

It is appropriately in the passages of childhood—veritable childhood, in which the famous Little Nell seems to me, I must reluctantly confess, to have little or no part—that Dickens writes those words of perception of which literature would do well to be proud. Take the passages of several of the novels in which the heart of a child is uttered by the humorist, in whose heart nothing ceases to live. These passages are too full for citation. But here, in the last word of the phrase, is a most characteristic stroke of literature. Pip, in *Great Expectations*, as every one knows, has taken food to give to his convict; and he goes to church on Christmas morning: Dickens puts these words into his mouth:—

"Under the weight of my wicked secret, I pondered whether the Church would be powerful enough to shield me from the vengeance of the terrible young man, if I divulged to that establishment." The word "establishment" is precisely the one that proves the hopelessness of such a project. A child confessing to an "establishment"! Another word of precision is this: "Trabb's boy, when I had entered, was sweeping the shop; and he had sweetened his labors by sweeping over me." Here is another, and it repeats the effect of Mr. Vholes's sleeve, in a child's apprehension: "Miss Murdstone, who was busy at her writing-desk, gave me her cold finger-nails." Then there is "a sobbing gaslight"; and, again, Mrs. Wilfer's "darkling state," and "lurid indications of the better marriages she might have made" (wherewith she celebrates her silver wedding)—these serve to remind a reader of the thousands of their kind.

I cannot think that the telling of a violent action (most difficult of narrative writing) could be done more dramatically than it is done in the passage that tells the murder in *Martin Chuzzlewit*. So with the half-told murder in *Edwin Drood*. As by strong dramatic drawing in a picture the thing is held. These passages of extreme action are never without dignity. Literary dignity is rarer in the pathetic mood; but it is frequent in landscape. Here is an example: "All beyond his figure was a vast dark curtain, in solemn movement towards one quarter of the heavens."

Nor is dignity absent from this composed thought of Esther Summerson, in that passage of her life where she had resolved to forego an unavowed love: "There was nothing to be undone; no chain for him to drag, or for me to break." This has a quality not unworthy of Bolingbroke, and resembling him by nobility. For when Bolingbroke says of the gifts and benefits of Fortune, that she might take, but that she should not snatch, them from him, meaning that his own detaining hold upon them should not be violent, he uses a phrase hardly more majestic than that of Dickens. Thus it is to an eighteenth-century classic, and a master of style; it is to the friend of Pope, and the inspirer of the *Essay on Man*, that we may liken Dickens the man of letters. And this is the author whom so many readers have charged with vulgarity. The vulgarity that is attributable to his early ignorance of social manners is a very unimportant thing in comparison with the high literary distinction of authorship. The pathetic writer, the humorist, the observer, the describer, we all know, but surely the world has not yet done justice to the man of letters and the man of style, who has not only told us stories, but has borne the responsibilities of English authorship.

It is surely worth mentioning that on the point of grammar Dickens is above criticism. Ignorant of those languages which are held to furnish the foundations of grammatical construction he assuredly was. Nevertheless, he knew how to construct. He grasped the language, as it were, from within. I believe that throughout all those volumes of his there is not one example, I will not say of bad grammar, but of weak grammar. Hardly another author is thus infallible. Those critics who think Thackeray to be, in some sort, more literary than Dickens, would be dismayed if they compared the two authors upon this point. No comparison of any kind, perhaps, need be made between them; but it is the Thackeray party that is to blame for first making a kind of rivalry. And I intend no disrespect to that truly great author when I note that Thackeray's grammar is often strangely to seek. Not only so, but he puts, all unconsciously, a solecism into the mouth of Dr. Johnson himself, in the course of the few words which he makes Johnson speak, in his novel, *The Virginians*.

Security of grammar is surely much more than a mere correctness and knowledge of the rules of a language. It is strength, it is logic. It even proves imagination; because loose sentences nearly always imply vagueness of image,—visual and mental uncertainty, something merely rhetorical or ready made. Strong grammar is like strong drawing, and proves a capable grasp of the substance of things. In this matter Dickens is on the heights of authorship. When Dickens was learning to write, English prose, as commonly printed, was in bad condition. There were the great exceptions, as Americans remember, but one does not think of them as coming Dickens's way. The writer at once popular and literary was Macaulay. But in the matter of style Macaulay was little else than an energetic follower of Gibbon; and the following of Gibbon became, through the fine practice of Macaulay, a harmful habit in English prose. Macaulay unfortunately had not the copyright. And as the authors of the articles of the English Church speak, in theology, of a corrupt following of the Apostles, so also was there a corrupt following of Gibbon. The style of Mr. Micawber himself was a corrupt following of Gibbon, and the style of the daily paper and the style of the grocer's circular to-day are also a corrupt following of Gibbon. Gibbon was a master, but it was through a second-hand admiration that Gibbon was placed where he eclipsed the past, so that the early eighteenth-century and the seventeenth-century were neglected for his sake. It was to the broad face of astonishment that Gibbon addressed his phrase. The shortened sentence (for it was he and not Macaulay who introduced the frequent full stop, the pause for historical surprise) was Gibbon's. His was the use, at once weak and rigid, of "the latter and the former," which the corrupt follower at once adopted: "Oh, do not doom me to the latter!" says a lover in one of Mrs. Inchbald's stories after presenting to his mistress the alternative of his hopes and fears. The grocer to-day diffuses (Gibbon himself would write "diffuses") the last ruins of the master's prose by post; and when the author of a work, recently published, on the *Divine Comedy*, says that Paolo and Francesca were to receive from Dante "such alleviation as circumstances would allow," this also is a distant, a shattered Gibbon, a drift of Gibbon.

That last is the innocent burlesque of the far-off corrupt follower. The burlesque so gayly undertaken by Dickens rallies a lofty and a distant Gibbon less innocently, and with an exquisite intelligence. And our admiration of Dickens's warm, living, and unrhetorical writing should surely be increased by our remembrance of the fact that this wreck of a master's style strewed the press in his day. It was everywhere. Dickens not only was clear of the wreckage—he saw it to be the refuse it was; he laughed at it, and even as he laughed he formed a Style.

—Alice Meynell, "Charles Dickens as a Man of Letters," (1903)

G.K. Chesterton
"On the Alleged Optimism of Dickens" (1906)

G.K. Chesterton, Christian apologist, convert to Roman Catholicism, essayist, biographer, and mystery writer, is the most important early-twentieth-century writer on Dickens. T.S. Eliot, who taught Dickens's novels as a young man and who originally titled *The Waste Land* after a phrase from *Our Mutual Friend*, and Peter Ackroyd, also a biographer of Dickens, regard Chesterton's biography as the best book on Dickens ever written, despite some important factual errors.

Chesterton advances two important arguments about Dickensian optimism. The first is that his optimism must be understood as a tactic in his effort to ameliorate social ills. Dickens's optimism can be seen as reconciling "two apparently antagonistic emotions" in our view of reform: "We must think the oppressed man intensely miserable, and at the same time intensely attractive and important." On the one hand, we must believe that there is a serious problem to be solved; on the other, we must think the afflicted worth saving. Chesterton's great example is the members of the Cratchit family, who bear their poverty so stoically that one cannot help but want to see and make them prosperous. A darker example is the contrast between Mrs. Jellyby's "telescopic philanthropy" in *Bleak House* and Jo the street sweeper, who can be safely ignored because he is in London, and not Borrioboola-Gha. Chesterton sees Dickens's vision as essentially "religious," because "it rests upon his perpetual assertion of the value of the human soul and of human daily life."

By making Dickens's grotesques a tribute to humanity, Chesterton also refutes Frederic Harrison's complaint that the comedy in Dickens remains simply farce. Chesterton explains that the villains in Dickens are farcical in order to bring them into view. Ordinarily, the banality of evil allows us to tolerate the intolerable. So, in *Oliver Twist*, "As long as Bumble was merely inhuman, he was allowed. When he became human, humanity wiped him right out." What Harrison sees as exhausting, repetitive distortion, Chesterton affirms as a corrective to our workaday blindness. This conflict between Harrison and Chesterton raises a fundamental question about Dickens, one that can be profitably explored in any of his novels: In what sense can he be called "realistic"? Given that no one has ever met a man like Micawber, or a nurse like Sarah Gamp, how does Dickens make us feel that we recognize his characters?

The second important argument, addressed briefly at the end, is about Dickens's melodramatic aesthetic, termed "streaky bacon" in *Oliver*

Twist. Chesterton defends Dickens as making evil itself visible. Dickens does not seek to understand or to justify evil actions; he represents evil because in its wake, "good things, in a blazing apocalypse, become good." Dickens's optimism and his desire for reform require an enemy, which is for Chesterton a crucial philosophical, even existential, point: "This life of ours is a very enjoyable fight, but a very miserable truce." Chesterton's view of Dickens, fighting in the name of humanity for social reform, is the most common frame through which modern readers have encountered his works.

In one of the plays of the decadent period, an intellectual expressed the atmosphere of his epoch by referring to Dickens as "a vulgar optimist." I have in a previous chapter suggested something of the real strangeness of such a term. After all, the main matter of astonishment (or rather of admiration) is that optimism should be vulgar. In a world in which physical distress is almost the common lot, we actually complain that happiness is too common. In a world in which the majority is physically miserable we actually complain of the sameness of praise; we are bored with the abundance of approval. When we consider what the conditions of the vulgar really are, it is difficult to imagine a stranger or more splendid tribute to humanity than such a phrase as vulgar optimism. It is as if one spoke of "vulgar martyrdom" or "common crucifixion."

First, however, let it be said frankly that there is a foundation for the charge against Dickens which is implied in the phrase about vulgar optimism. It does not concern itself with Dickens's confidence in the value of existence and the intrinsic victory of virtue; that is not optimism but religion. It is not concerned with his habit of making bright occasions bright, and happy stories happy; that is not optimism, but literature. Nor is it concerned even with his peculiar genius for the description of an almost bloated joviality; that is not optimism, it is simply Dickens. With all these higher variations of optimism I deal elsewhere. But over and above all these there is a real sense in which Dickens laid himself open to the accusation of a vulgar optimism, and I desire to put the admission of this first, before the discussion that follows. Dickens did have a disposition to make his characters at all costs happy, or, to speak more strictly, he had a disposition to make them comfortable rather than happy. He had a sort of literary hospitality; he too often treated his characters as if they were his guests. From a host is always expected, and always ought to be expected as long as human civilisation is healthy, a strictly physical benevolence, if you will, a kind of coarse benevolence. Food and fire and such things should always be the symbols of the man entertaining men; because they are things which all men beyond question have in common. But something more than this is needed from a man who is imagining and making men, the artist, the man who is not receiving men, but rather sending them forth.

As I shall remark in a moment in the matter of the Dickens villains, it is not true that he made every one thus at home. But he did do it to a certain wide class of incongruous characters, he did it to all who had been in any way unfortunate. It had needed its origin (a very beautiful origin) in his realisation of how much a little pleasure was to such people. He knew well that the greatest happiness that has been known since Eden is the happiness of the unhappy. So far he is admirable. And as long as he was describing the ecstasy of the poor, the borderland between pain and pleasure, he was at his highest. Nothing that has ever been written about human delights, no Earthly Paradise, no Utopia has ever come so near the quick nerve of happiness as his descriptions of the rare extravagances of the poor; such an admirable description, for instance, as that of Kit Nubbles taking his family to the theatre. For he seizes on the real source of the whole pleasure; a holy fear. Kit tells the waiter to bring the beer. And the waiter, instead of saying, "Did you address that language to me," said, "Pot of beer, sir; yes, sir." That internal and quivering humility of Kit is the only way to enjoy life or banquets; and the fear of the waiter is the beginning of dining. People in this mood "take their pleasures sadly"; which is the only way of taking them at all.

So far Dickens is supremely right. As long as he was dealing with such penury and such festivity his touch was almost invariably sure. But when he came to more difficult cases, to people who for one reason or another could not be cured with one good dinner, he did develop this other evil, this genuinely vulgar optimism of which I speak. And the mark of it is this: that he gave the characters a comfort that had no especial connection with themselves; he threw comfort at them like alms. There are cases at the end of his stories in which his kindness to his characters is a careless and insolent kindness. He loses his real charity and adopts the charity of the Charity Organisation Society; the charity that is not kind, the charity that is puffed up, and that does behave itself unseemly. At the end of some of his stories he deals out his characters a kind of out-door relief.

I will give two instances. The whole meaning of the character of Mr. Micawber is that a man can be always almost rich by constantly expecting riches. The lesson is a really important one in our sweeping modern sociology. We talk of the man whose life is a failure; but Micawber's life never is a failure, because it is always a crisis. We think constantly of the man who if he looked back would see that his existence was unsuccessful; but Micawber never does look back; he always looks forward, because the bailiff is coming to-morrow. You cannot say he is defeated, for his absurd battle never ends; he cannot despair of life, for he is so much occupied in living. All this is of immense importance in the understanding of the poor; it is worth all the slum novelists that ever insulted democracy. But how did it happen that the man who created this Micawber could pension him off at the end of the story and make him a successful colonial mayor? Micawber never did succeed, never ought to succeed; his kingdom is not of this world. But this is an excellent instance of Dickens's disposition to make his characters grossly and incongruously comfortable. There is another instance in the same book. Dora, the first wife of David Copperfield, is a very genuine and amusing figure; she has certainly far more force of character than Agnes. She represents the infinite and divine irrationality of the human heart. What possessed Dickens to make her such a dehumanised prig as to recommend her husband to marry another woman? One could easily respect a husband who after time and development made such a marriage, but surely not a wife who desired it. If Dora had died hating Agnes we should know that everything was right, and that God would reconcile the irreconcilable. When Dora dies recommending Agnes we know that everything is wrong, at least if hypocrisy and artificiality and moral vulgarity are wrong. There, again, Dickens yields to a mere desire to give comfort. He wishes to pile up pillows round Dora; and he smothers her with them, like Othello.

This is the real vulgar optimism of Dickens: it does exist; and I have deliberately put it first. Let us admit that Dickens's mind was far too much filled with pictures of satisfaction and cosiness and repose. Let us admit that he thought principally of the pleasures of the oppressed classes; let us admit that it hardly cost him any artistic pang to make out human beings as much happier than they are. Let us admit all this, and a curious fact remains.

For it was this too easily contented Dickens, this man with cushions at his back and (it sometimes seems) cotton wool in his ears; it was this happy dreamer, this vulgar optimist who alone of modern writers did really destroy some of the wrongs he hated and bring about some of the reforms he desired. Dickens did help to pull down the debtors' prisons; and if he was too much of an optimist he was quite enough of a destroyer. Dickens did drive Squeers out of his Yorkshire den; and if Dickens was too contented, it was more than Squeers was. Dickens did leave his mark on parochialism, on nursing, on funerals, on public executions, on workhouses, on the Court of Chancery. These things were altered; they are different. It may be that such reforms are not adequate remedies; that is another question altogether. The next sociologists may think these old Radical reforms quite narrow or accidental. But such as they were, the old Radicals got them done; and the new sociologists cannot get anything done at all. And in the practical doing of them Dickens played a solid and quite demonstrable part; that is the plain matter that concerns us here. If Dickens was an optimist he was an uncommonly active and useful kind of optimist. If Dickens was a sentimentalist he was a very practical sentimentalist.

And the reason of this is one that goes deep into Dickens's social reform, and like every other real and desirable thing, involves a kind of mystical contradiction. If we are to save the oppressed, we must have two apparently antagonistic emotions in us at the same time. We must think the oppressed man intensely miserable, and at the same time intensely attractive and important. We must insist with violence upon his degradation; we must insist with the same violence upon his dignity. For if we relax by one inch the one assertion, men will say he does not need saving. And if we relax by one inch the other assertion, men will say he is not worth saving. The optimists will say that reform is needless. The pessimists will say that reform is hopeless. We must apply both simultaneously to the same oppressed man; we must say that he is a worm and a god; and we must thus lay ourselves open to the accusation (or the compliment) of transcendentalism. This is, indeed, the strongest argument for the religious conception of life. If the dignity of man is an earthly dignity we shall be tempted to deny his earthly degradation. If it is a heavenly dignity we can admit the earthly degradation with all the candour of Zola. If we are idealists about the other world we can be realists about this world. But that is not here the point. What is quite evident is that if a logical praise of the poor man is pushed too far, and if a logical distress about him is pushed too far, either will involve wreckage to the central paradox of reform. If the poor man is made too admirable he ceases to be pitiable; if the poor man is made too pitiable he becomes merely contemptible. There is a school of smug optimists who will deny that he is a poor man. There is a school of scientific pessimists who will deny that he is a man.

Out of this perennial contradiction arises the fact that there are always two types of the reformer. The first we may call for convenience the pessimistic, the second the optimistic reformer. One dwells upon the fact that souls are being lost; the other dwells upon the fact that they are worth saving. Both, of course, are (so far as that is concerned) quite right, but they naturally tend to a difference of method, and sometimes to a difference of perception.

The pessimistic reformer points out the good elements that oppression has destroyed; the optimistic reformer, with an even fiercer joy, points out the good elements that it has not destroyed. It is the case for the first reformer that slavery has made men slavish. It is the case for the second reformer that slavery has not made men slavish. The first describes how bad men are under bad conditions. The second describes how good men are under bad conditions. Of the first class of writers, for instance, is Gorky. Of the second class of writers is Dickens.

But here we must register a real and somewhat startling fact. In the face of all apparent probability, it is certainly true that the optimistic reformer reforms much more completely than the pessimistic reformer. People produce violent changes by being contented, by being far too contented. The man who said that "revolutions are not made with rose-water" was obviously inexperienced in practical human affairs. Men like Rousseau and Shelley do make revolutions, and do make them with rose-water; that is, with a too rosy and sentimental view of human goodness. Figures that come before and create convulsion and change (for instance, the central figure of the New Testament) always have the air of walking in an unnatural sweetness and calm. They give us their peace ultimately in blood and battle and division; not as the world giveth give they unto us.

Nor is the real reason of the triumph of the too-contented reformer particularly difficult to define. He triumphs because he keeps alive in the human soul an invincible sense of the thing being worth doing, of the war being worth winning, of the people being worth their deliverance. I remember that Mr. William Archer, some time ago, published in one of his interesting series of interviews, an interview with Mr. Thomas Hardy. That powerful writer was represented as saying, in the course of the conversation, that he did not wish at the particular moment to define his opinion with regard to the ultimate problem of whether life itself was worth living. There are, he said, hundreds of remediable evils in this world. When we have remedied all these (such was his argument), it will be time enough to ask whether existence itself under its best possible conditions is valuable or desirable. Here we have presented, with a considerable element of what can only be called unconscious humour, the plain reason of the failure of the pessimist as a reformer. Mr. Hardy is asking us, I will not say to buy a pig in a poke; he is asking us to buy a poke on the remote chance of there being a pig in it. When we have for some few frantic centuries tortured ourselves to save mankind, it will then be "time enough" to discuss whether they can possibly be saved. When, in the case of infant mortality, for example, we have exhausted ourselves with the earthshaking efforts required to save the life of every individual baby, it will then be time enough to consider whether every individual baby would not have been happier dead. We are to remove mountains and bring the millennium, because then we can have a quiet moment to discuss whether the millennium is at all desirable. Here we have the low-water mark of the impotence of the sad reformer. And here we have the reason of the paradoxical triumph of the happy one. His triumph is a religious triumph; it rests upon his perpetual assertion of the value of the human soul and of human daily life. It rests upon his assertion that human life is enjoyable because it is human. And he will never admit, like so many compassionate pessimists, that human life ever ceases to be human. He does not merely pity the lowness of men; he feels an insult to their elevation. Brute pity should be given only to brutes. Cruelty to animals is cruelty and a vile thing; but cruelty to a man is not cruelty, it is treason. Tyranny over a man is not tyranny, it is rebellion, for man is royal. Now, the practical weakness of the vast mass of modern pity for the poor and the oppressed is precisely that it is merely pity; the pity is pitiful, but not respectful. Men feel that the cruelty to the poor is a kind of cruelty to animals. They never feel that it is justice to equals; nay, it is treachery to comrades. This dark scientific pity, this brutal pity, has an elemental sincerity of its own; but it is entirely useless for all ends of social reform. Democracy swept Europe with the sabre when it was founded upon the Rights of Man. It has done literally nothing at all since it has been founded only upon the wrongs of man. Or, more strictly speaking, its recent failure has been due to its not admitting the existence of any rights, or wrongs, or indeed of any humanity. Evolution (the sinister enemy of revolution) does not especially deny the existence of God; what it does deny is the existence of man. And all the despair about the poor, and the cold and repugnant pity for them, has been largely due to the vague sense that they have literally relapsed into the state of the lower animals.

A writer sufficiently typical of recent revolutionism—Gorky—has called one of his books by the eerie and effective title "Creatures that once were Men." That title explains the whole failure of the Russian revolution. And the reason why the English writers, such as Dickens, did with all their limitations achieve so many of the actual things at which they aimed was that they could not possibly have put such a title upon a human hook. Dickens really helped the unfortunate in the matters to which he set himself. And the reason is that across all his books and sketches about the unfortunate might be written the common title, "Creatures that Still are Men."

There does exist, then, this strange optimistic reformer; the man whose work begins with approval and ends with earthquake. Jesus Christ was destined to found a faith which made the rich poorer and the poor rich; but even when He was going to enrich them, He began with the phrase, "Blessed are the poor." The Gissings and the Gorkys say, as an universal literary motto, "Cursed are the poor." Among a million who have faintly followed Christ in this divine contradiction, Dickens stands out especially. He said, in all his reforming utterances, "Cure poverty;" but he said in all his actual descriptions, "Blessed are the poor." He described their happiness, and men rushed to remove their sorrow. He described them as human, and men resented the insults to their humanity. It is not difficult to see why, as I said at an earlier stage of this book, Dickens's denunciations have had so much more practical an effect than the denunciations of such a man as Gissing. Both agreed that the souls of the people were in a kind of prison. But Gissing said that the prison was full of dead souls. Dickens said that the prison was full of living souls. And the fiery cavalcade of rescuers felt that they had not come too late.

Of this general fact about Dickens's descriptions of poverty there will not, I suppose, be any serious dispute. The dispute will only be about the truth of those descriptions. It is clear that whereas Gissing would say, "See how their poverty depresses the Smiths or the Browns," Dickens says, "See how little, after all, their poverty can depress the Cratchits." No one will deny that he made a special feature of the poor. We will come to the discussion of the veracity of these scenes in a moment. It is here sufficient to register in conclusion of our examination of the reforming optimist, that Dickens certainly was such an optimist, and that he made it his business to insist upon what happiness there is in the lives of the unhappy. His poor man is always a Mark Tapley, a man the optimism of whose spirit increases if anything with the pessimism of his experience. It can also be registered as a fact equally solid and quite equally demonstrable that this optimistic Dickens did effect great reforms.

The reforms in which Dickens was instrumental were indeed, from the point of view of our sweeping social panaceas, special and limited. But perhaps, for that reason especially, they afford a compact and concrete instance of the psychological paradox of which we speak. Dickens did definitely destroy—or at the very least help to destroy—certain institutions; he destroyed those institutions simply by describing them. But the crux and peculiarity of the whole matter is this, that, in a sense, it can really be said that he described these things too optimistically. In a real sense, he described

Dotheboys Hall as a better place than it is. In a real sense, he made out the workhouse as a pleasanter place than it can ever be. For the chief glory of Dickens is that he made these places interesting; and the chief infamy of England is that it has made these places dull. Dullness was the thing that Dickens's genius could never succeed in describing; his vitality was so violent that he could not introduce into his books the genuine impression even of a moment of monotony. If there is anywhere in his novels an instant of silence, we only hear more clearly the hero whispering with the heroine, the villain sharpening his dagger, or the creaking of the machinery that is to give out the god from the machine. He could splendidly describe gloomy places, but he could not describe dreary places. He could describe miserable marriages, but not monotonous marriages. It must have been genuinely entertaining to be married to Mr. Quilp. This sense of a still incessant excitement he spreads over every inch of his story, and over every dark tract of his landscape. His idea of a desolate place is a place where anything can happen, he has no idea of that desolate place where nothing can happen. This is a good thing for his soul, for the place where nothing can happen is hell. But still, it might reasonably be maintained by the modern mind that he is hampered in describing human evil and sorrow by this inability to imagine tedium, this dullness in the matter of dullness. For, after all, it is certainly true that the worst part of the lot of the unfortunate is the fact that they have long spaces in which to review the irrevocability of their doom. It is certainly true that the worst days of the oppressed man are the nine days out of ten in which he is not oppressed. This sense of sickness and sameness Dickens did certainly fail or refuse to give. When we read such a description as that excellent one—in detail—of Dotheboys Hall, we feel that, while everything else is accurate, the author does, in the words of the excellent Captain Nares in Stevenson's "Wrecker," "draw the dreariness rather mild." The boys at Dotheboys were, perhaps, less bullied, but they were certainly more bored. For, indeed, how could anyone be bored with the society of so sumptuous a creature as Mr. Squeers? Who would not put up with a few illogical floggings in order to enjoy the conversation of a man who could say, "She's a rum 'un is Natur'. . . . Natur' is more easier conceived than described." The same principle applies to the workhouse in "Oliver Twist." We feel vaguely that neither Oliver nor anyone else could be entirely unhappy in the presence of the purple personality of Mr. Bumble. The one thing he did not describe in any of the abuses he denounced was the soul-destroying potency of routine. He made out the bad school, the bad parochial system, the bad debtor's prison as very much jollier and more exciting than they may really have been. In a sense, then, he flattered them; but he destroyed them with the flattery. By making Mrs. Gamp delightful he made her impossible. He gave every one an interest in Mr. Bumble's existence; and by the same act gave every one an interest in his destruction. It would be difficult to find a stronger instance of the utility and energy of the method which we have, for the sake of argument, called the method of the optimistic reformer. As long as low Yorkshire schools were entirely colourless and dreary, they continued quietly tolerated by the public and quietly intolerable to the victims. So long as Squeers was dull as well as cruel he was permitted; the moment he became amusing as well as cruel he was destroyed. As long as Bumble was merely inhuman he was allowed. When he became human, humanity wiped him right out. For in order to do these great acts of justice we must always realise not only the humanity of the oppressed, but even the humanity of the oppressor. The satirist had, in a sense, to create the images in the mind before, as an iconoclast, he could destroy them. Dickens had to make Squeers live before be could make him die.

In connection with the accusation of vulgar optimism, which I have taken as a text for this chapter, there is another somewhat odd thing to notice. Nobody in the world was ever less optimistic than Dickens in his treatment of evil or the evil man. When I say optimist in this matter I mean optimism, in the modern sense, of an attempt to whitewash evil. Nobody ever made less attempt to whitewash evil than Dickens. Nobody black was ever less white than Dickens's black. He painted his villains and lost characters more black than they really are. He crowds his stories with a kind of villain rare in modern fiction—the villain really without any "redeeming point." There is no redeeming point in Squeers, or in Monks, or in Ralph Nickleby, or in Bill Sikes, or in Quilp, or in Brass, or in Mr. Chester, or in Mr. Pecksniff, or in Jonas Chuzzlewit, or in Carker, or in Uriah Heep, or in Blandois, or in a hundred more. So far as the balance of good and evil in human characters is concerned, Dickens certainly could not be called a vulgar optimist. His emphasis on evil was melodramatic. He might be called a vulgar pessimist.

Some will dismiss this lurid villainy as a detail of his artificial romance. I am not inclined to do so. He inherited, undoubtedly, this unqualified villain as he inherited so many other things, from the whole history of European literature. But he breathed into the blackguard a peculiar and vigorous life of his own. He did not show any tendency to modify his black-guardism in accordance with the increasing considerateness of the age; he did not seem to wish to make his villain less villainous; he did not wish to imitate the analysis of George Eliot, or the reverent scepticism of Thackeray. And all this works back, I think, to a real thing in him, that he wished to have an obstreperous and incalculable enemy. He wished to keep alive the idea of combat, which means, of necessity, a combat against something individual and alive. I do not know whether, in the kindly rationalism of his epoch, he kept any belief in a personal devil in his theology, but he certainly created a personal devil in every one of his books.

A good example of my meaning can be found, for instance, in such a character as Quilp. Dickens may, for all I know, have had originally some idea of describing Quilp as the bitter and unhappy cripple, a deformity whose mind is stunted along with his body. But if he had such an idea, he soon abandoned it. Quilp is not in the least unhappy. His whole picturesqueness consists in the fact that he has a kind of hellish happiness, an atrocious hilarity that makes him go bounding about like an indiarubber ball. Quilp is not in the least bitter; he has an unaffected gaiety, an expansiveness, an universality. He desires to hurt people in the same hearty way that a good-natured man desires to help them. He likes to poison people with the same kind of clamorous camaraderie with which an honest man likes to stand them drink. Quilp is not in the least stunted in mind; he is not in reality even stunted in body—his body, that is, does not in any way fall short of what he wants it to do. His smallness gives him rather the promptitude of a bird or the precipitance of a bullet. In a word, Quilp is precisely the devil of the Middle Ages; he belongs to that amazingly healthy period when even lost spirits were hilarious.

This heartiness and vivacity in the villains of Dickens is worthy of note because it is directly connected with his own cheerfulness. This is a truth little understood in our time, but it is a very essential one. If optimism means a general approval, it is certainly true that the more a man becomes an optimist the more he becomes a melancholy man. If he manages to praise everything, his praise will develop an alarming resemblance to a polite boredom. He will say that the marsh is as good as the garden; he will mean that the garden is as dull as the marsh. He may force himself to say that emptiness is good, but he will hardly prevent himself from asking what is the good of such good. This optimism does exist—this optimism which is more hopeless than pessimism—this optimism which is the very heart of hell.

Against such an aching vacuum of joyless approval there is only one antidote—a sudden and pugnacious belief in positive evil. This world can be made beautiful again by beholding it as a battlefield. When we have defined and isolated the evil thing, the colours come back into everything else. When evil things have become evil, good things, in a blazing apocalypse, become good. There are some men who are dreary because they do not believe in God; but there are many others who are dreary because they do not believe in the devil. The grass grows green again when we believe in the devil, the roses grow red again when we believe in the devil.

No man was more filled with the sense of this bellicose basis of all cheerfulness than Dickens. He knew very well the essential truth, that the true optimist can only continue an optimist so long as he is discontented. For the full value of this life can only be got by fighting; the violent take it by storm. And if we have accepted everything, we have missed something—war. This life of ours is a very enjoyable fight, but a very miserable truce. And it appears strange to me that so few critics of Dickens or of other romantic writers have noticed this philosophical meaning in the undiluted villain. The villain is not in the story to be a character; he is there to be a danger—a ceaseless, ruthless, and uncompromising menace, like that of wild beasts or the sea. For the full satisfaction of the sense of combat, which everywhere and always involves a sense of equality, it is necessary to make the evil thing a man; but it is not always necessary, it is not even always artistic, to make him a mixed and probable man. In any tale, the tone of which is at all symbolic, he may quite legitimately be made an aboriginal and infernal energy. He must be a man only in the sense that he must have a wit and will to be matched with the wit and will of the man chiefly fighting. The evil may be inhuman, but it must not be impersonal, which is almost exactly the position occupied by Satan in the theological scheme.

But when all is said, as I have remarked before, the chief fountain in Dickens of what I have called cheerfulness, and some prefer to call optimism, is something deeper than a verbal philosophy. It is, after all, an incomparable hunger and pleasure for the vitality and the variety, for the infinite eccentricity of existence. And this word "eccentricity" brings us, perhaps, nearer to the matter than any other. It is, perhaps, the strongest mark of the divinity of man that he talks of this world as "a strange world," though he has seen no other. We feel that all there is is eccentric, though we do not know what is the centre. This sentiment of the grotesqueness of the universe ran through Dickens's brain and body like the mad blood of the elves. He saw all his streets in fantastic perspectives, he saw all his cockney villas as top heavy and wild, he saw every man's nose twice as big as it was, and very man's eyes like saucers. And this was the basis of his gaiety—the only real basis of any philosophical gaiety. This world is not to be justified as it is justified by the mechanical optimists; it is not to be justified as the best of all possible worlds. Its merit is not that it is orderly and explicable; its merit is that it is wild and utterly unexplained. Its merit is precisely that none of us could have conceived such a thing, that we should have rejected the bare idea of it as miracle and unreason. It is the best of all impossible worlds.

—G.K. Chesterton, "On the Alleged Optimism of Dickens," *Charles Dickens*, 1906

George Santayana (1921)

George Santayana was an influential American philosopher and man of letters, best known for the ubiquitous aphorism "Those who cannot remember the past are condemned to repeat it." Like G.K. Chesterton, Santayana is interested in redeeming Dickens's moral vision; both writers emphasize that Dickens not only "put the distinction between good and evil in the right place," but further "that he felt this distinction intensely." Students discussing Dickens's moral vision should perhaps start with this essay and Chesterton's "On the Alleged Optimism of Dickens." What is perhaps surprising about this ostensibly moral argument is the way it rehabilitates Dickens's comedy and psychology.

Santayana sees in Dickens's sympathy the virtual apotheosis of Christian charity, albeit drained of its explicitly religious content. From the philosopher's point of view, the novelist "had no *ideas* on any subject," only sympathy for the lived experience of humanity, and a hatred for any institution that impeded or overshadowed that experience. Even Christmas becomes "a feast of overflowing simple kindness and good cheer" rather than "the celebration of a metaphysical misery." As a result, he suggests, Dickens is one of the few moral writers able to overcome the moralist's curse: most moralists "do not wish mankind to be happy in its own way, but in theirs." Instead, what we find in Dickens is simply "love of the good of others."

What Santayana opens up here is a new perspective on the so-called grotesquerie, exaggeration, or caricature in Dickens. George Henry Lewes had said that Dickens's most famous characters, such as Wilkins Micawber, Sarah Gamp, or Sam Weller, are masks only, and not people. Santayana takes the exact opposite approach, noting that our everyday selves are already masks, behind which we do nothing but hide what we really want or feel. If caricature is what you want, "the world is a perpetual caricature of itself," forever distorting some authentic emotion in order to bring it into accord with propriety and convention. High-minded people pretend that there are not such individuals as Dickens's creations in the world, but "there *are* such people; we are such people ourselves." George Henry Lewes had been surprised that we seem to remember in reading Dickens things that have never existed in the world. Santayana observes that what we remember is our own stifled impulse, and we are able, through Dickens's comedy, to survive the tension between what we are and what we are required to be. Taken together, the defense of Dickens's psychology and craft offered by Chesterton, Santayana, Meynell, and Swinburne makes a natural contrast to such contemporaries as Bagehot, Harrison, Lewes, and George Eliot.

If Christendom should lose everything that is now in the melting-pot, human life would still remain amiable and quite adequately human. I draw this comforting assurance from the pages of Dickens. Who could not be happy in his world? Yet there is nothing essential to it which the most destructive revolution would be able to destroy. People would still be as different, as absurd, and as charming as are his characters; the springs of kindness and folly in their lives would not be dried up. Indeed, there is much in Dickens which communism, if it came, would only emphasise and render universal. Those schools, those poorhouses, those prisons, with those surviving shreds of family life in them, show us what in the coming age (with some sanitary improvements) would be the nursery and home of everybody. Everybody would be a waif, like Oliver Twist, like Smike, like Pip, and like David Copperfield; and amongst the agents and underlings of social government, to whom all these waifs would be entrusted, there would surely be a goodly sprinkling of Pecksniffs, Squeers's, and Fangs; whilst the Fagins would be everywhere commissioners of the people. Nor would there fail to be, in high places and in low, the occasional sparkle of some Pickwick or Cherryble Brothers or Sam Weller or Mark Tapley; and the voluble Flora Finchings would be everywhere in evidence, and the strong-minded Betsey Trotwoods in office. There would also be, among the inefficient, many a Dora and Agnes and Little Emily—with her charm but without her tragedy, since this is one of the things which the promised social reform would happily render impossible; I mean, by removing all the disgrace of it. The only element in the world of Dickens which would become obsolete would be the setting, the atmosphere of material instrumentalities and arrangements, as travelling by coach is obsolete; but travelling by rail, by motor, or by airship will emotionally be much the same thing. It is worth noting how such instrumentalities, which absorb modern life, are admired and enjoyed by Dickens, as they were by Homer. The poets ought not to be afraid of them; they exercise the mind congenially, and can be played with joyfully. Consider the black ships and the chariots of Homer, the coaches and river-boats of Dickens, and the aeroplanes of to-day; to what would an unspoiled young mind turn with more interest? Dickens tells us little of English sports, but he shares the sporting nature of the Englishman, to whom the whole material world is a playing-field, the scene giving ample scope to his love of action, legality, and pleasant achievement. His art is to sport according to the rules of the game, and to do things for the sake of doing them, rather than for any ulterior motive.

It is remarkable, in spite of his ardent simplicity and openness of heart, how insensible Dickens was to the greater themes of the human imagination—religion, science, politics, art. He was a waif himself, and utterly disinherited. For example, the terrible heritage of contentious religions which fills the world seems not to exist for him. In this matter he was like a sensitive child, with a most religious disposition, but no religious ideas. Perhaps, properly speaking, he had no *ideas* on any subject; what he had was a vast sympathetic participation in the daily life of mankind; and what he saw of ancient institutions made him hate them, as needless sources of oppression, misery, selfishness, and rancour. His one political passion was philanthropy, genuine but felt only on its negative, reforming side; of positive utopias, or enthusiasms we hear nothing. The political background of Christendom is only, so to speak, an old faded back-drop for his stage; a castle, a frigate, a gallows, and a large female angel with white wings standing above an orphan by an open grave—a decoration which has to serve for all the melodramas in his theatre, intellectually so provincial and poor. Common life as it is lived was varied and lovable enough for Dickens, if only the pests and cruelties could be removed from it. Suffering wounded him, but not vulgarity; whatever pleased his senses and whatever shocked them filled his mind alike with romantic wonder, with the endless delight of observation. Vulgarity—and what can we relish, if we recoil at vulgarity?—was innocent and amusing; in fact, for the humourist, it was the spice of life. There was more piety in being human than in being pious. In reviving Christmas, Dickens transformed it from the celebration of a metaphysical mystery into a feast of overflowing simple kindness and good cheer; the church bells were still there—in the orchestra; and the angels of Bethlehem were still there—painted on the back-curtain. Churches, in his novels, are vague, desolate places where one has ghastly experiences, and where only the pew-opener is human; and such religious and political conflicts as he depicts in *Barnaby Rudge* and in *A Tale of Two Cities* are street brawls and prison scenes and conspiracies in taverns, without any indication of the contrasts in mind or interests between the opposed parties. Nor had Dickens any lively sense for fine art, classical tradition, science, or even the manners and feelings of the upper classes in his own time and country: in his novels we may almost say there is no army, no navy, no church, no sport, no distant travel, no daring adventure, no feeling for the watery wastes and the motley nations of the planet, and—luckily, with his notion of them—no lords and ladies. Even love of the traditional sort is hardly in Dickens's sphere—I mean the soldierly passion in which a rather rakish gallantry was sobered by devotion, and loyalty rested on pride. In Dickens love is sentimental or benevolent or merry or sneaking or canine; in his last book he was going to describe a love that was passionate and criminal; but love for him was never chivalrous, never poetical. What he paints most tragically is a quasi-paternal devotion in the old to the young, the love of Mr. Peggotty for Little Emily, or of Solomon Gills for Walter Gay. A series of shabby little adventures, such as might absorb the interest of an average youth, were romantic enough for Dickens.

I say he was disinherited, but he inherited the most terrible negations. Religion lay on him like the weight of the atmosphere, sixteen pounds to the square inch, yet never noticed nor mentioned. He lived and wrote in the shadow of the most awful prohibitions. Hearts petrified by legality and falsified by worldliness offered, indeed, a good subject for a novelist, and Dickens availed himself of it to the extent of always contrasting natural goodness and happiness with whatever is morose; but his morose people were wicked, not virtuous in their own way; so that the protest of his temperament against his environment never took a radical form nor went back to first principles. He needed to feel, in his writing, that he was carrying the sympathies of every man with him. In him conscience was single, and he could not conceive how it could ever be divided in other men. He denounced scandals without exposing shams, and conformed willingly and scrupulously to the proprieties. Lady Dedlock's secret, for instance, he treats as if it were the sin of Adam, remote, mysterious, inexpiable. Mrs. Dombey is not allowed to deceive her husband except by pretending to deceive him. The seduction of Little Emily is left out altogether, with the whole character of Steerforth, the development of which would have been so important in the moral experience of David Copperfield himself. But it is not public prejudice alone that plays the censor over Dickens's art; his own kindness and even weakness of heart act sometimes as marplots. The character of Miss Mowcher, for example, so brilliantly introduced, was evidently intended to be shady, and to play a very important part in the story; but its original in real life, which was recognised, had to be conciliated, and the sequel was omitted and patched up with an apology—itself admirable—for the poor dwarf. Such a sacrifice does honour to Dickens's heart; but artists should meditate on their works in time, and it is easy to remove any too great likeness in a portrait by a few touches making it more consistent than real people are apt to be; and in this case, if the little creature had been really guilty, how much more subtle and tragic her apology for herself might have been, like that of the bastard Edmund in *King Lear*! So, too, in *Dombey and Son*, Dickens could not bear to let Walter Gay turn out badly, as he had been meant to do, and to break his uncle's heart as well as the heroine's; he was accordingly transformed into a stage hero miraculously saved from shipwreck, and Florence was not allowed to reward the admirable Toots, as she should have done, with her trembling hand. But Dickens was no free artist; he had more genius than taste, a warm fancy not aided by a thorough understanding of complex characters. He worked under pressure, for money and applause, and often had to cheapen in execution what his inspiration had so vividly conceived.

What, then, is there left, if Dickens has all these limitations? In our romantic disgust we might be tempted to say, Nothing. But in fact almost everything is left, almost everything that counts in the daily life of mankind, or that by its presence or absence can determine whether life shall be worth living or not; because a simple good life is worth living, and an elaborate bad life is not. There remain in the first place eating and drinking; relished not bestially, but humanly, jovially, as the sane and exhilarating basis for everything else. This is a sound English beginning; but the immediate sequel, as the England of that day presented it to Dickens, is no less delightful. There is the ruddy glow of the hearth; the sparkle of glasses and brasses and well-scrubbed pewter; the savoury fumes of the hot punch, after the tingle of the wintry air; the coaching-scenes, the motley figures and absurd incidents of travel; the changing sights and joys of the road. And then, to balance this, the traffic of ports and cities, the hubbub of crowded streets, the luxury of shop-windows and of palaces not to be entered; the procession of the passers-by, shabby or ludicrously genteel; the dingy look and musty smell of their lodgings; the labyrinth of back-alleys, courts, and mews, with their crying children, and scolding old women, and listless, half-drunken loiterers. These sights, like fables, have a sort of moral in them to which Dickens was very sensitive; the important airs of nobodies on great occasions, the sadness and preoccupation of the great as they hasten by in their mourning or on their pressing affairs; the sadly comic characters of the tavern; the diligence of shop-keepers, like squirrels turning in their cages; the children peeping out everywhere like grass in an untrodden street; the charm of humble things, the nobleness of humble people, the horror of crime, the ghastliness of vice, the deft hand and shining face of virtue passing through the midst of it all; and finally a fresh wind of indifference and change blowing across our troubles and clearing the most lurid sky.

I do not know whether it was Christian charity or naturalistic insight, or a mixture of both (for they are closely akin) that attracted Dickens particularly to the deformed, the half-witted, the abandoned, or those impeded or misunderstood by virtue of some singular inner consecration. The visible moral of these things, when brutal prejudice does not blind us to it, comes very near to true philosophy; one turn of the screw, one flash of reflection, and we have understood nature and human morality and the relation between them.

In his love of roads and wayfarers, of river-ports and wharves and the idle or sinister figures that lounge about them, Dickens was like Walt Whitman; and I think a second Dickens may any day appear in America, when it is possible in that land of hurry to reach the same degree of saturation, the same unquestioning pleasure in the familiar facts. The spirit of Dickens would be better able to do justice to America than was that of Walt Whitman; because America, although it may seem nothing but a noisy nebula to the impressionist, is not a nebula but a concourse of very distinct individual bodies, natural and social, each with its definite interest and story. Walt Whitman had a sort of transcendental philosophy which swallowed the universe whole, supposing there was a universal spirit in things identical with the absolute spirit that observed them; but Dickens was innocent of any such clap-trap, and remained a true spirit in his own person. Kindly and clear-sighted, but self-identical and unequivocally human, he glided through the slums like one of his own little heroes, uncontaminated by their squalor and confusion, courageous and firm in his clear allegiances amid the flux of things, a pale angel at the Carnival, his heart aflame, his voice always flute-like in its tenderness and warning. This is the true relation of spirit to existence, not the other which confuses them; for this earth (I cannot speak for the universe at large) has no spirit of its own, but brings forth spirits only at certain points, in the hearts and brains of frail living creatures, who like insects flit through it, buzzing and gathering what sweets they can; and it is the spaces they traverse in this career, charged with their own moral burden, that they can report on or describe, not things rolling on to infinity in their vain tides. To be hypnotised by that flood would be a heathen idolatry. Accordingly Walt Whitman, in his comprehensive democratic vistas, could never see the trees for the wood, and remained incapable, for all his diffuse love of the human herd, of ever painting a character or telling a story; the very things in which Dickens was a master. It is this life of the individual, as it may be lived in a given nation, that determines the whole value of that nation to the poet, to the moralist, and to the judicious historian. But for the excellence of the typical single life, no nation deserves to be remembered more than the sands of the sea; and America will not be a success, if every American is a failure.

Dickens entered the theatre of this world by the stage door; the shabby little adventures of the actors in their private capacity replace for him the mock tragedies which they enact before a dreaming public. Mediocrity of circumstances and mediocrity of soul forever return to the centre of his stage; a more wretched or a grander existence is sometimes broached, but the pendulum soon swings back, and we return, with the relief with which we put on our slippers after the most romantic excursion, to a golden mediocrity—to mutton and beer, and to love and babies in a suburban villa with one frowsy maid. Dickens is the poet of those acres of yellow brick streets which the traveller sees from the railway viaducts as he approaches London; they need a poet, and they deserve one, since a complete human life may very well be lived there. Their little excitements and sorrows, their hopes and humours are like those of the Wooden Midshipman in *Dombey and Son*; but the sea is not far off, and the sky—Dickens never forgets it—is above all those brief troubles. He had a sentiment in the presence of this vast flatness of human fates, in spite of their individual pungency, which I think might well be the dominant sentiment of mankind in the future; a sense of happy freedom in littleness, an open-eyed reverence and religion without words. This universal human anonymity is like a sea, an infinitive democratic desert, chock-full and yet the very image of emptiness, with nothing in it for the mind, except, as the Moslems say, the presence of Allah. Awe is the counterpart of humility—and this is perhaps religion enough. The atom in the universal vortex ought to be humble; he ought to see that, materially, he doesn't much matter, and that morally his loves are merely his own, without authority over the universe. He can admit without obloquy that he is what he is; and he can rejoice in his own being, and in that of all other things in so far as he can share it sympathetically. The apportionment of existence and of fortune is in Other Hands; his own portion is contentment, vision, love, and laughter.

Having humility, that most liberating of sentiments, having a true vision of human existence and joy in that vision, Dickens had in a superlative degree the gift of humour, of mimicry, of unrestrained farce. He was the perfect comedian. When people say Dickens exaggerates, it seems to me they can have no eyes and no ears. They probably have only *notions* of what things and people are; they accept them conventionally, at their diplomatic value. Their minds run on in the region of discourse, where there are masks only and no faces, ideas and no facts; they have little sense for those living grimaces that play from moment to moment upon the countenance of the world. The world is a perpetual caricature of itself; at every moment it is the mockery and the contradiction of what it is pretending to be. But as it nevertheless intends all the time to be something different and highly dignified, at the next moment it correct and checks and tries to cover up the absurd thing it was; so that a conventional world, a world of masks, is superimposed on the reality, and passes in every sphere of human interest for the reality itself. Humour is the perception of this illusion, the fact allowed to pierce here and there through the convention, whilst the convention continues to be maintained, as if we had not observed its absurdity. Pure comedy is more radical, cruder, in a certain sense less human; because comedy throws the convention over altogether, revels for a moment in the fact, and brutally says to the notions of mankind, as if it slapped them in the face, There, take that! That's what you really are! At this the polite world pretends to laugh, not tolerantly as it does at humour, but a little angrily. It does not like to see itself by chance in the glass, without having had time to compose its features for demure self-contemplation. "What a bad mirror," it exclaims; "it must be concave or convex; for surely I never looked like that. Mere caricature, farce, and horse play. Dickens exaggerates; *I* never was so sentimental as that; *I* never saw anything so dreadful; *I* don't believe there were ever any people like Quilp, or Squeers, or Serjeant Buzfuz." But the polite world is lying; there *are* such people; we are such people ourselves in our true moments, in our veritable impulses; but we are careful to stifle and to hide those moments from ourselves and from the world; to purse and pucker ourselves into the mask of our conventional personality; and so simpering, we profess that it is very coarse and inartistic of Dickens to undo our life's work for us in an instant, and remind us of what we are. And as to other people, though we may allow that considered superficially they are often absurd, we do not wish to dwell on their eccentricities, nor to mimic them. On the contrary, it is good manners to look away quickly, to suppress a smile, and to say to ourselves that the ludicrous figure in the street is not at all comic, but a dull ordinary Christian, and that it is foolish to give any importance to the fact that its hat has blown off, that it has slipped on an orange-peel and unintentionally sat on the pavement, that it has a pimple on its nose, that its one tooth projects over its lower lip, that it is angry with things in general, and that it is looking everywhere for the penny which it holds tightly in its hand. That may fairly represent the moral condition of most of us at most times; but we do not want to think of it; we do not want to see; we gloss the fact over; we console ourselves before we are grieved, and reassert our composure before we have laughed. We are afraid, ashamed, anxious to be spared. What displeases us in Dickens is that he does not spare us; he mimics things to the full; he dilates and exhausts and repeats; he wallows. He is too intent on the passing experience to look over his shoulder, and consider whether we have not already understood, and had enough. He is not thinking of us; he is obeying the impulse of the passion, the person, or the story he is enacting. This faculty, which renders him a consummate comedian, is just what alienated from him a later generation in which people of taste were aesthetes and virtuous people were higher snobs; they wanted a mincing art, and he gave them copious improvisation, they wanted analysis and development, and he gave them absolute comedy. I must confess, though the fault is mine and not his, that sometimes his absoluteness is too much for me. When I come to the death of Little Nell, or to What the Waves were always Saying, or even to the incorrigible perversities of the pretty Dora, I skip. I can't take my liquor neat in such draughts, and my inner man says to Dickens, Please don't. But then I am a coward in so many ways! There are so many things in this world that I skip, as I skip the undiluted Dickens! When I reach Dover on a rough day, I wait there until the Channel is smoother; am I not travelling for pleasure? But my prudence does not blind me to the admirable virtue of the sailors that cross in all weathers, nor even to the automatic determination of the seasick ladies, who might so easily have followed my example, if they were not the slaves of their railway tickets and of their labelled luggage. They are loyal to their tour, and I to my philosophy. Yet as wrapped in my great-coat and sure of a good dinner, I pace the windy pier and soliloquise, I feel the superiority of the bluff tar, glad of breeze, stretching a firm arm to the unsteady passenger, and watching with a masterful thrill of emotion the home cliffs receding and the foreign coasts ahead. It is only courage (which Dickens had without knowing it) and universal kindness (which he knew he had) that are requisite to nerve us for a true vision of this world. And as some of us are cowards about crossing the Channel, and others about "crossing the bar," so almost everybody is a coward about his own humanity. We do not consent to be absurd, though absurd we are. We have no fundamental humility. We do not wish the moments of our lives to be caught by a quick eye in their grotesque initiative, and to be pilloried in this way before our own eyes. For that reason we don't like Dickens, and don't like comedy, and don't like the truth. Dickens could don the comic mask with innocent courage; he could wear it with a grace, ease, and irresistible vivacity seldom given to men. We must go back for anything like it to the very greatest comic poets, to Shakespeare or to Aristophanes. Who else, for instance, could have penned this:

> "It was all Mrs. Bumble. She *would* do it," urged Mr. Bumble; first looking round to ascertain that his partner had left the room.
> "That is no excuse," replied Mr. Brownlow. "You were present on the occasion of the destruction of these trinkets, and indeed are the more guilty of the two, in the eye of the law; for the law supposes that your wife acts under your direction."
> "If the law supposes that," said Mr. Bumble, squeezing his hat emphatically in both hands, "the law is a ass, a idiot. If that's the eye of the law, the law is a bachelor; and the worse I wish the law is, that his eye may be opened by experience—by experience."
> Laying great stress on the repetition of these two words, Mr. Bumble fixed his hat on very tight, and putting his hands in his pockets, followed his helpmate downstairs.

This is high comedy; the irresistible, absurd, intense dream of the old fool, personifying the law in order to convince and to punish it. I can understand that this sort of thing should not be common in English literature, nor much relished; because pure comedy is scornful, merciless, devastating, holding no door open to anything beyond. Cultivated English feeling winces at this brutality, although the common people love it in clowns and in puppet shows; and I think they are right. Dickens, who surely was tender enough, had so irresistible a comic genius that it carried him beyond the gentle humour which most Englishmen possess to the absolute grotesque reality. Squeers, for instance, when he sips the wretched dilution which he has prepared for his starved and shivering little pupils, smacks his lips and cries: "Here's richness!" It is savage comedy; humour would come in if we understood (what Dickens does not tell us) that the little creatures were duly impressed and thought the thin liquid truly delicious. I suspect that English sensibility prefers the humour and wit of Hamlet to the pure comedy of Falstaff; and that even in Aristophanes it seeks consolation in the lyrical poetry for the flaying of human life in the comedy itself. Tastes are free; but we should not deny that in merciless and rollicking comedy life is caught in the act. The most grotesque creatures of Dickens are not exaggerations or mockeries of something other than themselves; they arise because nature generates them, like toadstools; they exist because they can't help it, as we all do. The fact that these perfectly self-justified beings are absurd appears only by comparison, and from outside; circumstances, or the expectations of other people, make them ridiculous and force them to contradict themselves; but in nature it is no crime to be exceptional. Often, but for the savagery of the average man, it would not even be a misfortune. The sleepy fat boy in *Pickwick* looks foolish; but in himself he is no more foolish, nor less solidly self-justified, than a pumpkin lying on the ground. Toots seems ridiculous; and we laugh heartily at his incoherence, his beautiful waistcoats, and his extreme modesty; but when did anybody more obviously grow into what he is because he couldn't grow otherwise? So with Mr. Pickwick, and Sam Weller, and Mrs. Gamp, and Micawber, and all the rest of this wonderful gallery; they are ridiculous only by accident, and in a context in which they never intended to appear. If Oedipus and Lear and Cleopatra do not seem ridiculous, it is only because tragic reflection has taken them out of the context in which, in real life, they would have figured. If we saw them as facts, and not as emanations of a poet's dream, we should laugh at them till doomsday; what grotesque presumption, what silly whims, what mad contradiction of the simplest realities! Yet we should not laugh at them without feeling how real their griefs were; as real and terrible as the griefs of children and of dreams. But facts, however serious inwardly, are always absurd outwardly; and the just critic of life sees both truths at once, as Cervantes did in *Don Quixote*. A pompous idealist who does not see the ridiculous in all things is the dupe of his sympathy and abstraction; and a clown, who does not see that these ridiculous creatures are living quite in earnest, is the dupe of his egotism. Dickens saw the absurdity, and understood the life; I think he was a good philosopher.

It is usual to compare Dickens with Thackeray, which is like comparing the grape with the gooseberry; there are obvious points of resemblance, and the gooseberry has some superior qualities of its own; but you can't make red wine of it. The wine of Dickens is of the richest, the purest, the sweetest, the most fortifying to the blood; there is distilled in it, with the perfection of comedy, the perfection of morals. I do not mean, of course, that Dickens appreciated all the values that human life has or might have; that is beyond any man. Even the greatest philosophers, such as Aristotle, have not always much imagination to conceive forms of happiness or folly other than those which their age or their temperament reveals to them; their insight runs only to discovering the *principle* of happiness, that it is spontaneous life of any sort harmonised with circumstances. The sympathies and imagination of Dickens, vivid in their sphere, were no less limited in range; and of course it was not his business to find philosophic formulas; nevertheless I call his the perfection of morals for two reasons: that he put the distinction between good and evil in the right place, and that he felt this distinction intensely. A moralist might have excellent judgment, he might see what sort of life is spontaneous in a given being and how far it may be harmonised with circumstances, yet his heart might remain cold, he might not suffer nor rejoice with the suffering or joy he foresaw. Humanitarians like Bentham and Mill, who talked about the greatest happiness of the greatest number, might conceivably be moral prigs in their own persons, and they might have been chilled to the bone in their theoretic love of mankind, if they had had the wit to imagine in what, as a matter of fact, the majority would place their happiness. Even if their theory had been correct (which I think it was in intention, though not in statement) they would then not have been perfect moralists, because their maxims would not have expressed their hearts. In expressing their hearts, they ought to have embraced one of those forms of "idealism" by which men fortify themselves in their bitter passions or in their helpless commitments; for they do not wish mankind to be happy in its own way, but in theirs. Dickens was not one of those moralists who summon every man to do himself the greatest violence so that he may not offend them, nor defeat their ideals. Love of the good of others is something that shines in every page of Dickens with a truly celestial splendour. How entirely limpid is his sympathy with life—a sympathy uncontaminated by dogma or pedantry or snobbery or bias of any kind! How generous is this keen, light spirit, how pure this open heart! And yet, in spite of this extreme sensibility, not the least wobbling; no deviation from a just severity of judgment, from an uncompromising distinction between white and black. And this happens as it ought to happen; sympathy is not checked by a flatly contrary prejudice or commandment, by some categorical imperative irrelevant to human nature; the check, like the cheer, comes by tracing the course of spontaneous impulse amid circumstances that inexorably lead it to success or to failure. There is a bed to this stream, freely as the water may flow; when it comes to this precipice it must leap, when it runs over these pebbles it must sing, and when it spreads into that marsh it must become livid and malarial. The very sympathy with human impulse quickens in Dickens the sense of danger; his very joy in joy makes him stern to what kills it. How admirably drawn are his surly villains! No rhetorical vilification of them, as in a sermon; no exaggeration of their qualms or fears; rather a sense of how obvious and human all their courses seem from their own point of view; and yet no sentimental apology for them, no romantic worship of rebels in their madness or crime. The pity of it, the waste of it all, are seen not by a second vision but by the same original vision which revealed the lure and the drift of the passion. Vice is a monster here of such sorry mien, that the longer we see it the more we deplore it; that other sort of vice which Pope found so seductive was perhaps only some innocent impulse artificially suppressed, and called a vice because it broke out inconveniently and displeased the company. True vice is human nature strangled by the suicide of attempting the impossible. Those so self-justified villains of Dickens never elude their fates. Bill Sikes is not let off, neither is Nancy; the oddly benevolent Magwitch does not escape from the net, nor does the unfortunate young Richard Carstone, victim of the Circumlocution Office. The horror and ugliness of their fall are rendered with the hand of a master; we see here, as in the world, that in spite of the romanticists it is not virtue to rush enthusiastically along any road. I think Dickens is one of the best friends mankind has ever had. He has held the mirror up to nature, and of its reflected fragments has composed a fresh world, where the men and women differ from real people only in that they live in a literary medium, so that all ages and places may know them. And they are worth knowing, just as one's neighbours are, for their picturesque characters and their pathetic fates. Their names should be in every child's mouth; they ought to be adopted members of every household. Their stories cause the merriest and the sweetest chimes to ring in the fancy, without confusing our moral judgment or alienating our interest from the motley commonplaces of daily life. In every English-speaking home, in the four quarters of the globe, parents and children will do well to read Dickens aloud of a winter's evening; they will love winter, and one another, and God the better for it. What a wreath that will be of ever-fresh holly, thick with bright berries, to hang to this poet's memory—the very crown he would have chosen.

—George Santayana, "Dickens," (1921)

WORKS

THE PICKWICK PAPERS

John Wilson Croker
"*The Pickwick Papers*" (1837)

John Wilson Croker was a politician, scholar, and critic now infamous for the review that "killed Keats." The brief excerpt here attests to the Pickwick craze that swept London, launching a protomodern version of celebrity.

The popularity of this writer is one of the most remarkable literary phenomena of recent times, for it has been fairly earned without resorting to any of the means by which most other writers have succeeded in attracting the attention of their contemporaries. He has flattered no popular prejudice and profited by no passing folly: he has attempted no caricature sketches of the manners or conversation of the aristocracy; and there are very few political or personal allusions in his works. Moreover, his class of subjects are such as to expose him at the outset to the fatal objection of vulgarity; and, with the exception of occasional extracts in the newspapers, he received little or no assistance from the press. Yet, in less than six months from the appearance of the first number of the *Pickwick Papers,* the whole reading public were talking about them—the names of Winkle, Wardell, Weller, Snodgrass, Dodson and Fogg, had become familiar in our mouths as household terms; and Mr. Dickens was the grand object of interest to the whole tribe of 'Leo-hunters,' male and female, of the metropolis. Nay, Pickwick chintzes figured in linendrapers' windows, and Weller corduroys in breeches-makers' advertisements; Boz cabs might be seen rattling through the streets, and the portrait of the author of *Pelham* or *Crichton* was scraped down or pasted over to make room for that of the new popular favourite in the omnibusses. This is only to be accounted for on the supposition that a fresh vein of humour had been opened; that a new and decidedly original genius had sprung up.

—John Wilson Croker, *"The Pickwick Papers,"*
Quarterly Review, December 1837, p. 484

Richard Grant White
"The Styles of Dickens and Disraeli" (1870)

Richard Grant White was an American Shakespearean and anglophile. White's judgment of Dickens is characteristic of a tendency in late Victorian culture to value the apparently improvisational *Pickwick* over what some readers saw as Dickens's self-imitation.

It has been said that *The Pickwick Papers* was its author's best book; and, in certain respects, this judgment is sound. Humor was Mr. Dickens's great distinctive trait; and for humor, pure and simple, he produced in all his life nothing quite equal to *Pickwick*—nothing so sustained, so varied, so unstrained. He afterwards became more conscious of his humor as he wrote, and showed his consciousness. He let us see the preparation of his fun; he made points like an actor who feels that the points are expected by his audience, and also feels, and shows that he feels, that by the use of certain means he can make them. The spontaneous humor of *Pickwick* was never equalled, even by its author. He afterwards gave to too many of his humorous characters certain peculiarities of person, manner, or speech, on which he rung a limited range of changes; and this degenerated into a trick, like the giving of what in stage cant is called a gag to a comic actor, which he uses deliberately to force a laugh. This was a needless device in Mr. Dickens, whose humor seemed exhaustless.

—Richard Grant White, "The Styles of Dickens and Disraeli," *Galaxy*, August 1870, p. 258

S.C. Hall (1883)

Samuel Carter Hall, the journalist and notable art critic, is an apparent source for Seth Pecksniff in *Martin Chuzzlewit*.

I well remember my sensations of astonishment and interest when the first number of *Pickwick* was brought me, and I looked it over. Forster was with me at the time. How, on the introduction of Sam Weller, the work took the town by storm, and its author, who, only a short time before, had been an unnoticed parliamentary reporter, reached at a bound the summit of success, and became the literary lion of the day, I need not here describe.

No man since Walter Scott has so amply and efficiently supplied in fiction the intellectual need of the age; but that great man did not do a tithe of what Dickens has done to quicken its social and moral progress.

—S.C. Hall, *Retrospect of a Long Life,*
1883, p. 394

Margaret Oliphant (1892)

Author of more than two hundred books and countless more articles, Margaret Oliphant was a fiction writer and influential critic for *Blackwood's Magazine*. Her interest in *The Pickwick Papers* arises from its national character, and especially its ability to capture "the strictly English quality of fun."

The first numbers of the book—which was issued in twenty monthly parts—at once took the public fancy, laying the foundation of a popularity which has never decreased. There is perhaps no book more widely known in the English language, nor, strangely enough, many which have been received with such favour on the Continent, though it is intensely national in character. It is, indeed, an almost perfect specimen of the strictly English quality of fun—using English in its very narrowest sense as applying only to that part of her Majesty's dominions called England—which differs as greatly from the humour of Scotland and Ireland as from French wit or American extravagance. We could quote instances of more genuinely humorous scenes than that of the trial in *Pickwick,* but we cannot think of anything so irresistibly funny. It is hardly high comedy, but neither is it merely farcical; and it has the great qualities of being always good-humoured and hardly ever grotesque.

Another secret of the success of *Pickwick,* perhaps, is that it is not in the ordinary sense of the word, a novel. There is no continuous story to speak of, only a collection of amusing scenes of high average excellence, though of course containing some that are of inferior merit. Nor do we find in *Pickwick* any real delineation of character, with the exception, perhaps, of the Wellers, who are, however, as little real as they are always amusing.

—Margaret Oliphant, *The Victorian Age of English Literature,* 1892, Vol. 1, pp. 251–52

BARNABY RUDGE

Edgar Allan Poe "Charles Dickens" (1841)

Master of suspense and the macabre, inventor of the detective story, journalist, and poet, Edgar Allan Poe was also an important theorist of fiction. What is noteworthy here is his discussion of causality in plots: Poe admires Dickens's ability to create suspense, but observes that the effect would be heightened if there were no resolution, because "the anticipation must surpass the reality." Poe suggests that Dickens leaves us wanting something more—that effects seem disproportionate to their causes.

His opening chapters assure us that he has at length discovered the secret of his true strength, and that *Barnaby Rudge* will appeal principally to the *imagination*. Of this faculty we have many striking instances in the few numbers already issued. We see it where the belfry man in the lonely church at midnight, about to toll the "passing-bell," is struck with horror at hearing the solitary note of another, and awaits, aghast, a repetition of the sound. We recognise it more fully where this single note is discovered, in the morning, to have been that of an alarm pulled by the hand of one in the death-struggle with a murderer:—also in the expression of countenance which is so strikingly attributed to Mrs. Rudge—"the capacity for expressing terror"—something only dimly seen, but never absent for a moment—"the shadow of some look to which an instant of intense and most unutterable horror only could have given rise." This is a conception admirably adapted to whet curiosity in respect to the character of that event which is hinted at as forming the ground-work of the novel; and so far is well suited to the purposes of a periodical story. But this observation should not fail to be made—that the anticipation must surpass the reality; that no matter how terrific be the circumstances which, in the *denouement,* shall appear to have occasioned the expression of countenance worn habitually by Mrs. Rudge, still they will not be able to satisfy the mind of the reader. He will surely be disappointed. The skilful intimation of horror held out by the artist produces an effect which will deprive his conclusion, of all. These intimations—these dark hints of some uncertain evil—are often rhetorically praised as effective—but are only justly so praised where there is *no denouement* whatever—where the reader's imagination is left to clear up the mystery for itself—and this, we suppose, is not the design of Mr. Dickens.

But the chief points in which the ideality of this story is apparent are the creation of the hero Barnaby Rudge, and the commingling with his character, as accessory, that of the human-looking raven. Barnaby we regard as an original idea altogether, so far as novel-writing is concerned. He is peculiar, inasmuch as he is an idiot endowed with the fantastic qualities of the madman, and has been born possessed with a maniacal horror of blood—the result of some terrible spectacle seen by his mother during pregnancy. The design of Mr. Dickens is here two-fold—first that of increasing our anticipation in regard to the deed committed—exaggerating our impression of its atrocity—and, secondly, that of causing this horror of blood on the part of the idiot, to bring about, in consistence with poetical justice, the condemnation of the murderer:—for it is a murder that has been committed. We say in accordance with poetical justice—and, in fact, it will be seen hereafter that Barnaby, the idiot, is the murderer's own son. The horror of blood which he feels is the mediate result of the atrocity, since this atrocity it was which impressed the imagination of the pregnant mother; and poetical justice will therefore be well fulfilled when this horror shall urge on the son to the conviction of the father in the perpetrator of the deed.

—Edgar Allan Poe, "Charles Dickens" (1841), Essays and Reviews, ed. G.R. Thompson, 1984, pp. 218–19

THE OLD CURIOSITY SHOP

Edgar Allan Poe "Charles Dickens" (1841)

Students exploring Dickens's grotesques, caricatures, and exaggerated humor will find an important foil in Poe, who insists that Dickens is not a caricaturist. Poe makes two complementary claims: first, that by exaggeration one arrives at truth—one cannot artistically capture truth directly. Poe's second claim is that Dickens is inventing his characters, creating them as much out of his genius as any found materials, and so it is unfair to call them exaggerations.

But if the conception of this story deserves praise, its execution is beyond all—and here the subject naturally leads us from the generalisation which is the proper province of the critic, into details among which it is scarcely fitting that he should venture. . . .

When we speak in this manner of the *Old Curiosity Shop,* we speak with entire deliberation, and know quite well what it is we assert. We do not mean to say that it is perfect, as a whole—this could not well have been the case under the circumstances of its composition. But we know that, in all the higher elements which go to make up literary greatness, it is supremely excellent. We think, for instance, that the introduction of Nelly's brother (and here we address those who have read the work) is supererogatory—that the character of Quilp would have been more in keeping had he been confined to petty and grotesque acts of malice—that his death should have been made the *immediate* consequence of his attempt at revenge upon Kit; and that after matters had been put fairly in train for this poetical justice, he should not have perished by an accident inconsequential upon his villainy. We think, too, that there is an air of ultra-accident in the finally discovered relationship between Kit's master and the bachelor of the old church—that the sneering politeness put into the mouth of Quilp, with his manner of commencing a question which he wishes answered in the affirmative, with an affirmative interrogatory, instead of the ordinary negative one—are fashions borrowed from the author's own Fagin—that he has repeated himself in many other instances—that the practical tricks and love of mischief of the dwarf's boy are too nearly consonant with the traits of the master—that so much of the propensities of Swiveller as relate to his inapposite appropriation of odds and ends of verse, is stolen from the generic loafer of our fellow-townsman, Neal—and that the writer has suffered the overflowing kindness of his own bosom to mislead him in a very important point of art, when he endows so many of his *dramatis personal* with a warmth of feeling so very rare in reality. Above all, we acknowledge that the death of Nelly is excessively painful—that it leaves a most distressing oppression of spirit upon the reader—and should, therefore, have been avoided.

But when we come to speak of the excellences of the tale these defects appear really insignificant. It embodies more *originality* in every point, but in character especially, than any single work within our knowledge. There is the grandfather—a truly profound conception; the gentle and lovely Nelly—we have discoursed of her before; Quilp, with mouth like that of the panting dog—(a bold idea which the engraver has neglected to embody) with his hilarious antics, his cowardice, and his very petty and spoilt-child-like malevolence; Dick Swiveller, that prince of good-hearted, good-for-nothing, lazy, luxurious, poetical, brave, romantically generous, gallant, affectionate, and not over-and-above honest, "glorious Apollos;" the marchioness, his bride; Tom Codlin and his partner; Miss Sally Brass, that "fine fellow;" the pony that had an opinion of its own; the boy that stood upon his head; the sexton; the man at the forge; not forgetting the dancing dogs and baby Nubbles. There are other admirably drawn characters—but we note these for their remarkable originality, as well as for their wonderful keeping, and the glowing colors in which they are painted. We have heard some of them called caricatures—but the charge is grossly ill-founded. No critical principle is more firmly based in reason than that a certain amount of exaggeration is essential to the proper depicting of truth itself. We do not paint an object to be true, but to appear true to the beholder. Were we to copy nature with accuracy the object copied would seem unnatural. The columns of the Greek temples, which convey the idea of absolute proportion, are very considerably thicker just beneath the capital than at the base. We regret that we have not left ourselves space in which to examine this whole question as it deserves. We must content ourselves with saying that caricature seldom exists (unless in so gross a form as to disgust at once) where the component parts are *in keeping;* and that the laugh excited by it, in any case, is radically distinct from that induced by a properly artistical *incongruity*—the source of all mirth. Were these creations of Mr. Dickens' really caricatures they would not live in public estimation beyond the hour of their first survey. We regard them as *creations*—(that is to say as original combinations of character) only not all of the highest order, because the elements employed are not always of the highest. In the instances of Nelly, the grandfather, the Sexton, and the man of the furnace, the force of the creative intellect could scarcely have been engaged with nobler material, and the result is that these personages belong to the most august regions of the *Ideal.*

In truth, the great feature of the *Curiosity Shop* is its chaste, vigorous, and glorious *imagination*. This is the one charm, all potent, which alone would suffice to compensate for a world more of error than Mr. Dickens ever committed. It is not only seen in the conception, and general handling of the story, or in the invention of character; but it pervades every sentence of the book. We recognise its prodigious influence in every inspired word. It is this which induces the reader who is at all ideal, to pause frequently, to re-read the occasionally quaint phrases, to muse in uncontrollable delight over thoughts which, while he wonders he has never hit upon them before, he yet admits that he never has encountered. In fact it is the wand of the enchanter. . . .

Upon the whole we think the *Curiosity Shop* very much the best of the works of Mr. Dickens. It is scarcely possible to speak of it too well.

It is in all respects a tale which will secure for its author the enthusiastic admiration of every man of genius.

—Edgar Allan Poe, "Charles Dickens" (1841),
Essays and Reviews, ed. G.R. Thompson,
1984, pp. 213–17

THOMAS DE QUINCEY (1847)

Thomas De Quincey, known for his *Confessions of an English Opium-Eater* (1822), was a journalist, essayist, and critic. De Quincey mounts two different complaints about Dickens. The first is that Dickens's tendency to exaggerate provokes frustration because the exaggerations are too close to reality—it makes them seem like a mistake, rather than fun. The second charge is more serious and speaks to Dickens as a moral optimist: De Quincey suggests that Dickens fails to understand the self-lacerating rage and despair that animates true gamblers.

Whatever may be the separate beauty of Nell's position as to character and situation in relation to her grandfather, it is dreadfully marred to me by the extravagance and caricature (as so often happens in Dickens) of the gambling insanity in the old man. Dickens, like all novelists anxious only for effect, misunderstands the true impulse in obstinate incorrigible gamesters: it is not faith, unconquerable faith, in their luck; it is the very opposite principle—a despair of their own luck—rage and hatred in consequence, as at a blind enemy working in the dark, and furious desire to affront this dark malignant power; just as in the frenzy of hopeless combat you will see a man without a chance, and knowing that he does but prolong his adversary's triumph, yet still flying again with his fists at the face which he can never reach. Without love on the old man's part to Nell, hers for him would be less interesting; and *with* love of any strength, the old fool could not *but* have paused. The risk was *instant:* it ruined Nell's hopes of a breakfast; it tended to a jail. Now Alnaschar delusions take a different flight—they settle on the future. Extravagance and want of fidelity to nature and the possibilities of life are what everywhere mar Dickens to me; and these faults are fatal, because the *modes* of life amongst which these extravagances intrude are always the absolute realities of vulgarised life as it exists in plebeian ranks amongst our countrymen at this moment. Were the mode of life one more idealised or removed from our own, I might be less sensible of the insupportable extravagances.

—Thomas De Quincey, Letter to His Daughter
(September 19, 1847), cited in Alexander Hay Japp
(as "H.A. Page"), *Thomas De Quincey:*
His Life and Writings, 1877, Vol. 1, pp. 348–49

Sara Coleridge (1849)

I admire Nell in the *Old Curiosity Shop* exceedingly. No doubt the whole thing is a good deal borrowed from Wilhelm Meister. But little Nell is a far purer, lovelier, more *English* conception than Mignon, treasonable as the saying would seem to some. No doubt it was suggested by Mignon.

—Sara Coleridge, Letter to Aubrey De Vere
(October 2, 1849), *Memoir and Letters of Sara Coleridge*,
ed. Edith Coleridge, 1874, Vol. 2, p. 407

Bret Harte
"Dickens in Camp" (1870)

Above the pines the moon was slowly drifting,
    The river sang below;
The dim Sierras, far beyond, uplifting
    Their minarets of snow.

The roaring camp-fire, with rude humor, painted
    The ruddy tints of health
On haggard face and form that drooped and fainted
    In the fierce race for wealth;

Till one arose, and from his pack's scant treasure
    A hoarded volume drew,
And cards were dropped from hands of listless leisure
    To hear the tale anew.

And then, while round them shadows gathered faster,
    And as the firelight fell,
He read aloud the book wherein the Master
    Had writ of "Little Nell."

Perhaps 't was boyish fancy,—for the reader
    Was youngest of them all,—
But, as he read, from clustering pine and cedar
    A silence seemed to fall;

The fir-trees, gathering closer in the shadows,
    Listened in every spray,
While the whole camp with "Nell" on English meadows
    Wandered and lost their way.

And so in mountain solitudes—o'ertaken
    As by some spell divine—
Their cares dropped from them like the needles shaken
    From out the gusty pine.

Lost is that camp and wasted all its fire;
    And he who wrought that spell?
Ah! towering pine and stately Kentish spire,
    Ye have one tale to tell!

Lost is that camp, but let its fragrant story
    Blend with the breath that thrills
With hop-vine's incense all the pensive glory
    That fills the Kentish hills.

And on that grave where English oak and holly
And laurel wreaths entwine,
Deem it not all a too presumptuous folly,
This spray of Western pine!

                  —Bret Harte, "Dickens in Camp," 1870

GEORGE GISSING "DICKENS IN MEMORY" (1902)

Because most readers are accustomed to thinking of Dickens as quintessentially a London novelist, it is helpful to recall Gissing's attention to the "atmosphere of rural peace" in the early novels. Likewise, the contrast he draws between mere sentiment and Dickens's transfiguring sympathetic love will also help students think about the emotion and tone of the novels.

I believe that the first book—the first real, substantial book—I read through was *The Old Curiosity Shop*. At all events, it was the first volume of Dickens which I made my own. And I could not have lighted better in my choice. At ten years old, or so, one is not ready for *Pickwick*. I remember very well the day when I plunged into that sea of mirth; I can hear myself, half choked with laughter, clamoring for the attention of my elders whilst I read aloud this and that passage from the great Trial. But *The Old Curiosity Shop* makes strong appeal to a youthful imagination, and contains little that is beyond its scope. Dickens's sentiment, however it may distress the mature mind of our later day, is not unwholesome, and, at all events in this story, addresses itself naturally enough to feelings unsubdued by criticism. His quality of picturesqueness is here seen at its best, with little or nothing of that melodrama which makes the alloy of *Nicholas Nickleby* and *Oliver Twist*—to speak only of the early books. The opening scene, that dim-lighted storehouse of things old and grotesque, is the best approach to Dickens's world, where sights of every day are transfigured in the service of romance. The kindliness of the author's spirit, his overflowing sympathy with poor and humble folk, set one's mind to a sort of music which it is good to live with; and no writer of moralities ever showed triumphant virtue in so cheery a light as that which falls upon these honest people when rascality has got its deserts. Notably good, too, whether for young or old, is the atmosphere of rural peace breathed in so many pages of this book; I know that it helped to make conscious in me a love of English field and lane and village, one day to become a solacing passion. In *The Old Curiosity Shop*, town is set before you only for effect of contrast; the aspiration of the story is to the country road winding along under a pure sky. Others have pictured with a closer fidelity the scenes of English rustic life, but who succeeds better than Dickens in throwing a charm upon the wayside inn and the village church? Among his supreme merits is that of having presented in abiding form one of the best of our national ideals—rural homeliness. By the way of happiest emotions, the child reader takes this ideal into mind and heart; and perhaps it is in great part because Dickens's books are still so much read, because one sees edition after edition scattered over town and country homes, that one cannot wholly despair of this new England which tries so hard to be unlike the old.

—George Gissing, "Dickens in Memory,"
Critic, January 1902, pp. 48–49

AMERICAN NOTES

Henry Wadsworth Longfellow (1842)

I have read Dickens's book. It is jovial and good-natured, and at times very severe. You will read it with delight and, for the most part, approbation. He has a grand chapter on Slavery. *Spitting* and *politics at Washington* are the other topics of censure. Both you and I would censure them with equal severity, to say the least.

—Henry Wadsworth Longfellow, Letter to Charles Sumner (October 16, 1842), cited in Samuel Longfellow, *Life of Henry Wadsworth Longfellow,* 1891, Vol. 1, p. 421

Thomas Babington Macaulay (1842)

This morning I received Dickens's book. I have now read it. It is impossible for me to review it; nor do I think that you would wish me to do so. I can not praise it, and I will not cut it up. I can not praise it, though it contains a few lively dialogues and descriptions; for it seems to me to be, on the whole, a failure. It is written like the worst parts of *Humphrey's Clock.* What is meant to be easy and sprightly is vulgar and flippant, as in the first two pages. What is meant to be fine is a great deal too fine for me, as the description of the Fall of Niagara. A reader who wants an amusing account of the United States had better go to Mrs. Trollope, coarse and malignant as she is. A reader who wants information about American politics, manners, and literature had better go even to so poor a creature as Buckingham. In short, I pronounce the book, in spite of some gleams of genius, at once frivolous and dull.

Therefore I will not praise it. Neither will I attack it; first, because I have eaten salt with Dickens; secondly, because he is a good man, and a man of real talent; thirdly, because he hates slavery as heartily as I do; and, fourthly, because I wish to see him enrolled in our blue-and-yellow corps, where he may do excellent service as a skirmisher and sharpshooter.

—Thomas Babington Macaulay, Letter to Macvey Napier (October 19, 1842), cited in G. Otto Trevelyan, *The Life and Letters of Lord Macaulay,* 1876, Vol. 2, p. 109

JAMES SPEDDING
"DICKENS'S *AMERICAN NOTES*" (1843)

James Spedding was a critic and scholar whose most important work centered on Francis Bacon, including a fourteen-volume collected works and biography. Here he dismisses *American Notes* as, in effect, private grumblings—perhaps charming or amusing, but not of sufficient interest to warrant publication.

Such being our opinion of Mr. Dickens's faculties and opportunities for observation, we expected from him a book, not without large defects both positive and negative, but containing some substantial and valuable addition to our stock of information with regard to this most interesting country—interesting not only for the indissoluble connexion of its interests with our own, but likewise as the quarter from which we must look for light on the great question of these times,—What is to become of *Democracy*, and how is it to be dealt with? We cannot say that our expectations are justified by the result. Though the book is said to have given great offence on the other side of the Atlantic, we cannot see any sufficient reason for it. To us it appears that Mr. Dickens deserves great praise for the care with which he has avoided all-offensive topics, and abstained from amusing his readers at the expense of his entertainers; and if we had an account of the temptations in this kind which he has resisted, we do not doubt that the reserve and self-control which he has exercised would appear scarcely less than heroical. But, on the other hand, we cannot say that his book throws any new light on his subject. He has done little more than confide to the public what should have been a series of letters for the entertainment of his private friends. Very agreeable and amusing letters they would have been; and as such, had they been posthumously published, would have been read with interest and pleasure. As it is, in the middle of our amusement at the graphic sketches of life and manners, the ludicrous incidents, the wayside conversations about nothing, so happily told, and the lively remarks, with which these *Notes* abound—in the middle of our respect for the tone of good sense and good humour which runs through them—and in spite of a high appreciation of the gentlemanly feeling which has induced him to refrain from all personal allusions and criticisms, and for the modesty which has kept him silent on so many subjects, concerning which most persons in the same situation (not being reminded of the worthlessness of their opinions by the general inattention of mankind to what they say) are betrayed into the delivery of oracles—in the middle of all this we cannot help feeling that we should have respected Mr. Dickens more if he had kept his book to himself; if he had been so far dissatisfied with these *American Notes* as to shrink from the "general circulation" of them; if he had felt unwilling to stand by and see his nothings trumpeted to all corners of the earth, quoted and criticised in every newspaper, passing through edition after edition in England, and settling in clouds of sixpenny copies all over the United States. That he had nothing better to say is no reproach to him. He had much to say about international copyright, and that, we doubt not, was well worth hearing; we only wish it had been heard with more favour. But, having nothing better to say, why say anything? Or why, at least, sound a trumpet before him to call men away from their business to listen? To us it seems to imply a want of respect either for himself or for his subject, that he should be thus prompt to gratify the prurient public appetite for novelty, by bringing the fruits of his mind into the market unripe. This, however, is a matter of taste. In reputation, so easy and abundant a writer will suffer little from an occasional mistake. Though this book should only live till New Year's Day, it will have lived long enough for his fame; for on that day we observe that he is himself to come forth again in a series of monthly numbers, so that none but himself will be his extinguisher.

—James Spedding, "Dickens's *American Notes*" (1843), *Reviews and Discussions,* 1849, pp. 247–48

Lord Jeffrey Francis (1852)

A thousand thanks to you for your charming book! and for all the pleasure, profit, and *relief* it has afforded me. You *have* been very tender to our sensitive friends beyond sea, and really said nothing which should give any serious offence to any moderately rational patriot among them. The *Slavers,* of course, will give you no quarter, and I suppose you did not expect they should. But I do not think you could have said less, and my whole heart goes along with every word you have written. Some people will be angry too, that you have been so strict to observe their *spitting,* and neglect of ablutions, &c. And more, that you should have spoken with so little reverence of their courts of law and state legislature, and even of their grand Congress itself. But all this latter part is done in such a spirit of good-humoured playfulness, and so mixed up with clear intimations that you have quite as little veneration for things of the same sort *at home,* that it will not be easy to represent it as the fruit of *English* insolence and envy.

—Lord Jeffrey Francis, Letter to Charles Dickens (October 16, 1842), cited in Lord Henry Cockburn, *Life of Lord Jeffrey,* 1852, Vol. 2, p. 294

A CHRISTMAS CAROL

WILLIAM MAKEPEACE THACKERAY "A BOX OF NOVELS" (1844)

The author of *Vanity Fair* (1847–48) and *Pendennis* (1848–50), among many other novels, William Makepeace Thackeray (1811–63) was one of the most important novelists of the mid-Victorian period. During his lifetime, he rivaled Dickens in reputation among critics. Unlike Dickens, who focused his attention on the middle and laboring classes, Thackeray developed a style—classical, satirical, and ironic—that was best suited for novels of society and the aristocracy; he also wrote insightfully about historical change. The excerpt here offers a good example of Thackeray's humor and complex narratorial stance, though it mainly attests to the universal popularity of *A Christmas Carol.*

I do not mean that the *Christmas Carol* is quite as brilliant or self-evident as the sun at noonday; but it is so spread over England by this time, that no sceptic, no *Fraser's Magazine,*—no, not even the godlike and ancient *Quarterly* itself (venerable, Saturnian, bigwigged dynasty!) could review it down.

In fact, one might as well detail the plot of the *Merry Wives of Windsor,* or *Robinson Crusoe,* as recapitulate here the adventures of Scrooge the miser, and his Christmas conversion. I am not sure that the allegory is a very complete one, and protest, with the classics, against the use of blank verse in prose; but here all objections stop. Who can listen to objections regarding such a book as this? It seems to me a national benefit, and to every man or woman who reads it a personal kindness. The last two people I heard speak of it were women; neither knew the other, or the author, and both said, by way of criticism, "God bless him!" A Scotch philosopher, who nationally does not keep Christmas-day, on reading the book, sent out for a turkey, and asked two friends to dine—this is a fact! Many men were known to sit down after perusing it, and write off letters to their friends, not about business, but out of their fulness of heart, and to wish old acquaintances a happy Christmas. Had the book appeared a fortnight earlier, all the prize cattle would have been gobbled up in pure love and friendship, Epping denuded of sausages, and not a turkey left in Norfolk. His royal highness's fat stock would have fetched unheard-of prices, and Alderman Bannister would have been tired of slaying. But there is a Christmas for 1844, too; the book will be as early then as now, and so let speculators look out.

As for Tiny Tim, there is a certain passage in the book regarding that young gentleman, about which a man should hardly venture to speak in print or in public, any more than he would of any other affections of his private heart. There is not a reader in England but that little creature will be a bond of union between the author and him; and he will say of Charles Dickens, as the woman just now, "God Bless Him!" What a feeling is this for a writer to be able to inspire, and what a reward to reap!

—William Makepeace Thackeray, "A Box of Novels," *Fraser's Magazine,* February 1844, pp. 168–69

Julia C.R. Dorr
"Christmas and Its Literature" (1868)

Julia Caroline Ripley Dorr was an American poet and novelist. Her slightly overwrought excerpt underscores the powerful sense that Scrooge is everyman, Dickens's invitation to his readers to revisit their own Christmases past, present, and to come.

It is easy, too, to say of Dickens that he makes us acquainted with many unsavory characters—people whom we would hardly care to associate with in real life, or to touch without gloves; and it is easy to ask why one need be so familiar with them and their disreputable haunts on paper. But what a thrill ran through the whole English-speaking race when A *Christmas Carol in Prose* announced to it that Marley was dead, to begin with—as dead as a door-nail! No carol that ever was sung so stirred the deep heart of humanity. The world laughed and cried over it, and Scrooge and Scrooge's nephew, and old Fezziwig, and Bob Cratchit, and Tiny Tim, became household words in a million homes. It was not Scrooge only that the Ghost of Christmas Past led backward over the pathway of the years, showing him the wasted opportunities, the graves of buried loves and hopes, the monuments raised to pride and hatred, the littlenesses, the meannesses, the barrenness that made "the shadows of the things that have been" so terrible. It was not to him only that the Ghost of Christmas Present revealed the things that were, the light struggling with darkness, patience and faith and hope and innocent merrymaking in lowliest homes, the love that sweetens penury, and, side by side with it, the degradation that is unutterable. And not to Scrooge alone, thank God, did Christmas Future show that the past, with all its records of sin and misery, could be blotted out, and a new page written.

—Julia C.R. Dorr, "Christmas and Its Literature," *Book Buyer,* December 1868, pp. 284–85

MARTIN CHUZZLEWIT

Philip Hone (1843)

Philip Hone is perhaps most famous for his meticulous diary, which he kept from 1828 until his death. He was a successful merchant and auctioneer, and, briefly, mayor of New York City (1826–27). His reaction is characteristic of many Americans who had feted Dickens upon his arrival in 1842.

Dickens, Boz—For Shame. Dickens has just published as one of the chapters of *Martin Chuzzlewit* an account of the arrival of his hero in New York, and what he saw, and heard, and did, and suffered, in this land of pagans, brutes, and infidels. I am sorry to see it. Thinking that Mr. Dickens has been ungenerously treated by my countrymen, I have taken his part on most occasions; but he has now written an exceedingly foolish libel upon us, from which he will not obtain credit as an author, nor as a man of wit, any more than as a man of good taste, good nature, or good manners. It is difficult to believe that such unmitigated trash should have flown from the same pen that drew the portrait of the immortal *Pickwick* and his expressive gaiters, the honest locksmith and his pretty Dolly of Clerkenwell, and poor little Nell, who has caused so many tears to flow. Shame, Mr. Dickens! Considering all that we did for you, if, as some folks say, I and others made fools of ourselves to make much of you, you should not afford them the triumph of saying, "There! We told you so!" "It serves you right!" and such other consolatory phrases. If we were fools you were the cause of it, and should have stood by us. "Et *tu,* Brute."

—Philip Hone, *Diary,* July 29, 1843

Sara Coleridge (1874)

Daughter of Samuel Taylor Coleridge, Sara Coleridge was a poet in her own right, as well as a proponent of her father's work when it fell out of favor. Implicitly registering the furious pace of Dickens's publications, Coleridge links the characters in *Chuzzlewit* to his earlier works.

This last work contains, besides all the fun, some very marked and available morals. I scarce know any book in which the evil and odiousness of selfishness is more forcibly brought out, or in a greater variety of exhibitions. In the midst of the merry quotations, or at least on any fair opportunity, I draw the boys' attention to these points, bid them remark how *unmanly* is the selfishness of young Martin, and I insist upon it that Tom Pinch's character, if it could really exist, would be a very beautiful one. But I doubt, as I do in regard to *Pickwick,* that so much sense, and deep, solid goodness, could coexist with such want of discernment and liability to be gulled. Tigg is very clever, and the boys roar with laughter at the "what's-his-name place whence no thingumbob ever came back;" but this is only a new edition of Jingle and Smangles; Mark Tapley, also, is a second Sam Weller. The new characters are Pecksniff, and the thrice-notable Sairey Gamp, with Betsy Prig to show her off.

—Sara Coleridge, Letter to Mrs. H.M. Jones
(August 17, 1848), *Memoir and Letters of Sara Coleridge,*
ed. Edith Coleridge, 1874, Vol. 2, p. 346

William Dean Howells "Dickens" (1895)

I liked *Martin Chuzzlewit,* . . . and the other day I read a great part of it again, and found it roughly true in the passages that referred to America, though it was surcharged in the serious moods, and caricatured in the comic. The English are always inadequate observers; they seem too full of themselves to have eyes and ears for any alien people; but as far as an Englishman could, Dickens had caught the look of our life in certain aspects. His report of it was clumsy and farcical; but in a large, loose way it was like enough; at least he had caught the note of our self-satisfied, intolerant, and hypocritical provinciality, and this was not altogether lost in his mocking horseplay.

—William Dean Howells, "Dickens,"
My Literary Passions, 1895

DAVID COPPERFIELD

Charlotte Brontë (1849)

I have read *David Copperfield*; it seems to me very good—admirable in some parts. You said it had affinity to *Jane Eyre*. It has, now and then—only what an advantage has Dickens in his varied knowledge of men and things!

—Charlotte Brontë,
Letter to W.S. Williams (September 13, 1849)

Charles Dickens (1850)

I did not find it easy to get sufficiently far away from it, in the first sensations of having finished it, to refer to it with the composure which this formal heading would seem to require. My interest in it was so recent and strong, and my mind was so divided between pleasure and regret—pleasure in the achievement of a long design, regret in the separation from many companions—that I was in danger of wearying the reader with personal confidences and private emotions.

Besides which, all that I could have said of the Story to any purpose, I had endeavoured to say in it.

It would concern the reader little, perhaps, to know how sorrowfully the pen is laid down at the close of a two-years' imaginative task; or how an Author feels as if he were dismissing some portion of himself into the shadowy world, when a crowd of the creatures of his brain are going from him for ever. Yet, I had nothing else to tell; unless, indeed, I were to confess (which might be of less moment still), that no one can ever believe this Narrative in the reading more than I believed it in the writing.

So true are these avowals at the present day, that I can now only take the reader into one confidence more. Of all my books, I like this the best. It will be easily believed that I am a fond parent to every child of my fancy, and that no one can ever love that family as dearly as I love them. But, like many fond parents, I have in my heart of hearts a favourite child. And his name is David Copperfield.

—Charles Dickens, "Preface" to
David Copperfield, 1850

William Makepeace Thackeray "Mr. Brown the Elder Takes Mr. Brown the Younger to a Club" (1850)

Have you read *David Copperfield*, by the way? How beautiful it is—how charmingly fresh and simple! In those admirable touches of tender humour—and I should call humour, Bob, a mixture of love and wit—who can equal this great genius? There are little words and phrases in his books which are like personal benefits to the reader. What a place it is to hold in the affections of men! What an awful responsibility hanging over a writer! What man holding such a place, and knowing that his words go forth to vast congregations of mankind,—to grown folks—to their children, and perhaps to their children's children,—but must think of his calling with a solemn and humble heart! May love and truth guide such a man always! It is an awful prayer; may heaven further its fulfilment!

—William Makepeace Thackeray, "Mr. Brown the Elder Takes Mr. Brown the Younger to a Club," *Sketches and Travels in London,* 1850

Hans Christian Andersen "A Visit to Charles Dickens" (1870)

As I was stepping into the house Dickens came out to meet me, with bright looks and a hearty greeting. He looked a little older than when we said goodbye ten years ago; but that was partly owing to the beard he had grown. His eyes were bright as ever; the smile on his lips was the same; his frank voice was just as friendly,—ay, and if possible, more winning still. He was now in the prime of manhood in his 45th year; full of youth and life and eloquence, and rich in a rare humour that glowed with kindliness. I know not how to describe him better than in the words of one of my first letters home: "Take the best out of all Dickens's writings, combine them into the picture of a man, and there thou hast Charles Dickens." And such as in the first hour he stood before me, the very same he remained all the time of my visit; ever genuine, and cheerful, and sympathetic.

—Hans Christian Andersen, "A Visit to Charles Dickens," *Temple Bar,* December 1870, p. 29

Mowbray Morris "Charles Dickens" (1882)

Mowbray Morris was a critic and a writer, as well as a reader for the publishing house Macmillan. Following Coleridge's distinction between mere fancy and the idealizing power of the imagination, Morris sees in *David Copperfield* a reversal of Dickens's typical procedure. Usually Dickens must make his readers believe in something essentially unreal, a fancy that he grounds through various comic or bathetic tics. In *David Copperfield*, however, Dickens works from his own life, aiming to find the ideal meaning and expression of the underlying realities. This distinction is worth pursuing in studies of Dickens's characterization and realism.

I have said that in *David Copperfield* Dickens is freer from defect than in any other of his works. It is rarely that public opinion has ratified an author's judgment so completely as it has here. As we all know, this was Dickens's favourite, and the reason we all know. It may be noted in passing how characteristic of the two men is their choice. To Dickens *David Copperfield* was, to use his own words, his favourite child, because in its pages he saw the reflection of his own youth. Thackeray, though he never spoke out on such matters, is generally believed to have looked not a little into his own heart when he wrote *Pendennis*. Yet his favourite was *Esmond*, for *Esmond* he rightly felt to be the most complete and perfect of his works; in that exquisite book his *art* touched its highest point. With *David Copperfield,* no doubt the secret of the writer's partiality is in some sense the secret of the reader's. Though none, perhaps, have been so outspoken as Hogg, every man takes pleasure in writing about himself, and we are always pleased to hear what he has to say; egotism, as Macaulay says, so unpopular in conversation, is always popular in writing. But not in the charm of autobiography alone lies the fascination which this delightful book has exercised on every class of readers. It is not only Dickens's most attractive work, but it is his best work. And it is his best for this reason, that whereas in all his others he is continually striving to realise the conception of his fancy, in this alone his business is to idealise the reality; in this alone, as it seems to me, his imagination prevails over his fancy. In this alone he is never grotesque, or for him so rarely that we hardly care to qualify the adverb. Nowhere else is his pathos so tender and so sure; nowhere else is his humour, though often more boisterous and more abundant, so easy and so fine; nowhere else is his observation so vivid and so deep; nowhere else has he held with so sure a hand the balance between the classes. If in the character of Daniel Pegotty more eloquently and more reasonably than he has ever done elsewhere, even in honest Joe Gargery, he has enlarged on his favourite abiding-place for virtue, he has also nowhere else been so ready and so glad to welcome her in those more seemly places wherein for the most part he can find no resting-place for her feet. Weak-minded as Doctor Strong is, fatuous, if the reader pleases, we are never asked to laugh at the kindly, chivalrous old scholar, as we are at Sir Leicester Dedlock; Clara Pegotty is no better woman than Agnes Wickfield. And even in smaller matters, and in the characters of second-rate importance, we may find the same sureness of touch. It has been made a reproach against him that his characters are too apt to be forgotten in the externals of their callings, that they never speak without some allusion to their occupations, and cannot be separated from them. In the extraordinary number and variety of characters that he has drawn, no doubt one can find instances of this. For so many of these characters, nearly all, indeed, of the comic ones, real as he has made them to us, are not, when we come to examine them, realities, but rather conceptions of his fancy, which he has to shape into realities by the use of certain traits and peculiarities of humanity with which his extraordinary observation has supplied him. Major Pendennis, and Costigan, and Becky Sharp *are* realities whom Thackeray idealises, makes characters of fiction out of. But Sam Weller and Mrs. Gamp are the children of fancy whom Dickens makes real, partly by the addition of sundry human attributes, but even more so by the marvellous skill and distinctness with which he brings them and keeps them before us. But in order to do this he is obliged never to lose sight, or to suffer us to lose sight, of those peculiarities, whether of speech, or manner, or condition, which make them for us the realities that they are. And in so doing it cannot but happen that he seems to thrust those peculiarities at times somewhat too persistently upon us. In *David Copperfield* this is not so, or much less so than anywhere else, except, of course, in *The Tale of Two Cities,* Dickens's only essay at the romance proper, where the characters are subordinate to the story. We may see this, for example, by comparing Omer, the undertaker, in *David Copperfield,* with Mould, the undertaker, in *Martin Chuzzlewit.* Mould and all his family live in a perpetual atmosphere of funerals; his children are represented as solacing their young existences by "playing at buryin's down in the shop, and follerin' the order-book to its long home in the iron safe;" and Mr. Mould's own idea of fellowship is of a person "one would almost feel disposed to bury for nothing, and do it neatly, too!" On his first introduction, after old Anthony's death, he sets the seal on his personality by the remark that Jonas's liberal orders for the funeral prove "what was so forcibly observed by the lamented theatrical poet—*buried at Stratford*—that there is good in everything." That touch is very comical, but also very grotesque; it is a touch of fancy, not of nature. But when David Copperfield, as a man, recalls himself to the recollection of the good-hearted Omer, who had known him as a boy, the undertaker is revealed in a very different fashion. "To be sure," said Mr. Omer, touching my waistcoat with his forefinger; "and there was a little child too! *There was two parties. The little party was laid along with the other party.* Over at Blunderstone it was, of course. Dear me! And how have you been since?" Every one must be conscious of the difference here.

—Mowbray Morris, "Charles Dickens,"
Fortnightly Review, December 1882, pp. 776–77

JAMES RUSSELL LOWELL (1887)

I am trying to get rested by reading Dickens, and am over *David Copperfield* now. I had never read it, I find, though Mr. Micawber has become so proverbial that, finding his name in it, I thought I had. Dickens says in his preface that David Copperfield was his "favorite child," and I don't wonder, for it is amazingly well done so far as I have got.

—James Russell Lowell, Letter to
Charles Eliot Norton (April 8, 1887)

G.K. CHESTERTON
"DAVID COPPERFIELD" (1911)

Chesterton's commentary on *David Copperfield* is noteworthy for two reasons: his claim that the novel marks a transition in Dickens's fiction, and his stunning defense of David's marriage to Dora. Students addressing the topics of love, marriage, characterization, or plot will find this brief essay a valuable resource.

Chesterton notes that the opening chapters of the novel are something entirely new in Dickens: a systematic elaboration of a coherent world. As Dickens reworks the material from his own life, David looks less like a grotesque and more like an actual person. As the novel proceeds, however, Chesterton notices that this newfound humanity falls off, and characters such as Micawber and Heep take over. More than this, the novel becomes indiscriminately cruel in its treatment of even Copperfield's friends. Chesterton arrives at a basic question: to what extent can David Copperfield be said to mature, when anything that is a possible check to his happiness is, in effect, sent to Australia? Micawber, Little Emily, and Peggotty all end up in Australia. Chesterton jokes about having "a horrible feeling that David Copperfield will send even his aunt to Australia if she worries him too much about donkeys."

The ruthless excision of all obstacles to David's happiness is, for Chesterton, a sign of either fatigue or moral cowardice. He opts for the former. Particularly troubling to Chesterton is the death of Dora, or, rather, David's subsequent marriage to Agnes, which is presented largely as a *fait accompli*. On the one hand, Chesterton believes it is clear that Copperfield and Dickens "looked at the marriage with Dora merely as a flirtation." On the other hand, the discontent that readers may feel at the end of the novel attests, despite Dickens's apparent intention, to "the primary human instinct and principle that a marriage is a marriage and irrevocable." Though Dora is dismissed within the novel as "silly" and as a child bride, she nevertheless persists stubbornly at the novel's end in David's memory. From this point of view, it is striking that Dora does not go to Australia—because she has died, she cannot be exiled, and because she expressly sanctions David's marriage to Agnes, the second couple cannot satisfactorily replace the first. For contemporary students, Chesterton's essay both highlights Dickens's own proto-imperialism (Australia as a sort of imperial sewer) and the conflict between traditional social relations and modern, secular cultures (a conflict driving both Dickens and Chesterton).

In this book Dickens is really trying to write a new kind of book, and the enterprise is almost as chivalrous as a cavalry charge. He is making a romantic attempt to be realistic. That is almost the definition of *David Copperfield*. In his last book, *Dombey and Son*, we see a certain maturity and even a certain mild exhaustion in his earlier farcical method. He never failed to have fine things in any of his books, and Toots is a very fine thing. Still, I could never find Captain Cuttle and Mr. Sol Gills very funny, and the whole Wooden Midshipman seems to me very wooden. In *David Copperfield* he suddenly unseals a new torrent of truth, the truth out of his own life. The impulse of the thing is autobiography; he is trying to tell all the absurd things that have happened to himself, and not the least absurd thing is himself. Yet though it is Dickens's ablest and clearest book, there is in it a falling away of a somewhat singular kind.

Generally speaking there was astonishingly little of fatigue in Dickens's books. He sometimes wrote bad work; he sometimes wrote even unimportant work; but he wrote hardly a line which is not full of his own fierce vitality and fancy. If he is dull it is hardly ever because he cannot think of anything; it is because, by some silly excitement or momentary lapse of judgment, he has thought of something that was not worth thinking of. If his joke is feeble, it is as an impromptu joke at an uproarious dinner-table may be feeble; it is no indication of any lack of vitality. The joke is feeble, but it is not a sign of feebleness. Broadly speaking, this is true of Dickens. If his writing is not amusing us, at least it is amusing him. Even when he is tiring he is not tired.

But in the case of *David Copperfield* there is a real reason for noting an air of fatigue. For although this is the best of all Dickens's books, it constantly disappoints the critical and intelligent reader. The reason is that Dickens began it under his sudden emotional impulse of telling the whole truth about himself and gradually allowed the whole truth to be more and more diluted, until towards the end of the book we are back in the old pedantic and decorative art of Dickens, an art which we justly admired in its own place and on its own terms, but which we resent when we feel it gradually returning through a tale pitched originally in a more practical and piercing key. Here, I say, is the one real example of the fatigue of Dickens. He begins his story in a new style and then slips back into an old one. The earlier part is in his later manner. The later part is in his earlier manner.

There are many marks of something weak and shadowy in the end of *David Copperfield*. Here, for instance, is one of them which is not without its bearing on many tendencies of modern England. Why did Dickens at the end of this book give way to that typically English optimism about emigration? He seems to think that he can cure the souls of a whole cartload, or rather boatload, of his characters by sending them all to the Colonies. Peggotty is a desolate and insulted parent whose house has been desecrated and his pride laid low; therefore let him go to Australia. Emily is a woman whose heart is broken and whose honour is blasted; but she will be quite happy if she goes to Australia. Mr. Micawber is a man whose soul cannot be made to understand the tyranny of time or the limits of human hope; but he will understand all these things if he goes to Australia. For it must be noted that Dickens does not use this emigration merely as a mode of exit. He does not send these characters away on a ship merely as a symbol suggesting that they pass wholly out of his hearer's life. He does definitely suggest that Australia is a sort of island Valley of Avalon, where the soul may heal it of its grievous wound. It is seriously suggested that Peggotty finds peace in Australia. It is really indicated that Emily regains her dignity in Australia. It is positively explained of Mr. Micawber not that he was happy in Australia (for he would be that anywhere), but that he was definitely prosperous and practically successful in Australia; and that he would certainly be nowhere. Colonising is not talked of merely as a coarse, economic expedient for going to a new market. It is really offered as something that will cure the hopeless tragedy of Peggotty; as something that will cure the still more hopeless comedy of Micawber.

I will not dwell here on the subsequent adventures of this very sentimental and extremely English illusion. It would be an exaggeration to say that Dickens in this matter is something of a forerunner of much modern imperialism. His political views were such that he would have regarded modern imperialism with horror and contempt. Nevertheless there is here something of that hazy sentimentalism which makes some Imperialists prefer to talk of the fringe of the empire of which they know nothing, rather than of the heart of the empire which they know is diseased. It is said that in the twilight and decline of Rome, close to the dark ages, the people in Gaul believed that Britain was a land of ghosts (perhaps it was foggy), and that the dead were ferried across to it from the northern coast of France. If (as is not entirely impossible) our own century appears to future ages as a time of temporary decay and twilight, it may be said that there was attached to England a blessed island called Australia to which the souls of the socially dead were ferried across to remain in bliss for ever.

This element which is represented by the colonial optimism at the end of *David Copperfield* is a moral element. The truth is that there is something a little mean about this sort of optimism. I do not like the notion of David Copperfield sitting down comfortably to his tea-table with Agnes, having got rid of all the inconvenient or distressing characters of the story by sending them to the other side of the world. The whole thing has too much about it of the selfishness of a family which sends a scapegrace to the Colonies to starve with its blessing. There is too much in the whole thing of that element which was satirised by an ironic interpretation of the epitaph "Peace, perfect peace, with loved ones far away." We should have thought more of David Copperfield (and also of Charles Dickens) if he had endeavoured for the rest of his life, by conversation and comfort, to bind up the wounds of his old friends from the seaside. We should have thought more of David Copperfield (and also of Charles Dickens) if he had faced the possibility of going on till his dying day lending money to Mr. Wilkins Micawber. We should have thought more of David Copperfield (and also of Charles Dickens) if he had not looked upon the marriage with Dora merely as a flirtation, an episode which he survived and ought to survive. And yet the truth is that there is nowhere in fiction where we feel so keenly the primary human instinct and principle that a marriage is a marriage and irrevocable, that such things do leave a wound and also a bond as in this case of David's short connection with his silly little wife. When all is said and done, when Dickens has done his best and his worst, when he has sentimentalised for pages and tried to tie up everything in the pink tape of optimism, the fact, in the psychology of the reader, still remains. The reader does still feel that David's marriage to Dora was a real marriage; and that his marriage to Agnes was nothing, a middle-aged compromise, a taking of the second best, a sort of spiritualised and sublimated marriage of convenience. For all the readers of Dickens Dora is thoroughly avenged. The modern world (intent on anarchy in everything, even in Government) refuses to perceive the permanent element of tragic constancy which inheres in all passion, and which is the origin of marriage. Marriage rests upon the fact that you cannot have your cake and eat it; that you cannot lose your heart and have it. But, as I have said, there is perhaps no place in literature where we feel more vividly the sense of this monogamous instinct in man than in David Copperfield. A man is monogamous even if he is only monogamous for a month; love is eternal even if it is only eternal for a month. It always leaves behind it the sense of something broken and betrayed.

But I have mentioned Dora in this connection only because she illustrates the same fact which Micawber illustrates; the fact that there is at the end of this book too much tendency to bless people and get rid of them. Micawber is a nuisance. Dickens the despot condemns him to exile. Dora is a nuisance. Dickens the despot condemns her to death. But it is the whole business of Dickens in the world to express the fact that such people are the spice and interest of life. It is the whole point of Dickens that there is nobody more worth living with than a strong, splendid, entertaining, immortal nuisance. Micawber interrupts practical life; but what is practical life that it should venture to interrupt Micawber? Dora confuses the housekeeping; but we are not angry with Dora because she confuses the housekeeping. We are angry with the housekeeping because it confuses Dora. I repeat, and it cannot be too much repeated that the whole lesson of Dickens is here. It is better to know Micawber than not to know the minor worries that arise out of knowing Micawber. It is better to have a bad debt and a good friend. In the same way it is better to marry a human and healthy personality which happens to attract you than to marry a mere housewife; for a mere housewife is a mere housekeeper. All this was what Dickens stood for; that the very people who are most irritating in small business circumstances are often the people who are most delightful in long stretches of experience of life. It is just the man who is maddening when he is ordering a cutlet or arranging an appointment who is probably the man in whose company it is worth while to journey steadily towards the grave. Distribute the dignified people and the capable people and the highly business-like people among all the situations which their ambition or their innate corruption may demand; but keep close to your heart, keep deep in your inner councils the absurd people. Let the clever people pretend to govern you, let the unimpeachable people pretend to advise you, but let the fools alone influence you; let the laughable people whose faults you see and understand be the only people who are really inside your life, who really come near you or accompany you on your lonely march towards the last impossibility. That is the whole meaning of Dickens; that we should keep the absurd people for our friends. And here at the end of *David Copperfield* he seems in some dim way to deny it. He seems to want to get rid of the preposterous people simply because they will always continue to be preposterous. I have a horrible feeling that David Copperfield will send even his aunt to Australia if she worries him too much about donkeys.

I repeat, then, that this wrong ending of *David Copperfield* is one of the very few examples in Dickens of a real symptom of fatigue. Having created splendid beings for whom alone life might be worth living, he cannot endure the thought of his hero living with them. Having given his hero superb and terrible friends, he is afraid of the awful and tempestuous vista of their friendship. He slips back into a more superficial kind of story and ends it in a more superficial way. He is afraid of the things he has made; of that terrible figure Micawber; of that yet more terrible figure Dora. He cannot make up his mind to see his hero perpetually entangled in the splendid tortures and sacred surprises that come from living with really individual and unmanageable people. He cannot endure the idea that his fairy prince will not have henceforward a perfectly peaceful time. But the wise old fairy tales (which are the wisest things in the world, at any rate the wisest things of worldly origin), the wise old fairy tales never were so silly as to say that the prince and the princess lived peacefully ever afterwards. The fairy tales said that the prince and princess lived happily ever afterwards: and so they did. They lived happily, although it is very likely that from time to time they threw the furniture at each other. Most marriages, I think, are happy marriages; but there is no such thing as a contented marriage. The whole pleasure of marriage is that it is a perpetual crisis. David Copperfield and Dora quarrelled over the cold mutton; and if they had gone on quarrelling to the end of their lives, they would have gone on loving each other to the end of their lives; it would have been a human marriage. But David Copperfield and Agnes would agree about the cold mutton. And that cold mutton would be very cold.

I have here endeavoured to suggest some of the main merits of Dickens within the framework of one of his faults. I have said that *David Copperfield* represents a rather sad transition from his strongest method to his weakest. Nobody would ever complain of Charles Dickens going on writing his own kind of novels, his old kind of novels. If there be anywhere a man who loves good books, that man wishes that there were four *Oliver Twists* and at least forty-four *Pickwicks*. If there be any one who loves laughter and creation, he would be glad to read a hundred of Nicholas Nickleby and two hundred of *The Old Curiosity Shop*. But while any one would have welcomed one of Dickens's own ordered and conventional novels, it was not in this spirit that they welcomed *David Copperfield*.

David Copperfield begins as if it were going to be a new kind of Dickens novel; then it gradually turns into an old kind of Dickens novel. It is here that many readers of this splendid book have been subtly and secretly irritated. Nicholas Nickleby is all very well; we accept him as something which is required to tie the whole affair together. Nicholas is a sort of string or clothesline on which are hung the limp figure of Smike, the jumping-jack of Mr. Squeers and the twin dolls named Cheeryble. If we do not accept Nicholas Nickleby as the hero of the story, at least we accept him as the title of the story. But in *David Copperfield* Dickens begins something which looks for the moment fresh and startling. In the earlier chapters (the amazing earlier chapters of this book) he does seem to be going to tell the living truth about a living boy and man. It is melancholy to see that sudden fire fading. It is sad to see David Copperfield gradually turning into Nicholas Nickleby. Nicholas Nickleby does not exist at all; he is a quite colourless primary condition of the story. We look through Nicholas Nickleby at the story just as we look through a plain pane of glass at the street. But David Copperfield does begin by existing; it is only gradually that he gives up that exhausting habit.

Any fair critical account of Dickens must always make him out much smaller than he is. For any fair criticism of Dickens must take account of his evident errors, as I have taken account of one of the most evident of them during the last two or three pages. It would not even be loyal to conceal them. But no honest criticism, no criticism, though it spoke with the tongues of men and angels, could ever really talk about Dickens. In all this that I have said I have not been talking about Dickens at all. I say it with equanimity; I say it even with arrogance. I have been talking about the gaps of Dickens. I have been talking about the omissions of Dickens. I have been talking about the slumber of Dickens and the forgetfulness and unconsciousness of Dickens. In one word, I have been talking not about Dickens, but about the absence of Dickens. But when we come to him and his work itself, what is there to be said? What is there to be said about earthquake and the dawn? He has created, especially in this book of *David Copperfield*, he has created, creatures who cling to us and tyrannise over us, creatures whom we would not forget if we could, creatures whom we could not forget if we would, creatures who are more actual than the man who made them.

This is the excuse for all that indeterminate and rambling and sometimes sentimental criticism of which Dickens, more than any one else, is the victim, of which I fear that I for one have made him the victim in this place. When I was a boy I could not understand why the Dickensians worried so wearily about Dickens, about where he went to school and where he ate his dinners, about how he wore his trousers and when he cut his hair. I used to wonder why they did not write something that I could read about a man like Micawber. But I have come to the conclusion that this almost hysterical worship of the man, combined with a comparatively feeble criticism on his works, is just and natural. Dickens was a man like ourselves; we can see where he went wrong, and study him without being stunned or getting the sunstroke. But Micawber is not a man; Micawber is the superman. We can only walk round and round him wondering what we shall say. All the critics of Dickens, when all is said and done, have only walked round and round Micawber wondering what they should say. I am myself at this moment walking round and round Micawber wondering what I shall say. And I have not found out yet.

—G.K. Chesterton, "David Copperfield," *Criticisms & Appreciations of the Works of Charles Dickens*, 1911

GREAT EXPECTATIONS

E.S. Dallas (1861)

Eneas Sweetland Dallas was an influential critic and journalist, who for many years was the main reviewer at the *Times*. In this review, Dallas emphasizes the constraints that the new form of weekly publication impose on novels. He notes that this is the second large shift in novelistic format in the century, indeed the second pioneered by Dickens. Earlier,

Dickens's serial work had shown that large numbers of readers would buy novels in monthly installments (though, Dallas wryly notes, he can find no one who admits to reading novels in this way). In moving to the weekly serial, Dickens is merely adopting for general readership a form associated with so-called penny dreadfuls, deliberately shocking stories of crime and vice. The question, which Dallas raises but obviously cannot yet answer, is whether the form absolutely requires such an illicit focus, or whether it can be adapted to a more inclusive taste. Students discussing the phenomenon of serial publication will want to consult Dallas and Margaret Oliphant as well.

Mr Dickens has good-naturedly granted to his hosts of readers the desire of their hearts. They have been complaining that in his later works he has adopted a new style, to the neglect of that old manner which first won our admiration. Give us back the old *Pickwick* style, they cried, with its contempt of art, its loose story, its jumbled characters, and all its jesting that made us laugh so lustily; give us back Sam Weller and Mrs Gamp and Bob Sawyer, and Mrs Nickleby, Pecksniff, Bumble, and the rest, and we are willing to sacrifice serious purpose, consistent plot, finished writing, and all else. Without calling upon his readers for any alarming sacrifices, Mr Dickens has in the present work given us more of his earlier fancies than we have had for years. *Great Expectations* is not, indeed, his best work, but it is to be ranked among his happiest. There is that flowing humour in it which disarms criticism, and which is all the more enjoyable because it defies criticism. Faults there are in abundance, but who is going to find fault when the very essence of the fun is to commit faults? . . .

The method of publishing an important work of fiction in monthly instalments was considered a hazardous experiment, which could not fail to set its mark upon the novel as a whole. Mr Dickens led the way in making the experiment, and his enterprise was crowned with such success that most of the good novels now find their way to the public in the form of a monthly dole. We cannot say that we have ever met with a man who would confess to having read a tale regularly month by month, and who, if asked how he liked Dickens's or Thackeray's last number, did not instantly insist upon the impossibility of his getting through a story piecemeal. Nevertheless, the monthly publication succeeds, and thousands of a novel are sold in minute doses, where only hundreds would have been disposed of in the lump. . . . On the whole, perhaps, the periodical publication of the novel has been of use to it, and has forced English writers to develop a plot and work up the incidents. Lingering over the delineation of character and of manners, our novelists began to lose sight of the story and to avoid action. Periodical publication compelled them to a different course. They could not afford, like Scheherazade, to let the devourers of their tales go to sleep at the end of a chapter. As modern stories are intended not to set people to sleep, but to keep them awake, instead of the narrative breaking down into a soporific dulness, it was necessary that it should rise at the close into startling incident. Hence a disposition to wind up every month with a melodramatic surprise that awakens curiosity in the succeeding number. Even the least melodramatic novelist of the day, Mr Thackeray, who, so far from feasting us with surprises, goes to the other extreme, and is at particular pains to assure us that the conduct and the character of his personages are not in the least surprising, falls into the way of finishing off his monthly work with a flourish of some sort to sustain the interest.

But what are we to say to the new experiment which is now being tried of publishing good novels week by week? Hitherto the weekly issue of fiction has been connected with publications of the lowest class—small penny and half-penny serials that found in the multitude some compensation for the degradation of their readers. The sale of these journals extended to hundreds of thousands, and so largely did this circulation depend on the weekly tale, that on the conclusion of a good story it has been known to suffer a fall of 40,000 or 50,000. The favourite authors were Mr J. F. Smith, Mr Pierce Egan, and Mr G. W. Reynolds, and the favourite subjects were stories from high life, in which the vices of an aristocracy were portrayed, now with withering sarcasm, and now with fascinating allurements. Lust was the alpha and murder the omega of these tales. When the attempt was made to introduce the readers of the penny journals to better authors and to a more wholesome species of fiction, it was an ignominious failure. And the question was naturally raised—is this failure due to the taste of the readers or to the form of the publication? One of the penny journals reproduced Sir Walter Scott's novels in its columns, and it was found that the fictions of Sir Walter were quite unsuited to the tastes of its weekly readers. Was this, however, entirely the fault of the readers? we ask. Was it not in a great measure due to the form of publication? Not one of Sir Walter's novels was intended to be read in weekly instalments, and it is not wonderful that appearing chapter by chapter in a penny journal they should suffer. Mr Dickens has tried another experiment. The periodical which he conducts is addressed to a much higher class of readers than any which the penny journals would reach, and he has spread before them novel after novel specially adapted to their tastes. The first of these fictions which achieved a decided success was that of Mr Wilkie Collins—*The Woman in White*. It was read with avidity by hosts of weekly readers, and the momentum which it acquired when published in fragments carried it through several large editions when published as a whole. The novel was most successful, but if we are from it to form a judgment of the sort of story which succeeds in a weekly issue our estimate will not be very high. Everything is sacrificed to the plot—character, dialogue, passion, description; and the plot, when we come to examine it, is not merely improbable—it is impossible. We are fascinated with a first reading of the tale, but, having once had our curiosity appeased, we never wish to take it up again. After Mr Wilkie Collins's tale, the next great hit was this story of Mr Dickens's to which we invite the attention of our readers. It is quite equal to *The Woman in White* in the management of the plot, but, perhaps, this is not saying much when we have to add that the story, though not impossible like Mr Wilkie Collins's, is very improbable. If Mr Dickens, however, chose to keep the common herd of readers together by the marvels of an improbable story, he attracted the better class of readers by his fancy, his fun, and his sentiment. Altogether, his success was so great as to warrant the conclusion, which four goodly editions already justify, that the weekly form of publication is not incompatible with a very high order of fiction. And now there is being published, in the same periodical another novel, which promises still more. It is by one who of all our novelists is the greatest master of construction, and who knows how to keep an exciting story within the bounds of probability. The *Strange Story* which Sir Edward Lytton is now relating week by week, is not only interesting as an experiment in hebdomadal publication, it is doubly interesting as a scientific novel. Scientific novels are generally dull, dead things. Sir Edward Lytton undertakes the most difficult of all tasks—to write a scientific novel in weekly parts. It appears to be the greatest of all the successes achieved by *All the Year Round*. Hundreds of thousands of readers rush to read "the fairy tales of science and the long results of time" as recorded by Sir E. B. Lytton.

Great Expectations is republished as a three-volume novel. Mr Dickens, we believe, only once before published a three-volume tale—*Oliver Twist*. We mention the fact because the resemblance between the two tales is not merely the superficial one that they are both in the same number of volumes, but is also one of subject very much and of treatment. The hero of the present tale, Pip, is a sort of Oliver. He is low-born, fatherless and motherless, and he rises out of the cheerless degradation of his childhood into quite another sphere. The thieves got a hold of Oliver, tried to make him a pickpocket, and were succeeded in their friendly intentions by Mr Brownlow, who thought that he could manage better for the lad. Pip's life is not less mixed up with the ways of convicts. He befriends a convict in his need, and henceforth his destiny is involved in that of the prisoner. The convict in the new story takes the place of Mr Brownlow in the old, and supplies Master Pip with every luxury. In either tale, through some unaccountable caprice of fortune, the puny son of poverty suddenly finds himself the child of affluence. If we are asked which of the tales we like best, the reply must be that the earlier one is the more fresh in style, and rich in detail, but that the later one is the more free in handling, and the more powerful in effect. It is so, even though we have to acknowledge in the work some of Mr Dickens's worst mannerisms. For example, it is a mere mannerism that in all his tales there should be introduced some one—generally a woman—who has been confined indoors for years, and who, either from compulsion or from settled purpose, should live in dirt and gloom, never breathing the fresh air and enjoying the sunshine. A lady who has a whim of this sort is here, as in most of Mr Dickens's tales, the blind of the story. Making every allowance, however, for repetitions, the tale is really worthy of its author's reputation, and is well worth reading.

—E.S. Dallas, Review in the *Times*, October 17, 1861

Margaret Oliphant (1862)

In this influential essay, Oliphant reviews *Great Expectations* and *The Woman in White*, as well as other "sensation novels." In the 1860s, sensation novels were lurid, provocative works that focused on crime, adultery, bigamy, and other scandalous topics. The label "sensation" could refer either to the "ripped-from-the-headlines" plots or to the way these writers manipulated suspense and other intense emotional responses in order to tantalize and grip their readers. In general, critics agreed that the sensation novelists, such as Wilkie Collins, Charles Reade, Mary Elizabeth Braddon, and others, were following closely on Dickens's energy and penchant for grotesques and for crime. In the full essay, Oliphant links the rise of the genre to the formal requirements of serial publication, which demanded that novelists provide a series of cliffhangers as well as a carefully defined set of emotional responses.

In the extract provided here, Oliphant finds Dickens's powers on the wane. (On that topic, students might compare Sir James Fitzjames Stephen and Henry James, each of whom locates Dickens's failure elsewhere.) Compared to a novel such as Collins's *The Woman in White*, she argues, Dickens is simply repeating old tricks, trusting on his readers to fill in what he no longer cares to provide. Worse, she claims that he has moved from representing character grotesquely to representing landscape and other descriptive elements that way.

Aside from her distaste for *Great Expectations* in particular, Oliphant's essay also makes a useful contrast to the many critics who insist that Dickens shows us everyday life. It is true that he "shifted the fashionable ground," so that instead of having novels about lords and ladies we now have novels about the genteel poor and the genuinely poor. However, she further observes that Dickens constantly flees from representing such poverty, or any other kind of experience, realistically, instead leaping immediately into a mode of farcical exaggeration. In particular, it might be helpful to compare Oliphant's perspective with that of Gissing, who viewed Dickens's intermingling of farce and pathos as necessary, rather than escapist.

There can scarcely be a greater contrast between two works which aim in their different individualities at something of a similar effect, than there exists between Mr Wilkie Collins's powerful story [*The Woman in White*] and the last work of his Master in Art. Mr Dickens's successes in sensation are great. Even in *Great Expectations*, which is far from being one of his best works, he manages to impress distinct images of horror, surprise and pain upon the mind of his reader with vivid power and distinctness; but his performances go on an entirely different principle, and use other agencies than those which, in the hands of his disciple, heighten the effect by the evident simplicity of the means. Mr Dickens was one of the first popular writers who brought pictures of what is called common life into fashion. It is he who has been mainly instrumental in leading the present generation of authors to disregard to a great extent the pictorial advantages of life on the upper levels of society, and to find a counter-picturesqueness in the experiences of the poor. But while this is the case, it is equally certain that Mr Dickens, for his own part, has never ventured to depend for his special effects upon the common incidents of life. He has shifted the fashionable ground, and sought his heroes among penniless clerks and adventurers, as little beholden to their ancestors as to fortune. He has made washerwomen as interesting as duchesses, and found domestic angels among the vagabonds of a circus, on the very edge between lawlessness and crime; but whenever he has aimed at a scene, he has hurried aside into regions of exaggeration, and shown his own distrust of the common and usual by fantastic eccentricities, and accumulations of every description of high-strained oddity. The characters upon which he depends are not individual only, with a due recognizable difference to distinguish them from their fellows, but always peculiar, and set forth with a quaintly exaggerated distortion, by which we identify in a moment, not the character described, but the author who has made it, and of whom these oddities are characteristic. If it were possible to quicken these curious originals into life, what an odd crowd of ragamuffins and monsters would that be which should pursue this Frankenstein through the world! In the flush of fresh life and invention, when Sam Wellers and Mark Tapleys led the throng, we all awaited with impatience and received with delight the new oddities with which the great novelist filled his pages; but it is impossible to deny that nowadays that fertile fullness has failed, and that the persistent devotion to the eccentric which has distinguished Mr Dickens through all his literary life, does now no longer produce fruits such as earn him our forgiveness for all the daring steps he takes beyond the modesty of nature. In his last work, symptoms of a dangerous adherence to, and departure from, his old habitudes, will strike most of his faithful readers. The oddity remains, but much of the character has evaporated. The personages in *Great Expectations* are less out of the way, and the circumstances more so. Strange situations and fantastic predicaments have very much taken the place of those quaint and overstrained but still lifelike phases of humanity in which the author used to delight. He now carves his furniture grotesquely, and makes quaint masks upon his friezes; but he has no longer patience to keep up the strain so long as is necessary for the perfection of a character. After an indication of what he means this and that figure to be, he goes on with his story, too indifferent about it, one could suppose, to enter into the old elaboration. The book reminds us of a painter's rapid memoranda of some picture, in which he uses his pencil to help his memory. After he has dashed in the outline and composition, he scribbles a hasty 'carmine' or 'ultramarine' where those colours come. So the reds and blues of Mr Dickens's picture are only written in. He means us to fill in the glow of the natural hue from the feeble symbol of the word which represents it, or perhaps to go back in our own memory to those forcible and abundant days when he wrought out his own odd conceptions minutely as if he loved them. Perhaps it was not at any time the wholesomest kind of art, but it was certainly much more satisfactory and piquant than now.

So far as *Great Expectations* is a sensation novel, it occupies itself with incidents all but impossible, and in themselves strange, dangerous and exciting; but so far as it is one of the series of Mr Dickens's works, it is feeble, fatigued and colourless. One feels that he must have got tired of it as the work went on, and that the creatures he had called into being, but who are no longer the lively men and women they used to be, must have bored him unspeakably before it was time to cut short their career, and throw a hasty and impatient hint of their future to stop the tiresome public appetite. Joe Gargery the blacksmith alone represents the ancient mood of the author. He is as good, as true, patient and affectionate, as ungrammatical and confused in his faculty of speech, as could be desired; and shields the poor little Pip when he is a child on his hands, and forgives him when he is a man too grand for the blacksmith, with all that affecting tenderness and refinement of affection with which Mr Dickens has the faculty of making his poor blacksmiths and fishermen much more interesting than anything he has ever produced in the condition of gentleman.

—Margaret Oliphant, "Sensation Novels," *Blackwood's Edinburgh Magazine* 91, May 1862, pp. 564–84

G.K. CHESTERTON "GREAT EXPECTATIONS" (1911)

Chesterton sees *Great Expectations* as using Dickensian means to achieve an almost shockingly non-Dickensian end. Chesterton admires the "real unconquerable rush and energy" that Dickens brings to characters, and so it is perhaps surprising that Pip is so thoroughly conquered by his expectations. As Justin McCarthy's entry suggests, most Dickens stories operate like fairy tales. In *Oliver Twist*, for example, the orphan Oliver is ultimately restored to his family; in *Our Mutual Friend*, John Harmon becomes his own doppelganger in order to win both a bride and a vast fortune. The reversal of *Great Expectations* is that the expectations will be thwarted and that merely possessing such expectations will be the ruin, rather than the making, of Pip.

Like Thackeray's *Vanity Fair*, then, *Great Expectations* is a "novel without a hero." As Chesterton observes, it is "a novel which aims chiefly at showing that the hero is unheroic." More broadly, Dickens uses Pip to expose the masquerade at the heart of masculinity, especially in its gentlemanly guise: Pip simultaneously is confident and yet crushed by even "the slightest breath of ridicule." Students discussing masculinity, heroism, or the portrayal of the gentleman will have much to glean here. Chesterton makes an interesting contrast to Stevenson and Mallock, who argued repeatedly that Dickens did not know how authentic gentlemen behaved. Chesterton's ingenious solution is to turn Pip's desire to be a gentleman into an allegory for actual gentlemanly conduct.

Great Expectations, which was written in the afternoon of Dickens's life and fame, has a quality of serene irony and even sadness, which puts it quite alone among his other works. At no time could Dickens possibly be called cynical, he had too much vitality; but relatively to the other books this book is cynical; but it has the soft and gentle cynicism of old age, not the hard cynicism of youth. To be a young cynic is to be a young brute; but Dickens, who had been so perfectly romantic and sentimental in his youth, could afford to admit this touch of doubt into the mixed experience of his middle age. At no time could any books by Dickens have been called Thackerayan. Both of the two men were too great for that. But relatively to the other Dickensian productions this book may be called Thackerayan. It is a study in human weakness and the slow human surrender. It describes how easily a free lad of fresh and decent instincts can be made to care more for rank and pride and the degrees of our stratified society than for old affection and for honour. It is an extra chapter to *The Book of Snobs*.

The best way of stating the change which this book marks in Dickens can be put in one phrase. In this book for the first time the hero disappears. The hero had descended to Dickens by a long line which begins with the gods, nay, perhaps if one may say so, which begins with God. First comes Deity and then the image of Deity; first comes the god and then the demi-god, the Hercules who labours and conquers before he receives his heavenly crown. That idea, with continual mystery and modification, has continued behind all romantic tales; the demi-god became the hero of paganism; the hero of paganism became the knight-errant of Christianity; the knight-errant who wandered and was foiled before he triumphed became the hero of the later prose romance, the romance in which the hero had to fight a duel with the villain but always survived, in which the hero drove desperate horses through the night in order to rescue the heroine, but always rescued her.

This heroic modern hero, this demi-god in a top-hat, may be said to reach his supreme moment and typical example about the time when Dickens was writing that thundering and thrilling and highly unlikely scene in *Nicholas Nickleby*, the scene where Nicholas hopelessly denounces the atrocious Gride in his hour of grinning triumph, and a thud upon the floor above tells them that the heroine's tyrannical father has died just in time to set her free. That is the apotheosis of the pure heroic as Dickens found it, and as Dickens in some sense continued it. It may be that it does not appear with quite so much unmistakable Youth, beauty, valour, and virtue as it does in Nicholas Nickleby. Walter Gay is a simpler and more careless hero, but when he is doing any of the business of the story he is purely heroic. Kit Nubbles is a humbler hero, but he is a hero; when he is good he is very good. Even David Copperfield, who confesses to boyish tremors and boyish evasions in his account of his boyhood, acts the strict stiff part of the chivalrous gentleman in all the active and determining scenes of the tale. But *Great Expectations* may be called, like *Vanity Fair*, a novel without a hero. Almost all Thackeray's novels except *Esmond* are novels without a hero, but only one of Dickens's novels can be so described. I do not mean that it is a novel without a *jeune premier*, a young man to make love; *Pickwick* is that and *Oliver Twist*, and, perhaps, *The Old Curiosity Shop*. I mean that it is a novel without a hero in the same far deeper and more deadly sense in which *Pendennis* is also a novel without a hero. I mean that it is a novel which aims chiefly at showing that the hero is unheroic.

All such phrases as these must appear of course to overstate the case. Pip is a much more delightful person than Nicholas Nickleby. Or to take a stronger case for the purpose of our argument, Pip is a much more delightful person than Sydney Carton. Still the fact remains. Most of Nicholas Nickleby's personal actions are meant to show that he is heroic. Most of Pip's actions are meant to show that he is not heroic. The study of Sydney Carton is meant to indicate that with all his vices Sydney Carton was a hero. The study of Pip is meant to indicate that with all his virtues Pip was a snob. The motive of the literary explanation is different. Pip and Pendennis are meant to show how circumstances can corrupt men. Sam Weller and Hercules are meant to show how heroes can subdue circumstances.

This is the preliminary view of the book which is necessary if we are to regard it as a real and separate fact in the life of Dickens. Dickens had many moods because he was an artist; but he had one great mood, because he was a great artist. Any real difference therefore from the general drift, or rather (I apologise to Dickens) the general drive of his creation is very important. This is the one place in his work in which he does, I will not say feel like Thackeray, far less think like Thackeray, less still write like Thackeray, but this is the one of his works in which he understands Thackeray. He puts himself in some sense in the same place; he considers mankind at somewhat the same angle as mankind is considered in one of the sociable and sarcastic novels of Thackeray. When he deals with Pip he sets out not to show his strength like the strength of Hercules, but to show his weakness like the weakness of Pendennis. When he sets out to describe Pip's great expectation he does not set out, as in a fairy tale, with the idea that these great expectations will be fulfilled; he sets out from the first with the idea that these great expectations will be disappointing. We might very well, as I have remarked elsewhere, apply to all Dickens's books the title *Great Expectations*. All his books are full of an airy and yet ardent expectation of everything; of the next person who shall happen to speak, of the next chimney that shall happen to smoke, of the next event, of the next ecstasy; of the next fulfilment of any eager human fancy. All his books might be called *Great Expectations*. But the only book to which he gave the name of *Great Expectations* was the only book in which the expectation was never realised. It was so with the whole of that splendid and unconscious generation to which he belonged. The whole glory of that old English middle class was that it was unconscious; its excellence was entirely in that, that it was the culture of the nation, and that it did not know it. If Dickens had ever known that he was optimistic, he would have ceased to be happy.

It is necessary to make this first point clear: that in *Great Expectations* Dickens was really trying to be a quiet, a detached, and even a cynical observer of human life. Dickens was trying to be Thackeray. And the final and startling triumph of Dickens is this: that even to this moderate and modern story, he gives an incomparable energy which is not moderate and which is not modern. He is trying to be reasonable; but in spite of himself he is inspired. He is trying to be detailed, but in spite of himself he is gigantic. Compared to the rest of Dickens this is Thackeray; but compared to the whole of Thackeray we can only say in supreme praise of it that it is Dickens.

Take, for example, the one question of snobbishness. Dickens has achieved admirably the description of the doubts and vanities of the wretched Pip as he walks down the street in his new gentlemanly clothes, the clothes of which he is so proud and so ashamed. Nothing could be so exquisitely human, nothing especially could be so exquisitely masculine as that combination of self-love and self-assertion and even insolence with a naked and helpless sensibility to the slightest breath of ridicule. Pip thinks himself better than every one else, and yet anybody can snub him; that is the everlasting male, and perhaps the everlasting gentleman. Dickens has described perfectly this quivering and defenceless dignity. Dickens has described perfectly how ill-armed it is against the coarse humour of real humanity—the real humanity which Dickens loved, but which idealists and philanthropists do not love, the humanity of cabmen and costermongers and men singing in a third-class carriage; the humanity of Trabb's boy. In describing Pip's weakness Dickens is as true and as delicate as Thackeray. But Thackeray might have been easily as true and as delicate as Dickens. This quick and quiet eye for the tremors of mankind is a thing which Dickens possessed, but which others possessed also. George Eliot or Thackeray could have described the weakness of Pip. Exactly what George Eliot and Thackeray could not have described was the vigour of Trabb's boy. There would have been admirable humour and observation in their accounts of that intolerable urchin. Thackeray would have given us little light touches of Trabb's boy, absolutely true to the quality and colour of the humour, just as in his novels of the eighteenth century, the glimpses of Steele or Bolingbroke or Doctor Johnson are exactly and perfectly true to the colour and quality of their humour. George Eliot in her earlier books would have given us shrewd authentic scraps of the real dialect of Trabb's boy, just as she gave us shrewd and authentic scraps of the real talk in a Midland country town. In her later books she would have given us highly rationalistic explanations of Trabb's boy; which we should not have read. But exactly what they could never have given, and exactly what Dickens does give, is the *bounce* of Trabb's boy. It is the real unconquerable rush and energy in a character which was the supreme and quite indescribable greatness of Dickens. He conquered by rushes; he attacked in masses; he carried things at the spear point in a charge of spears; he was the Rupert of Fiction. The thing about any figure of Dickens, about Sam Weller or Dick Swiveller, or Micawber, or Bagstock, or Trabb's boy,—the thing about each one of these persons is that he cannot be exhausted. A Dickens character hits you first on the nose and then in the waistcoat, and then in the eye and then in the waistcoat again, with the blinding rapidity of some battering engine. The scene in which Trabb's boy continually overtakes Pip in order to reel and stagger as at a first encounter is a thing quite within the real competence of such a character; it might have been suggested by Thackeray, or George Eliot, or any realist. But the point with Dickens is that there is a rush in the boy's rushings; the writer and the reader rush with him. They start with him, they stare with him, they stagger with him, they share an inexpressible vitality in the air which emanates from this violent and capering satirist. Trabb's boy is among other things a boy; he has a physical rapture in hurling himself like a boomerang and in bouncing to the sky like a ball. It is just exactly in describing this quality that Dickens is Dickens and that no one else comes near him. No one feels in his bones that Felix Holt was strong as he feels in his bones that little Quilp was strong. No one can feel that even Rawdon Crawley's splendid smack across the face of Lord Steyne is quite so living and life-giving as the "kick after kick" which old Mr. Weller dealt the dancing and quivering Stiggins as he drove him towards the trough.

This quality, whether expressed intellectually or physically, is the profoundly popular and eternal quality in Dickens; it is the thing that no one else could do. This quality is the quality which has always given its continuous power and poetry to the common people everywhere. It is life; it is the joy of life felt by those who have nothing else but life. It is the thing that all aristocrats have always hated and dreaded in the people. And it is the thing which poor Pip really hates and dreads in Trabb's boy.

A great man of letters or any great artist is symbolic without knowing it. The things he describes are types because they are truths. Shakespeare may, or may not, have ever put it to himself that Richard the Second was a philosophical symbol; but all good criticism must necessarily see him so. It may be a reasonable question whether the artist should be allegorical. There can be no doubt among sane men that the critic should be allegorical. Spenser may have lost by being less realistic than Fielding. But any good criticism of *Tom Jones* must be as mystical as the *Faery Queen*. Hence it is unavoidable in speaking of a fine book like *Great Expectations* that we should give even to its unpretentious and realistic figures a certain massive mysticism. Pip is Pip, but he is also the well-meaning snob. And this is even more true of those two great figures in the tale which stand for the English democracy. For, indeed, the first and last word upon the English democracy is said in Joe Gargery and Trabb's boy. The actual English populace, as distinct from the French populace or the Scotch or Irish populace, may be said to lie between those two types. The first is the poor man who does not assert himself at all, and the second is the poor man who asserts himself entirely with the weapon of sarcasm. The only way in which the English now ever rise in revolution is under the symbol and leadership of Trabb's boy. What pikes and shillelahs were to the Irish populace, what guns and barricades were to the French populace, that chaff is to the English populace. It is their weapon, the use of which they really understand. It is the one way in which they can make a rich man feel uncomfortable, and they use it very justifiably for all it is worth. If they do not cut off the heads of tyrants at least they sometimes do their best to make the tyrants lose their heads. The gutter boys of the great towns carry the art of personal criticism to so rich and delicate a degree that some well-dressed persons when they walk past a file of them feel as if they were walking past a row of omniscient critics or judges with a power of life and death. Here and there only is some ordinary human custom, some natural human pleasure suppressed in deference to the fastidiousness of the rich. But all the rich tremble before the fastidiousness of the poor.

Of the other type of democracy it is far more difficult to speak. It is always hard to speak of good things or good people, for in satisfying the soul they take away a certain spur to speech. Dickens was often called a sentimentalist. In one sense he sometimes was a sentimentalist. But if sentimentalism be held to mean something artificial or theatrical, then in the core and reality of his character Dickens was the very reverse of a sentimentalist. He seriously and definitely loved goodness. To see sincerity and charity satisfied him like a meal. What some critics call his love of sweet stuff is really his love of plain beef and bread. Sometimes one is tempted to wish that in the long Dickens dinner the sweet courses could be left out; but this does not make the whole banquet other than a banquet singularly solid and simple. The critics complain of the sweet things, but not because they are so strong as to like simple things. They complain of the sweet things because they are so sophisticated as to like sour things; their tongues are tainted with the bitterness of absinthe. Yet because of the very simplicity of Dickens's moral tastes it is impossible to speak adequately of them; and Joe Gargery must stand as he stands in the book, a thing too obvious to be understood. But this may be said of him in one of his minor aspects, that he stands for a certain long-suffering in the English poor, a certain weary patience and politeness which almost breaks the heart. One cannot help wondering whether that great mass of silent virtue will ever achieve anything on this earth.

—G.K. Chesterton, "Great Expectations," *Criticisms & Appreciations of the Works of Charles Dickens*, 1911

A TALE OF TWO CITIES

SIR JAMES FITZJAMES STEPHEN (1859)

Sir James Fitzjames Stephen was a well-known critic for the *Saturday Review*, which led a concerted counterstrike against Dickens's popularity, chiefly on the grounds of vulgarity. James's brother, Leslie Stephen, was also an influential literary figure, both in his own right and as the father of Virginia Woolf. Sir James Fitzjames Stephen's hilariously mean-spirited review of *A Tale of Two Cities* is characteristic of the *Saturday Review*'s aristocratic disdain for the upstart Dickens.

Like Henry James, Stephen finds Dickens's characterizations to be intolerably artificial and, indeed, "really mechanical." In addition Stephen claims that Dickens's vaunted sympathy is in fact quite easy to produce:

"The whole art is to take a melancholy subject, and rub the reader's nose in it." Stephen even goes so far as to mock Dickens's transliterated French, drawing attention to Dickens's attenuated formal schooling. Given Dickens's well-known anxieties about debt and money, there may even be some irony in Stephen's opening quip that "to pay debts is a higher duty than to write good novels."

While Stephen's defense of the French aristocracy is unlikely to win many modern converts, there is something bracing about his thoroughgoing disdain for Dickens.

There are few more touching books in their way than the last of the *Waverly Novels*. The readers of *Castle Dangerous* and *Count Robert of Paris* can hardly fail to see in those dreary pages the reflection of a proud and honourable man redeeming what he looked upon as his honour at the expense of his genius. Sir Walter Scott's desperate efforts to pay his debts by extracting the very last ounce of metal from a mine which had long been substantially worked out, deserve the respect and enlist the sympathy which is the due of high spirit and unflinching courage. The novels, to be sure, are as bad as bad can be; but to pay debts is a higher duty than to write good novels, and as monuments of what can be done in that direction by a determined man, they are not without their interest and value. They have, moreover, the negative value of being only bad. They are not offensive or insulting. The usual strong men, the usual terrific combats, and the usual upholstery are brought upon the stage. They are no doubt greatly the worse for wear; but if they were good of their kind, there would be nothing to complain of. The soup is cold, the mutton raw, and the fowls tough; but there are soup, mutton, and fowls for dinner, not puppy pie and stewed cat.

In the *Tale of Two Cities*, Mr. Dickens has reached the *Castle Dangerous* stage without Sir Walter Scott's excuse; and instead of wholesome food ill-dressed, he has put before his readers dishes of which the quality is not disguised by the cooking. About a year ago, he thought proper to break up an old and to establish a new periodical, upon grounds which, if the statement—and, as far as we are aware, the uncontradicted statement—of Messrs. Bradbury and Evans is true, were most discreditable to his character for good feeling, and we might almost say for common decency, and in order to extend the circulation of the new periodical he published in it the story which now lies before us. It has the merit of being much shorter than its predecessors, and the consequence is, that the satisfaction which both the author and his readers must feel at its conclusion was deferred for a considerably less period than usual. It is a most curious production, whether it is considered in a literary, in a moral, or in an historical point of view. If it had not borne Mr. Dickens's name, it would in all probability have hardly met with a single reader; and if it has any popularity at all, it must derive it from the circumstance that it stands in the same relation to his other books as salad dressing stands in towards a complete salad. It is a bottle of the sauce in which *Pickwick* and *Nicholas Nickleby* were dressed, and to which they owed much of their popularity; and though it has stood open on the sideboard for a very long time, and has lost a good deal of its original flavour, the philosophic inquirer who is willing to go through the penance of tasting it will be, to a certain extent, repaid. He will have an opportunity of studying in its elements a system of cookery which procured for its ingenious inventor unparalleled popularity, and enabled him to infect the literature of his country with a disease which manifests itself in such repulsive symptoms that it has gone far to invert the familiar doctrines of the Latin Grammar about ingenuous arts, and to substitute for them the conviction that the principal results of a persistent devotion to literature are an incurable vulgarity of mind and of taste, and intolerable arrogance of temper.

As, notwithstanding the popularity of its author, it might be an error to assume that our readers are at all acquainted with the *Tale of Two Cities*, it may be desirable to mention shortly the points of the story. The Two Cities are London and Paris. A French physician, who has just been released after passing many years in the Bastille, is brought over to England, where he lives with his pretty daughter. Five years elapse, and the doctor and his daughter appear as witnesses on the trial for treason of a young Frenchman, who is suspected of being a French spy, and acquitted. A year or two more elapses, and the doctor's daughter marries the acquitted man, refusing two barristers, one of whom had defended him, whilst the other was devil to the first. Then ten years elapse, and as the Revolution is in full bloom in Paris, all the characters go over there on various excuses. The Frenchman turns out to be a noble who had given up his estate because he was conscience-stricken at the misery of the population around him, and thought he had better live by his wits in London than have the responsibility of continuing to be a landowner in France. He gets into prison, and is in great danger of losing his head, but his father-in-law, on the strength of his Bastille reputation, gets him off. He is, however, arrested a second time, and turns out to be the son of the infamous Marquis who had put the father-in-law into the Bastille for being shocked at his having murdered a serf. On this discovery he is condemned to death, and his wife goes through the usual business—"If I might embrace him once,"

"My husband—No! A moment," "Dear darling of my soul," and so forth. Next day, before the time fixed for his execution, the rejected barrister—the devil, not the counsel for the prisoner—gets into the prison, changes clothes with the husband, stupefies him with something in the nature of chloroform, gets him passed out of the prison by a confederate before he revives, and is guillotined in his place.

Such is the story, and it would perhaps be hard to imagine a clumsier or more disjointed framework for the display of the tawdry wares which form Mr. Dickens's stock-in-trade. The broken-backed way in which the story maunders along from 1775 to 1792 and back again to 1760 or thereabouts, is an excellent instance of the complete disregard of the rules of literary composition which have marked the whole of Mr. Dickens's career as an author. No portion of his popularity is due to intellectual excellence. The higher pleasures which novels are capable of giving are those which are derived from the development of a skilfully constructed plot, or the careful and moderate delineation of character; and neither of these are to be found in Mr. Dickens's works, nor has his influence over his contemporaries had the slightest tendency to promote the cultivation by others of the qualities which produce them. The two main sources of his popularity are his power of working upon the feelings by the coarsest stimulants, and his power of setting common occurrences in a grotesque and unexpected light. In his earlier works, the skill and vigour with which these operations were performed were so remarkable as to make it difficult to analyse the precise means by which the effect was produced on the mind of the reader. Now that familiarity has deprived his books of the gloss and freshness which they formerly possessed, the mechanism is laid bare; and the fact that the means by which the effect is produced are really mechanical has become painfully apparent. It would not, indeed, be matter of much difficulty to frame from such a book as the *Tale of Two Cities* regular recipes for grotesque and pathetic writing, by which any required quantity of the article night be produced with infallible certainty. The production of pathos is the simpler operation of the two. With a little practice and a good deal of determination, it would really be as easy to harrow up people's feelings as to poke the fire. The whole art is to take a melancholy subject, and rub the reader's nose in it, and this does not require any particular amount either of skill or knowledge. Every one knows, for example, that death is a solemn and affecting thing. If, therefore, it is wished to make a pathetic impression on the reader, the proper course is to introduce a death-bed scene, and to river attention to it by specifying all its details. Almost any subject will do, because the pathetic power of the scene lies in the fact of the death; and the artifice employed consists simply in enabling the notion of death to be reiterated at short intervals by introducing a variety of irrelevant trifles which suspend attention for the moment, and allow it after an interval to revert to death with the additional impulse derived from the momentary contrast. The process of doing this to almost any conceivable extent is so simple that it becomes, with practice, almost mechanical. To describe the light and shade of the room in which the body lies, the state of the bedclothes, the conversation of the servants, the sound of the undertaker's footsteps, the noise of driving the coffin-screws, and any number of other minutiae, is in effect a device for working on the feelings by repeating at intervals, Death—death—death—death—death, just as feeling of another class might be worked upon by continually calling a man a liar or a thief. It is an old remark, that if dirt enough is thrown some of it will stick; and Mr. Dickens's career shows that the same is true of pathos.

To be grotesque is a rather more difficult trick than to be pathetic; but it is just as much a trick, capable of being learned and performed almost mechanically. One principal element of grotesqueness is unexpected incongruity; and inasmuch as most things are different from most other things, there is in nature a supply of this element of grotesqueness which is absolutely inexhaustible. Whenever Mr. Dickens writes a novel, he makes two or three comic characters just as he might cut a pig out of a piece of orange-peel. In the present story there are two comic characters, one of whom is amusing by reason of the facts that his name is Jerry Cruncher, that his hair sticks out like iron spikes, and that, having reproached his wife for "flopping down on her knees" to pray, he goes on for seventeen years speaking of praying as "flopping." If, instead of saying that his hair was like iron spikes, Mr. Dickens had said that his ears were like mutton-chops, or his nose like a Bologna sausage, the effect would have been much the same. One of his former characters was identified by a habit of staring at things and people with his teeth, and another by a propensity to draw his moustache up under his nose, and his nose down over his moustache. As there are many members in one body, Mr. Dickens may possibly live long enough to have a character for each of them, so that he may have one character identified by his eyebrows, another by his nostrils, and another by his toe-nails. No popularity can disguise the fact that this is the very lowest of low styles of art. It is a step below Cato's full wig and lacquered chair which shook the pit and made the gallery stare, and in point of artistic merit stands on precisely the same level with the deformities which inspire the pencils of the prolific artists who supply valentines to the million at a penny a-piece.

One special piece of grotesqueness introduced by Mr. Dickens into his present tale is very curious. A good deal of the story relates to France, and many of the characters are French. Mr. Dickens accordingly makes them talk a language which, for a few sentences, is amusing enough, but which becomes intolerably tiresome and affected when it is spread over scores of pages. He translates every French word by its exact English equivalent. For example, "Voilà votre passeport" becomes "Behold your passport"—"Je viens de voir," "I come to see," &c. Apart from the bad taste of this, it shows a perfect ignorance of the nature and principles of language. The sort of person who would say in English, "Behold," is not the sort of person who would say in French "Voilà"; and to describe the most terrible events in this misbegotten jargon shows a great want of sensibility to the real requirements of art. If an acquaintance with Latin were made the excuse for a similar display, Mr. Dickens and his disciples would undoubtedly consider such conduct as inexcusable pedantry. To show off familiarity with a modern language is not very different from similar conduct with respect to an ancient one.

The moral tone of the *Tale of Two Cities* is not more wholesome than that of its predecessors, nor does it display any nearer approach to a solid knowledge of the subject-matter to which it refers. Mr. Dickens observes in his preface—"It has been one of my hopes to add something to the popular and picturesque means of understanding that terrible time, though no one can hope to add anything to the philosophy of Mr. Carlyle's wonderful book." The allusion to Mr. Carlyle confirms the presumption which the book itself raises, that Mr. Dickens happened to have read the History of the French Revolution, and, being on the look-out for a subject, determined off hand to write a novel about it. Whether he has any other knowledge of the subject than a single reading of Mr. Carlyle's work would supply does not appear, but certainly what he has written shows no more. It is exactly the sort of story which a man would write who had taken down Mr. Carlyle's theory without any sort of inquiry or examination, but with a comfortable conviction that "nothing could be added to its philosophy." The people, says Mr. Dickens, in effect, had been degraded by long and gross misgovernment, and acted like wild beasts in consequence. There is, no doubt, a great deal of truth in this view of the matter, but it is such very elementary truth that, unless a man had something new to say about it, it is hardly worth mentioning; and Mr. Dickens supports it by specific assertions which, if not absolutely false, are at any rate so selected as to convey an entirely false impression. It is a shameful thing for a popular writer to exaggerate the faults of the French aristocracy in a book which will naturally find its way to readers who know very little of the subject except what he chooses to tell them; . . .

In the early part of his novel he introduces the trial of a man who is accused of being a French spy, and does his best to show how utterly corrupt and unfair everybody was who took part in the proceedings. The counsel for the Crown is made to praise the Government spy, who is the principal witness, as a man of exalted virtue, and is said to address himself with zeal to the task of driving the nails into the prisoner's coffin. In examining the witnesses he makes every sort of unfair suggestion which can prejudice the prisoner, and the judge shows great reluctance to allow any circumstance to come out which would be favourable to him, and does all in his power to get him hung, though the evidence against him is weak in the extreme. It so happens that in the State Trials for the very year (1780) in which the scene of Mr. Dickens's story is laid, there is a full report of the trial of a French spy—one De la Motte—for the very crime which is imputed to Mr. Dickens's hero. One of the principal witnesses in this case was an accomplice of very bad character; and in fact it is difficult to doubt that the one trial is merely a fictitious "rendering" of the other. The comparison between them is both curious and instructive. It would be perfectly impossible to imagine a fairer trial than De la Motte's, or stronger evidence than that on which he was convicted. The counsel for the Crown said not one word about the character of the approver, and so far was the judge from pressing hard on the prisoner, that he excluded evidence offered against him which in almost any other country would have been all but conclusive against him. It is surely a very disgraceful thing to represent such a transaction as an attempt to commit a judicial murder.

We must say one word in conclusion as to the illustrations. They are thoroughly worthy of the text. It is impossible to imagine faces and figures more utterly unreal, or more wretchedly conventional, than those by which Mr. Browne represents Mr. Dickens's characters. The handsome faces are caricatures, and the ugly ones are like nothing human.

—Sir James Fitzjames Stephen,
"A Tale of Two Cities," (1859)

G.K. Chesterton
"A Tale of Two Cities" (1911)

Chesterton implies but does not explicitly say that *A Tale of Two Cities* is born of the same impulse as *Oliver Twist*: a uniquely Dickensian fusion of the hatred of oppression, on the one hand, with a recognition of the joy of revolution, even of the joy in destruction. Comparing Dickens to a revolutionary mob, Chesterton notes that each has a "cheery and quite one-sided satisfaction" when they pull down symbols of oppression. By recognizing the true happiness behind this impulse, Dickens pins down both the appeal of revolution and its easy convertibility into indiscriminate violence.

As an example of Dickens's literary work, *A Tale of Two Cities* is not wrongly named. It is his most typical contact with the civic ideals of Europe. All his other tales have been tales of one city. He was in spirit a Cockney; though that title has been quite unreasonably twisted to mean a cad. By the old sound and proverbial test a Cockney was a man born within the sound of Bow bells. That is, he was a man born within the immediate appeal of high civilisation and of eternal religion. Shakespeare, in the heart of his fantastic forest, turns with a splendid suddenness to the Cockney ideal as being the true one after all. For a jest, for a reaction, for an idle summer love or still idler summer hatred, it is well to wander away into the bewildering forest of Arden. It is well that those who are sick with love or sick with the absence of love, those who weary of the folly of courts or weary yet more of their wisdom, it is natural that these should trail away into the twinkling twilight of the woods. Yet it is here that Shakespeare makes one of his most arresting and startling assertions of the truth. Here is one of those rare and tremendous moments of which one may say that there is a stage direction, "Enter Shakespeare." He has admitted that for men weary of courts, for men sick of cities, the wood is the wisest place, and he has praised it with his purest lyric ecstasy. But when a man enters suddenly upon that celestial picnic, a man who is not sick of cities, but sick of hunger, a man who is not weary of courts, but weary of walking, then Shakespeare lets through his own voice with a shattering sincerity and cries the praise of practical human civilisation:

> If ever you have looked on better days,
> If ever you have sat at good men's feasts,
> If ever been where bells have knolled to church,
> If ever from your eyelids wiped a tear
> Or know what 't is to pity and be pitied.

There is nothing finer even in Shakespeare than that conception of the circle of rich men all pretending to rough it in the country, and the one really hungry man entering, sword in hand, and praising the city. "If ever been where bells have knolled to church"; if you have ever been within sound of Bow bells; if you have ever been happy and haughty enough to call yourself a Cockney.

We must remember this distinction always in the case of Dickens. Dickens is the great Cockney, at once tragic and comic, who enters abruptly upon the Arcadian banquet of the aesthetics and says, "Forbear and eat no more," and tells them that they shall not eat "until necessity be served." If there was one thing he would have favoured instinctively it would have been the spreading of the town as meaning the spreading of civilisation. And we should (I hope) all favour the spreading of the town if it did mean the spreading of civilisation. The objection to the spreading of the modern Manchester or Birmingham suburb is simply that such a suburb is much more barbaric than any village in Europe could ever conceivably be. And again, if there is anything that Dickens would have definitely hated it is that general treatment of nature as a dramatic spectacle, a piece of scene-painting which has become the common mark of the culture of our wealthier classes. Despite many fine pictures of natural scenery, especially along the English roadsides, he was upon the whole emphatically on the side of the town. He was on the side of bricks and mortar. He was a citizen; and, after all, a citizen means a man of the city. His strength was, after all, in the fact that he was a man of the city. But, after all, his weakness, his calamitous weakness, was that he was a man of one city.

For all practical purposes he had never been outside such places as Chatham and London. He did indeed travel on the Continent; but surely no man's travel was ever so superficial as his. He was more superficial than the smallest and commonest tourist. He went about Europe on stilts; he never touched the ground. There is one good test and one only of whether a man has travelled to any profit in Europe. An Englishman is, as such, a European, and as he approaches the central splendours of Europe he ought to feel that he is coming home. If he does not feel at home he had much better have stopped at home. England is a real home; London is a real home; and all the essential feelings of adventure or the picturesque can easily be gained by going out at night upon the flats of Essex or the cloven hills of Surrey. Your visit to Europe is useless unless it gives you the sense of an exile returning. Your first sight of Rome is futile unless you feel that you have seen it before. Thus useless and thus futile were the foreign experiments and the continental raids of Dickens. He enjoyed them as he would have enjoyed, as a boy, a scamper out of Chatham into some strange meadows, as he would have enjoyed, when a grown man, a steam in a police boat out into the fens to the far east of London. But he was the Cockney venturing far; he was not the European coming home. He is still the splendid Cockney Orlando of whom I spoke above; he cannot but suppose that any strange men, being happy in some pastoral way, are mysterious foreign scoundrels. Dickens's real speech to the lazy and laughing civilisation of Southern Europe would really have run in the Shakespearean words:

> but whoe'er you be
> Who in this desert inaccessible,
> Under the shade of melancholy boughs
> Lose and neglect the creeping hours of time.
> If ever you have looked on better things,
> If ever been where bells have knolled to church.

If, in short, you have ever had the advantage of being born within the sound of Bow bells. Dickens could not really conceive that there was any other city but his own.

It is necessary thus to insist that Dickens never understood the Continent, because only thus can we appreciate the really remarkable thing he did in *A Tale of Two Cities*. It is necessary to feel, first of all, the fact that to him London was the centre of the universe. He did not understand at all the real sense in which Paris is the capital of Europe. He had never realised that all roads lead to Rome. He had never felt (as an Englishman can feel) that he was an Athenian before he was a Londoner. Yet with everything against him he did this astonishing thing. He wrote a book about two cities, one of which he understood; the other he did not understand. And his description of the city he did not know is almost better than his description of the city he did know. This is the entrance of the unquestionable thing about Dickens; the thing called genius; the thing which every one has to talk about directly and distinctly because no one knows what it is. For a plain word (as for instance the word fool) always covers an infinite mystery.

A Tale of Two Cities is one of the more tragic tints of the later life of Dickens. It might be said that he grew sadder as he grew older; but this would be false, for two reasons. First, a man never or hardly ever does grow sad as he grows old; on the contrary, the most melancholy young lovers can be found forty years afterwards chuckling over their port wine. And second, Dickens never did grow old, even in a physical sense. What weariness did appear in him appeared in the prime of life; it was due not to age but to overwork, and his exaggerative way of doing everything. To call Dickens a victim of elderly disenchantment would be as absurd as to say the same of Keats. Such fatigue as there was, was due not to the slowing down of his blood, but rather to its unremitting rapidity. He was not wearied by his age; rather he was wearied by his youth. And though *A Tale of Two Cities* is full of sadness, it is full also of enthusiasm; that pathos is a young pathos rather than an old one. Yet there is one circumstance which does render important the fact that *A Tale of Two Cities* is one of the later works of Dickens. This fact is the fact of his dependence upon another of the great writers of the Victorian era. And it is in connection with this that we can best see the truth of which I have been speaking; the truth that his actual ignorance of France went with amazing intuitive perception of the truth about it. It is here that he has most clearly the plain mark of the man of genius; that he can understand what he does not understand.

Dickens was inspired to the study of the French Revolution and to the writing of a romance about it by the example and influence of Carlyle. Thomas Carlyle undoubtedly rediscovered for Englishmen the revolution that was at the back of all their policies and reforms. It is an entertaining side joke that the French Revolution should have been discovered for Britons by the only British writer who did not really believe in it. Nevertheless, the most authoritative and the most recent critics on that great renaissance agree in considering Carlyle's work one of the most searching and detailed power. Carlyle had read a great deal about the French Revolution. Dickens had read nothing at all, except Carlyle. Carlyle was a man who collected his ideas by the careful collation of documents and the verification of references. Dickens was a man who collected his ideas from loose hints in the streets, and those always the same streets; as I have said, he was the citizen of one city. Carlyle was in his way learned; Dickens was in every way ignorant. Dickens was an Englishman cut off from France; Carlyle was a Scotsman, historically connected with France. And yet, when all this is said and certified, Dickens is more right than Carlyle. Dickens's French Revolution is probably more like the real French Revolution than Carlyle's. It is difficult, if not impossible, to state the grounds of this strong conviction. One can only talk of it by employing that excellent method which Cardinal Newman employed when he spoke of the "notes" of Catholicism. There were certain "notes" of the Revolution. One note of the Revolution was the thing which silly people call optimism, and sensible people call high spirits. Carlyle could never quite get it, because with all his spiritual energy he had no high spirits. That is why he preferred prose to poetry. He could understand rhetoric; for rhetoric means singing with an object. But he could not understand lyrics; for the lyric means singing without an object;

as every one does when he is happy. Now for all its blood and its black guillotines, the French Revolution was full of mere high spirits. Nay, it was full of happiness. This actual lilt and levity Carlyle never really found in the Revolution, because he could not find it in himself. Dickens knew less of the Revolution, but he had more of it. When Dickens attacked abuses, he battered them down with exactly that sort of cheery and quite one-sided satisfaction with which the French mob battered down the Bastille. Dickens utterly and innocently believed in certain things; he would, I think, have drawn the sword for them. Carlyle half believed in half a hundred things; he was at once more of a mystic and more of a sceptic. Carlyle was the perfect type of the grumbling servant; the old grumbling servant of the aristocratic comedies. He followed the aristocracy, but he growled as he followed. He was obedient without being servile, just as Caleb Balderstone was obedient without being servile. But Dickens was the type of the man who might really have rebelled instead of grumbling. He might have gone out into the street and fought, like the man who took the Bastille. It is somewhat nationally significant that when we talk of the man in the street it means a figure silent, slouching, and even feeble. When the French speak of the man in the street, it means danger in the street.

No one can fail to notice this deep difference between Dickens and the Carlyle whom he avowedly copied. Splendid and symbolic as are Carlyle's scenes of the French Revolution, we have in reading them a curious sense that everything is happening at night. In Dickens even massacre happens by daylight. Carlyle always assumes that because things were tragedies therefore the men who did them felt tragic. Dickens knows that the man who works the worst tragedies is the man who feels comic; as for example, Mr. Quilp. The French Revolution was a much simpler world than Carlyle could understand; for Carlyle was subtle and not simple. Dickens could understand it, for he was simple and not subtle. He understood that plain rage against plain political injustice; he understood again that obvious vindictiveness and that obvious brutality which followed. "Cruelty and the abuse of absolute power," he told an American slave-owner, "are two of the bad passions of human nature." Carlyle was quite incapable of rising to the height of that uplifted common-sense. He must always find something mystical about the cruelty of the French Revolution. The effect was equally bad whether he found it mystically bad and called the thing anarchy, or whether he found it mystically good and called it the rule of the strong. In both cases he could not understand the common-sense justice or the common-sense vengeance of Dickens and the French Revolution.

Yet Dickens has in this book given a perfect and final touch to this whole conception of mere rebellion and mere human nature. Carlyle had written the story of the French Revolution and had made the story a mere tragedy. Dickens writes the story about the French Revolution, and does not make the Revolution itself the tragedy at all. Dickens knows that an outbreak is seldom a tragedy; generally it is the avoidance of a tragedy. All the real tragedies are silent. Men fight each other with furious cries, because men fight each other with chivalry and an unchangeable sense of brotherhood. But trees fight each other in utter stillness; because they fight each other cruelly and without quarter. In this book, as in history, the guillotine is not the calamity, but rather the solution of the calamity. The sin of Sydney Carton is a sin of habit, not of revolution. His gloom is the gloom of London, not the gloom of Paris.

—G.K. Chesterton, "A Tale of Two Cities," *Criticisms & Appreciations of the Works of Charles Dickens*, 1911

OLIVER TWIST

QUEEN VICTORIA (1839)

The longest-reigning monarch in English history, Victoria (1819–1901) ascended the throne in 1837, the same year that *Oliver Twist* began appearing, and she presided over a time of imperial expansion, economic growth, and the rise of the middle class. In these conversations with Lord Melbourne and Baroness Lehzen (her former governess), we can see a conflict between Victoria's interest in Dickens's realism—the description of vice, the scandalous conditions of the workhouses—and Melbourne's insistence that literature be elevating and pure. (For a related argument, see the excerpt from Thackeray that follows.) That disagreement suggests that ostensibly Victorian prudery in fact predates Dickens and Victoria, and suggests the challenges Dickens would have faced in representing working class and criminal life.

1 January, 1839. Talked of my getting on in Oliver Twist; of the descriptions of "squalid vice" in it; of the accounts of starvation in the Workhouses and Schools, Mr. Dickens gives in his books. Lord M. says, in many schools they give children the worst things to eat, and bad beer, to save expense; told him Mamma admonished me for reading light books.

Sunday, 7th April 1839. Lord M. was talking of some dish or other, and alluded to something in Oliver Twist; he read half of the 1st vol. at Panshanger. "It's all among Workhouses, and Coffin Makers, and Pickpockets," he said; "I don't like that low debasing style; it's all slang; it's just like The Beggar's Opera; I shouldn't think it would tend to raise morals; I don't like that low debasing view of mankind." We defended Oliver very much, but in vain. "I don't like those things; I wish to avoid them; I don't like them in reality, and therefore I don't wish to see them represented," he continued; that everything one read should be pure and elevating. Schiller and Goethe would have been shocked at such things, he said. Lehzen said they would not have disliked reading them. "She don't know her own literature," said Lord M., for that Goethe said one ought never to see anything disagreeable; he wouldn't look upon the dead; "and that's just the same thing." "It's a bad taste," he continued, "which will pass away like any other, but depend upon it, while it lasts it's a bad, depraved, vicious taste; now just read Jonathan Wild," he said to Lord Torrington, "and Amelia, and see if it isn't just the same thing."

—Queen Victoria, *The Girlhood of Queen, Victoria: A Selection from Her Diaries, 1832–40*, ed. Viscount Esher, 1912, v. II

WILLIAM MAKEPEACE THACKERAY (1840)

In this extract, Thackeray points out that, because early Victorian conventions disallowed a truly realistic portrayal of criminal life, it was dishonest to attempt to represent criminal virtues.

"Going to See a Man Hanged" documents the strangely festive atmosphere that accompanied public executions—a popular form of entertainment. Registering first the rowdy presence of many criminals, especially brooding, threatening adolescent males, Thackeray encounters a girl whom "Cruikshank and Boz might have taken as a study for Nancy." Thackeray immediately acknowledges that, despite her immodest behavior and evident profession, "there was something good about the girl," associated with her "candour and simplicity." He comments that he observed her closely, because the noble prostitute is such as a staple of *Oliver Twist* and other works like it. He finds, however, the representation entirely false: if readerly squeamishness prevents an author from discussing the vices of a young woman, then, he implies, the author had better not extol her virtues. There is no way for the reader to judge accurately the character of such a woman, so long as the readerly conventions persist.

Students examining Dickens's representation of criminals, or his audience, will find Thackeray's extract helpful. Also, Thackeray connects *Twist* to crime ("Newgate") novels written by contemporaries such as William Harrison Ainsworth (*Jack Sheppard)* or Edward Bulwer Lytton (*Paul Clifford*). Finally, it is striking to contrast Thackeray's contemporaneous reaction to Dickens with the later judgment of Chesterton and Swinburne. For those later writers, what is remarkable about Dickens is his representations of malignity and violence, and not his subordination of these to any direct moral purpose.

Really the time passed away with extraordinary quickness. A thousand things of the sort related here came to amuse us. First the workmen knocking and hammering at the scaffold, mysterious clattering of blows was heard within it, and a ladder painted black was carried round, and into the interior of the edifice by a small side door. We all looked at this little ladder and at each other—things began to be very interesting. Soon came a squad of policemen; stalwart rosy-looking men, saying much for City feeding; well-dressed, well-limbed, and of admirable good-humour. They paced about the open space between the prison and the barriers which kept in the crowd from the scaffold. The front line, as far as I could see, was chiefly occupied by blackguards and boys—professional persons, no doubt, who saluted the policemen on their appearance with a volley of jokes and ribaldry. As far as I could judge from faces, there were more blackguards of sixteen and seventeen than of any maturer age; stunted, sallow, ill-grown lads, in ragged fustian, scowling about. There were a considerable number of girls, too, of the same age: one that Cruikshank and Boz might have taken as a study for Nancy. The girl was a young thief's mistress evidently; if attacked, ready to reply without a particle of modesty; could give as good ribaldry as she got; made no secret (and there were several inquiries) as to her profession and means of livelihood. But with all this, there was something good about the girl; a sort of devil-may-care candour and simplicity that one could not fail to see. Her answers to some of the coarse questions put to her, were very ready and good-humoured. She had a friend with her of the same age and class, of whom she seemed to be very fond, and who looked up to her for protection. Both of these women had beautiful eyes. Devil-may-care's were extraordinarily bright and blue, an admirably fair complexion, and a large red mouth full of white teeth. Au reste, ugly, stunted, thick-limbed, and by no means a beauty. Her friend could not be more than fifteen. They were not in rags, but had greasy cotton shawls, and old faded rag-shop bonnets. I was curious to look at them, having, in late fashionable novels, read many accounts of such personages. Bah! what figments these novelists tell us! Boz, who knows life well, knows that his Miss Nancy is the most unreal fantastical personage possible; no more like a thief's mistress than one of Gesner's shepherdesses resembles a real country wench. He dare not tell the truth concerning such young ladies. They have, no doubt, virtues like other human creatures; nay, their position engenders virtues that are not called into exercise among other women. But on these an honest painter of human nature has no right to dwell; not being able to paint the whole portrait, he has no right to present one or two favourable points as characterising the whole; and therefore, in fact, had better leave the picture alone altogether.

—William Makepeace Thackeray,
"Going to See a Man Hanged," August 1840

G.K. Chesterton "Oliver Twist" (1911)

Chesterton's aim in this essay is to account for the turn in Dickens's second novel. Compared with the uproarious fun of *The Pickwick Papers*, the gloom surrounding Oliver's birth makes for a much different mood. In *Oliver Twist*, Chesterton claims, we get the first inklings of Dickens's hatred of oppression. In addition to its interest for students of Dickens's politics, Chesterton's essay is also noteworthy for its emphasis on Dickens's democratic impulses, his suspicion of reformers, and most crucially, his humor. Because the excerpt focuses on Dickens's second novel, it makes an excellent foil to George Bernard Shaw's assertion that *Hard Times* marks a decisive turn in both humor and politics.

Chesterton begins by observing that what is distinctive about Dickens's work is the way humor and pathos coexist with darker elements and forces. Dickens's prose is also animated by "this other kind of energy, horrible, uncanny, barbaric, capable in another age of coarseness, greedy for the emblems of established ugliness, the coffin, the gibbet, the bones, the bloody knife." For a comparable argument, students might cite Swinburne's admiration for Dickens's malignity: the Catholic apologist and the flagellation enthusiast join in celebrating the democratic extremism of Dickens. The key to Dickens's appeal, Chesterton suggests, is his passionate all-consuming embrace of either happiness or malevolence. Happy mediums are for philosophers and aristocrats.

While Dickens is a moralist, Chesterton insists, this label means something different than the modern sense of the term. Dickens achieves morality by writing about immoral people and bringing them to a moral end. Students exploring morality or psychology may find suggestive the notion that Dickens enjoys punishing his villains.

Chesterton also provides details for the idea—voiced most cogently by Santayana—that Dickens hates oppression. In *Oliver Twist,* Dickens was challenging the work of ostensible reformers who, in his view, were insufficiently aware of and attentive to the suffering of their neighbors. What Chesterton admires about Dickens, then, is the way he converts politics into morality—the suffering of the poor is simply wrong.

In considering Dickens, as we almost always must consider him, as a man of rich originality, we may possibly miss the forces from which he drew even his original energy. It is not well for man to be alone. We, in the modern world, are ready enough to admit that when it is applied to some problem of monasticism or of an ecstatic life. But we will not admit that our modern artistic claim to absolute originality is really a claim to absolute unsociability; a claim to absolute loneliness. The anarchist is at least as solitary as the ascetic. And the men of very vivid vigour in literature, the men such as Dickens, have generally displayed a large sociability towards the society of letters, always expressed in the happy pursuit of pre-existent themes, sometimes expressed, as in the case of Molière or Sterne, in downright plagiarism. For even theft is a confession of our dependence on society. In Dickens, however, this element of the original foundations on which he worked is quite especially difficult to determine. This is partly due to the fact that for the present reading public he is practically the only one of his long line that is read at all. He sums up Smollett and Goldsmith, but he also destroys them. This one giant, being closest to us, cuts off from our view even the giants that begat him. But much more is this difficulty due to the fact that Dickens mixed up with the old material, materials so subtly modern, so made of the French Revolution, that the whole is transformed. If we want the best example of this, the best example is *Oliver Twist*.

Relatively to the other works of Dickens *Oliver Twist* is not of great value, but it is of great importance. Some parts of it are so crude and of so clumsy a melodrama, that one is almost tempted to say that Dickens would have been greater without it. But even if he had been greater without it he would still have been incomplete without it. With the exception of some gorgeous passages, both of humour and horror, the interest of the book lies not so much in its revelation of Dickens's literary genius as in its revelation of those moral, personal, and political instincts which were the make-up of his character and the permanent support of that literary genius. It is by far the most depressing of all his books; it is in some ways the most irritating; yet its ugliness gives the last touch of honesty to all that spontaneous and splendid output. Without this one discordant note all his merriment might have seemed like levity.

Dickens had just appeared upon the stage and set the whole world laughing with his first great story *Pickwick*. *Oliver Twist* was his encore. It was the second opportunity given to him by those who had rolled about with laughter over Tupman and Jingle, Weller and Dowler. Under such circumstances a stagey reciter will sometimes take care to give a pathetic piece after his humorous one; and with all his many moral merits, there was much that was stagey about Dickens. But this explanation alone is altogether inadequate and unworthy. There was in Dickens this other kind of energy, horrible, uncanny, barbaric, capable in another age of coarseness, greedy for the emblems of established ugliness, the coffin, the gibbet, the bones, the bloody knife. Dickens liked these things and he was all the more of a man for liking them; especially he was all the more of a boy. We can all recall with pleasure the fact that Miss Petowker (afterwards Mrs. Lillyvick) was in the habit of reciting a poem called "The Blood Drinker's Burial." I cannot express my regret that the words of this poem are not given; for Dickens would have been quite as capable of writing "The Blood Drinker's Burial" as Miss Petowker was of reciting it. This strain existed in Dickens alongside of his happy laughter; both were allied to the same robust romance. Here as elsewhere Dickens is close to all the permanent human things. He is close to religion, which has never allowed the thousand devils on its churches to stop the dancing of its bells. He is allied to the people, to the real poor, who love nothing so much as to take a cheerful glass and to talk about funerals. The extremes of his gloom and gaiety are the mark of religion and democracy; they mark him off from the moderate happiness of philosophers, and from that stoicism which is the virtue and the creed of aristocrats. There is nothing odd in the fact that the same man who conceived the humane hospitalities of Pickwick should also have imagined the inhuman laughter of Fagin's den. They are both genuine and they are both exaggerated. And the whole human tradition has tied up together in a strange knot these strands of festivity and fear. It is over the cups of Christmas Eve that men have always competed in telling ghost stories.

This first element was present in Dickens, and it is very powerfully present in *Oliver Twist*. It had not been present with sufficient consistency or continuity in *Pickwick* to make it remain on the reader's memory at all, for the tale of "Gabriel Grubb" is grotesque rather than horrible, and the two gloomy stories of the "Madman" and the "Queer Client" are so utterly irrelevant to the tale, that even if the reader remember them he probably does not remember that they occur in *Pickwick*. Critics have complained of Shakespeare and others for putting comic episodes into a tragedy. It required a man with the courage and coarseness of Dickens actually to put tragic episodes into a farce. But they are not caught up into the story at all. In *Oliver Twist*, however, the thing broke out with an almost brutal inspiration, and those who had fallen in love with Dickens for his generous buffoonery may very likely have been startled at receiving such very different fare at the next helping. When you have bought a man's book because you like his writing about Mr. Wardle's punch-bowl and Mr. Winkle's skates, it may very well be surprising to open it and read about the sickening thuds that beat out the life of Nancy, or that mysterious villain whose face was blasted with disease.

As a nightmare, the work is really admirable. Characters which are not very clearly conceived as regards their own psychology are yet, at certain moments, managed so as to shake to its foundations our own psychology. Bill Sikes is not exactly a real man, but for all that he is a real murderer. Nancy is not really impressive as a living woman; but (as the phrase goes) she makes a lovely corpse. Something quite childish and eternal in us, something which is shocked with the mere simplicity of death, quivers when we read of those repeated blows or see Sikes cursing the tell-tale cur who will follow his bloody foot-prints. And this strange, sublime, vulgar melodrama, which is melodrama and yet is painfully real, reaches its hideous height in that fine scene of the death of Sikes, the besieged house, the boy screaming within, the crowd screaming without, the murderer turned almost a maniac and dragging his victim uselessly up and down the room, the escape over the roof, the rope swiftly running taut, and death sudden, startling and symbolic; a man hanged. There is in this and similar scenes something of the quality of Hogarth and many other English moralists of the early eighteenth century. It is not easy to define this Hogarthian quality in words, beyond saying that it is a sort of alphabetical realism, like the cruel candour of children. But it has about it these two special principles which separate it from all that we call realism in our time. First, that with us a moral story means a story about moral people; with them a moral story meant more often a story about immoral people. Second, that with us realism is always associated with some subtle view of morals; with them realism was always associated with some simple view of morals. The end of Bill Sikes exactly in the way that the law would have killed him—this is a Hogarthian incident; it carries on that tradition of startling and shocking platitude.

All this element in the book was a sincere thing in the author, but none the less it came from old soils, from the graveyard and the gallows, and the lane where the ghost walked. Dickens was always attracted to such things, and (as Forster says with inimitable simplicity) "but for his strong sense might have fallen into the follies of spiritualism." As a matter of fact, like most of the men of strong sense in his tradition, Dickens was left with a half belief in spirits which became in practice a belief in bad spirits. The great disadvantage of those who have too much strong sense to believe in supernaturalism is that they keep last the low and little forms of the supernatural, such as omens, curses, spectres, and retributions, but find a high and happy supernaturalism quite incredible. Thus the Puritans denied the sacraments, but went on burning witches. This shadow does rest, to some extent, upon the rational English writers like Dickens; supernaturalism was dying, but its ugliest roots died last. Dickens would have found it easier to believe in a ghost than in a vision of the Virgin with angels. There, for good or evil, however, was the root of the old *diablerie* in Dickens, and there it is in *Oliver Twist*. But this was only the first of the new Dickens elements, which must have surprised those Dickensians who eagerly bought his second book. The second of the new Dickens elements is equally indisputable and separate. It swelled afterwards to enormous proportions in Dickens's work; but it really has its rise here. Again, as in the case of the element of *diablerie*, it would be possible to make technical exceptions in favour of *Pickwick*. Just as there were quite inappropriate scraps of the gruesome element in *Pickwick*, so there are quite inappropriate allusions to this other topic in *Pickwick*. But nobody by merely reading *Pickwick* would even remember this topic; no one by merely reading *Pickwick* would know what this topic is; this third great subject of Dickens; this second great subject of the Dickens of *Oliver Twist*.

This subject is social oppression. It is surely fair to say that no one could have gathered from *Pickwick* how this question boiled in the blood of the author of *Pickwick*. There are, indeed, passages, particularly in connection with Mr. Pickwick in the debtor's prison, which prove to us, looking back on a whole public career, that Dickens had been from the beginning bitter and inquisitive about the problem of our civilisation. No one could have imagined at the time that this bitterness ran in an unbroken river under all the surges of that superb gaiety and exuberance. With *Oliver Twist* this sterner side of Dickens was suddenly revealed. For the very first pages of *Oliver Twist* are stern even when they are funny. They amuse, but they cannot be enjoyed, as can the passages about the follies of Mr. Snodgrass or the humiliations of Mr. Winkle. The difference between the old easy humour and this new harsh humour is a difference not of degree but of kind. Dickens makes game of Mr. Bumble because he wants to kill Mr. Bumble; he made game of Mr. Winkle because he wanted him to live for ever. Dickens has taken the sword in hand; against what is he declaring war?

It is just here that the greatness of Dickens comes in; it is just here that the difference lies between the pedant and the poet. Dickens enters the social and political war, and the first stroke he deals is not only significant but even startling. Fully to see this we must appreciate the national situation. It was an age of reform, and even of radical reform; the world was full of radicals and reformers; but only too many of them took the line of attacking everything and anything that was opposed to some particular theory among the many political theories that possessed the end of the eighteenth century. Some had so much perfected the perfect theory of republicanism that they almost lay awake at night because Queen Victoria had a crown on her head. Others were so certain that mankind had hitherto been merely strangled in the bonds of the State that they saw truth only in the destruction of tariffs or of by-laws. The greater part of that generation held that clearness, economy, and a hard common-sense, would soon destroy the errors that had been erected by the superstitions and sentimentalities of the past. In pursuance of this idea many of the new men of the new century, quite confident that they were invigorating the new age, sought to destroy the old sentimental clericalism, the old sentimental feudalism, the old-world belief in priests, the old-world belief in patrons, and among other things the old-world belief in beggars. They sought among other things to clear away the old visionary kindliness on the subject of vagrants. Hence those reformers enacted not only a new reform bill but also a new poor law. In creating many other modern things they created the modern workhouse, and when Dickens came out to fight it was the first thing that he broke with his battle-axe.

This is where Dickens's social revolt is of more value than mere politics and avoids the vulgarity of the novel with a purpose. His revolt is not a revolt of the commercialist against the feudalist, of the Nonconformist against the Churchman, of the Free-trader against the Protectionist, of the Liberal against the Tory. If he were among us now his revolt would not be the revolt of the Socialist against the Individualist, or of the Anarchist against the Socialist. His revolt was simply and solely the eternal revolt; it was the revolt of the weak against the strong. He did not dislike this or that argument for oppression; he disliked oppression. He disliked a certain look on the face of a man when he looks down on another man. And that look on the face is, indeed, the only thing in the world that we have really to fight between here and the fires of Hell. That which pedants of that time and this time would have called the sentimentalism of Dickens was really simply the detached sanity of Dickens. He cared nothing for the fugitive explanations of the Constitutional Conservatives; he cared nothing for the fugitive explanations of the Manchester School. He would have cared quite as little for the fugitive explanations of the Fabian Society or of the modern scientific Socialist. He saw that under many forms there was one fact, the tyranny of man over man; and he struck at it when he saw it, whether it was old or new. When he found that footmen and rustics were too much afraid of Sir Leicester Dedlock, he attacked Sir Leicester Dedlock; he did not care whether Sir Leicester Dedlock said he was attacking England or whether Mr. Rouncewell, the Ironmaster, said he was attacking an effete oligarchy. In that case he pleased Mr. Rouncewell, the Ironmaster, and displeased Sir Leicester Dedlock, the Aristocrat. But when he found that Mr. Rouncewell's workmen were much too frightened of Mr. Rouncewell, then he displeased Mr. Rouncewell in turn; he displeased Mr. Rouncewell very much by calling him Mr. Bounderby. When he imagined himself to be fighting old laws he gave a sort of vague and general approval to new laws. But when he came to the new laws they had a bad time. When Dickens found that after a hundred economic arguments and granting a hundred economic considerations, the fact remained that paupers in modern workhouses were much too afraid of the beadle, just as vassals in ancient castles were much too afraid of the Dedlocks, then he struck suddenly and at once. This is what makes the opening chapters of *Oliver Twist* so curious and important. The very fact of Dickens's distance from, and independence of, the elaborate financial arguments of his time, makes more definite and dazzling his sudden assertion that he sees the old human tyranny in front of him as plain as the sun at noon-day. Dickens attacks the modern workhouse with a sort of inspired simplicity as a boy in a fairy tale who had wandered about, sword in hand, looking for ogres and who had found an indisputable ogre. All the other people of his time are attacking things because they are bad economics or because they are bad politics, or because they are bad science; he alone is attacking things because they are bad. All the others are Radicals with a large R; he alone is radical with a small one. He encounters evil with that beautiful surprise which, as it is the beginning of all real pleasure, is also the beginning of all righteous indignation. He enters the workhouse just as Oliver Twist enters it, as a little child.

This is the real power and pathos of that celebrated passage in the book which has passed into a proverb; but which has not lost its terrible humour even in being hackneyed. I mean, of course, the everlasting quotation about

Oliver Twist asking for more. The real poignancy that there is in this idea is a very good study in that strong school of social criticism which Dickens represented. A modern realist describing the dreary workhouse would have made all the children utterly crushed, not daring to speak at all, not expecting anything, not hoping anything, past all possibility of affording even an ironical contrast or a protest of despair. A modern, in short, would have made all the boys in the workhouse pathetic by making them all pessimists. But Oliver Twist is not pathetic because he is a pessimist. Oliver Twist is pathetic because he is an optimist. The whole tragedy of that incident is in the fact that he does expect the universe to be kind to him, that he does believe that he is living in a just world. He comes before the Guardians as the ragged peasants of the French Revolution came before the Kings and Parliaments of Europe. That is to say, he comes, indeed, with gloomy experiences, but he comes with a happy philosophy. He knows that there are wrongs of man to be reviled; but he believes also that there are rights of man to be demanded. It has often been remarked as a singular fact that the French poor, who stand in historic tradition as typical of all the desperate men who have dragged down tyranny, were, as a matter of fact, by no means worse off than the poor of many other European countries before the Revolution. The truth is that the French were tragic because they were better off. The others had known the sorrowful experiences; but they alone had known the splendid expectation and the original claims. It was just here that Dickens was so true a child of them and of that happy theory so bitterly applied. They were the one oppressed people that simply asked for justice; they were the one Parish Boy who innocently asked for more.

—G.K. Chesterton, "Oliver Twist," *Criticisms & Appreciations of the Works of Charles Dickens*, 1911

HARD TIMES

John Ruskin (1860)

This is a matched set with the following piece by George Bernard Shaw, which offers an elaborate rationale for Ruskin's claim that *Hard Times* is Dickens's greatest work. For Ruskin, as for Carlyle and others at midcentury, the novel's critique of laissez-faire economic practices signals a new profundity in Dickens's social views.

The essential value and truth of Dickens's writings have been unwisely lost sight of by many thoughtful persons, merely because he presents his truth with some colour of caricature. Unwisely, because Dickens's caricature, though often gross, is never mistaken. Allowing for his manner of telling them, the things he tells us are always true. I wish that he could think it right to limit his brilliant exaggeration to works written only for public amusement; and when he takes up a subject of high national importance, such as that which he handled in *Hard Times*, that he would use severer and more accurate analysis. The usefulness of that work (to my mind, in several respects, the greatest he has written) is with many persons seriously diminished because Mr. Bounderby is a dramatic monster, instead of a characteristic example of a worldly master; and Stephen Blackpool a dramatic perfection, instead of a characteristic example of an honest workman. But let us not lose the use of Dickens's wit and insight, because he chooses to speak in a circle of stage fire. He is entirely right in his main drift and purpose in every book he has written; and all of them, but especially *Hard Times*, should be studied with close and earnest care by persons interested in social questions. They will find much that is partial, and, because partial, apparently unjust; but if they examine all the evidence on the other side, which Dickens seems to overlook, it will appear, after all their trouble, that his view was the finally right one, grossly and sharply told.

—John Ruskin, "A Note on *Hard Times*," (1860)

GEORGE BERNARD SHAW (1912)

The Irish-born George Bernard Shaw was a renowned playwright (*Major Barbara, Pygmalion, Saint Joan*) and an activist who embraced such causes as feminism, socialism, and vegetarianism. Shaw picks up Ruskin's brief mention of *Hard Times* and argues that the novel represents a kind of conversion narrative, whereby Dickens—like such social critics as Ruskin, Carlyle, Marx, and William Morris—came to understand that the social ills of Victorian England were not the fault of individual malefactors. From the point of view of these critics, the woes arose directly from the organization of society. Society was not afflicted by oppressors; society was itself the oppressor.

The difference between *Bleak House* and *Hard Times*, according to Shaw, is the difference between Tom-All-Alone's and Coketown. In the earlier novel, Tom-All-Alone's is an anachronism, a blight on England's modernity that is maintained by the inherently corrupting Chancery system. Reform the law, Dickens suggests, and allow Tom-All-Alone's to join the nineteenth century. Coketown is different. While Dickens intended readers to recoil from the wearying toil and filth of Coketown, it is also clear that this toil and filth constitute modernity. Shaw suggests that this amounts to a wholesale moral revaluation: "Here you will find no more villains and heroes, but only oppressors and victims, oppressing and suffering in spite of themselves, driven by a huge machinery which grinds to pieces the people it should nourish and ennoble." For Shaw, that machinery is capitalism; for less sympathetic critics, such as Henry James, it was Dickens's own gift for exaggeration. Politically speaking, at least, *Hard Times* "was written to make you uncomfortable," not for amusement.

Shaw and James both emphasize that, in Dickens's later novels, this penchant for exaggeration becomes unmoored from any sense of restraint, and the playwright even agrees that, when the humor does not work, it is almost unreadable. The difference is that Shaw sees this exaggeration as "very nearly impossible, yet not quite impossible," arguing further that Dickens's complete abandonment of restraint helps make palatable the reader's discomfort with the political diagnosis.

It would be instructive to compare Shaw's praise for *Hard Times* with the scornful dismissals of Dickens's politics offered by Bagehot or Stephens. Even in Shaw this dismissive tone creeps into the discussion of Slackbridge, the union organizer. The radical playwright cannot understand Dickens's consistent rejection of democratic action, and so he waves his hands at it. In contrast to these writers' well-defined political agendas, a critic such as Santayana can argue that Dickens's generalized hatred of oppression is easily confused with a specific politics. Shaw's essay is a useful starting point for any discussion of the later novels' social critique, not just *Hard Times*.

John Ruskin once declared *Hard Times* Dickens's best novel. It is worth while asking why Ruskin thought this, because he would have been the first to admit that the habit of placing works of art in competition with one another, and wrangling as to which is the best, is the habit of the sportsman, not of the enlightened judge of art. Let us take it that what Ruskin meant was that *Hard Times* was one of his special favorites among Dickens's books. Was this the caprice of fancy? or is there any rational explanation of the preference? I think there is.

Hard Times is the first fruit of that very interesting occurrence which our religious sects call, sometimes conversion, sometimes being saved, sometimes attaining to conviction of sin. Now the great conversions of the XIX century were not convictions of individual, but of social sin. The first half of the XIX century considered itself the greatest of all the centuries. The second discovered that it was the wickedest of all the centuries. The first half despised and pitied the Middle Ages as barbarous, cruel, superstitious, ignorant. The second half saw no hope for mankind except in the recovery of the faith, the art, the humanity of the Middle Ages. In Macaulay's *History of England*, the world is so happy, so progressive, so firmly set in the right path, that the author cannot mention even the National Debt without proclaiming that the deeper the country goes into debt, the more it prospers. In Morris's *News from Nowhere* there is nothing left of all the institutions that Macaulay glorified except an old building, so ugly that it is used only as a manure market, that was once the British House of Parliament. *Hard Times* was written in 1854, just at the turn of the half century; and in it we see Dickens with his eyes newly open and his conscience newly stricken by the discovery of the real state of England. In the book that went immediately before, *Bleak House*, he was still denouncing evils and ridiculing absurdities that were mere symptoms of the anarchy that followed the industrial revolution of the XVIII and XIX centuries, and the conquest of political power by Commercialism in 1832. In *Bleak House* Dickens knows nothing of the industrial revolution: he imagines that what is wrong is that when a dispute arises over the division of the plunder of the nation, the Court of Chancery, instead of settling the dispute cheaply and promptly, beggars the disputants and pockets both their shares. His description of our party system, with its Coodle, Doodle, Foodle, etc., has never been surpassed for accuracy and for penetration of superficial pretence. But he had not dug down to the bed rock of the imposture. His portrait of the ironmaster who visits Sir Leicester Dedlock, and who is so solidly superior to him, might have been drawn by Macaulay: there is not a touch of Bounderby in it. His horrible and not untruthful portraits of the brickmakers whose abject and battered wives call them "master," and his picture of the now vanished slum between Drury Lane and Catherine Street which he calls Tom All Alone's, suggest (save in the one case of the outcast Jo, who is, like Oliver Twist, a child, and therefore outside the old self-help panacea of Dickens's time) nothing but individual delinquencies, local plague-spots, negligent authorities.

In *Hard Times* you will find all this changed. Coketown, which you can see to-day for yourself in all its grime in the Potteries (the real name of it is Hanley in Staffordshire on the London and North Western Railway), is not, like Tom All Alone's, a patch of slum in a fine city, easily cleared away, as Tom's actually was about fifty years after Dickens called attention to it. Coketown is the whole place; and its rich manufacturers are proud of its dirt, and declare that they like to see the sun blacked out with smoke, because it means that the furnaces are busy and money is being made; whilst its poor factory hands have never known any other sort of town, and are as content with it as a rat is with a hole. Mr. Rouncewell, the pillar of society who snubs Sir Leicester with such dignity, has become Mr. Bounderby, the self-made humbug. The Chancery suitors who are driving themselves mad by hanging about the Courts in the hope of getting a judgment in their favour instead of trying to earn an honest living, are replaced by factory operatives who toil miserably and incessantly only to see the streams of gold they set flowing slip through their fingers into the pockets of men who revile and oppress them.

Clearly this is not the Dickens who burlesqued the old song of the Fine Old English Gentleman, and saw in the evils he attacked only the sins and wickednesses and follies of a great civilization. This is Karl Marx, Carlyle, Ruskin, Morris, Carpenter, rising up against civilization itself as against a disease, and declaring that it is not our disorder but our order that is horrible; that it is not criminals but our magnates that are robbing and murdering us; and that it is not merely Tom All Alone's that must be demolished and abolished, pulled down, rooted up, and made for ever impossible so that nothing shall remain of it but History's record of its infamy, but our entire social system. For that was how men felt, and how some of them spoke, in the early days of the Great Conversion which produced, first, such books as the *Latter Day Pamphlets* of Carlyle, Dickens's *Hard Times*, and the tracts and sociological novels of the Christian Socialists, and later on the Socialist movement which has now spread all over the world, and which has succeeded in convincing even those who most abhor the name of Socialism that the condition of the civilized world is deplorable, and that the remedy is far beyond the means of individual righteousness. In short, whereas formerly men said to the victim of society who ventured to complain, "Go and reform yourself before you pretend to reform Society," it now has to admit that until Society is reformed, no man can reform himself except in the most insignificantly small ways. He may cease picking your pocket of half crowns; but he cannot cease taking a quarter of a million a year from the community for nothing at one end of the scale, or living under conditions in which health, decency, and gentleness are impossible at the other, if he happens to be born to such a lot.

You must therefore resign yourself, if you are reading Dickens's books in the order in which they were written, to bid adieu now to the light-hearted and only occasionally indignant Dickens of the earlier books, and get such entertainment as you can from him now that the occasional indignation has spread and deepened into a passionate revolt against the whole industrial order of the modern world. Here you will find no more villains and heroes, but only oppressors and victims, oppressing and suffering in spite of themselves, driven by a huge machinery which grinds to pieces the people it should nourish and ennoble, and having for its directors the basest and most foolish of us instead of the noblest and most farsighted.

Many readers find the change disappointing. Others find Dickens worth reading almost for the first time. The increase in strength and intensity is enormous: the power that indicts a nation so terribly is much more impressive than that which ridicules individuals. But it cannot be said that there is an increase of simple pleasure for the reader, though the books are not therefore less attractive. One cannot say that it is pleasanter to look at a battle than at a merry-go-round; but there can be no question which draws the larger crowd. To describe the change in the readers' feelings more precisely, one may say that it is impossible to enjoy Gradgrind or Bounderby as one enjoys Pecksniff or the Artful Dodger or Mrs. Gamp or Micawber or Dick Swiveller, because these earlier characters have nothing to do with us except to amuse us. We neither hate nor fear them. We do not expect ever to meet them, and should not be in the least afraid of them if we did. England is not full of Micawbers and Swivellers. They are not our fathers, our schoolmasters, our employers, our tyrants. We do not read novels to escape from them and forget them: quite the contrary. But England is full of Bounderbys and Podsnaps and Gradgrinds; and we are all to a quite appalling extent in their power. We either hate and fear them or else we are them, and resent being held up to odium by a novelist. We have only to turn to the article on Dickens in the current edition of the *Encyclopedia Britannica* to find how desperately our able critics still exalt all Dickens's early stories about individuals whilst ignoring or belittling such masterpieces as *Hard Times, Little Dorrit, Our Mutual Friend*, and even *Bleak House* (because of Sir Leicester Dedlock), for their mercilessly faithful and penetrating exposures of English social, industrial, and political life; to see how hard Dickens hits the conscience of the governing class; and how loth we still are to confess, not that we are so wicked (for of that we are rather proud), but so ridiculous, so futile, so incapable of making our country really prosperous. *The Old Curiosity Shop* was written to amuse you, entertain you, touch you; and it succeeded. *Hard Times* was written to make you uncomfortable; and it will make you uncomfortable (and serve you right) though it will perhaps interest you more, and certainly leave a deeper scar on you, than any two of its forerunners.

At the same time you need not fear to find Dickens losing his good humor and sense of fun and becoming serious in Mr. Gradgrind's way. On the contrary, Dickens in this book casts off, and casts off for ever, all restraint on his wild sense of humour. He had always been inclined to break loose: there are passages in the speeches of Mrs. Nickleby and Pecksniff which are impossible as well as funny. But now it is no longer a question of passages: here he begins at last to exercise quite recklessly his power of presenting a character to you in the most fantastic and outrageous terms, putting into its mouth from one end of the book to the other hardly one word which could conceivably be uttered by any sane human being, and yet leaving you with an unmistakable and exactly truthful portrait of a character that you recognize at once as not only real but typical. Nobody ever talked, or ever will talk, as Silas Wegg talks to Boffin and Mr. Venus, or as Mr. Venus reports Pleasant Riderhood to have talked, or as Rogue Riderhood talks, or as John Chivery talks. They utter rhapsodies of nonsense conceived in an ecstasy of mirth. And this begins in *Hard Times*. Jack Bunsby in *Dombey and Son* is absurd: the oracles he delivers are very nearly impossible, and yet not quite impossible. But Mrs. Sparsit in this book, though Rembrandt could not have drawn a certain type of real woman more precisely to the life, is grotesque from beginning to end in her way of expressing herself. Her nature, her tricks of manner, her way of taking Mr. Bounderby's marriage, her instinct for hunting down Louisa and Mrs. Pegler, are drawn with an unerring hand; and she says nothing that is out of character. But no clown gone suddenly mad in a very mad harlequinade could express all these truths in more extravagantly ridiculous speeches. Dickens's business in life has become too serious for troubling over the small change of verisimilitude, and denying himself and his readers the indulgence of his humour in inessentials. He even calls the schoolmaster McChoakumchild, which is almost an insult to the serious reader. And it was so afterwards to the end of his life. There are moments when he imperils the whole effect of his character drawing by some overpoweringly comic sally. For instance, happening in *Hard Times* to describe Mr. Bounderby as drumming on his hat as if it were a tambourine, which is quite correct and natural, he presently says that "Mr. Bounderby put his tambourine on his head, like an oriental dancer." Which similitude is so unexpectedly and excruciatingly funny that it is almost impossible to feel duly angry with the odious Bounderby afterwards.

This disregard of naturalness in Speech is extraordinarily entertaining in the comic method; but it must be admitted that it is not only not entertaining, but sometimes hardly bearable when it does not make us laugh. There are two persons in *Hard Times*, Louisa Gradgrind and Cissy Jupe, who are serious throughout. Louisa is a figure of poetic tragedy; and there is no question of naturalness in her case: she speaks from beginning to end as an inspired prophetess, conscious of her own doom and finally bearing to her father the judgment of Providence on his blind conceit. If you once consent to overlook her marriage, which is none the less an act of prostitution because she does it to obtain advantages for her brother and not for herself, there is nothing in the solemn poetry of her deadly speech that jars. But Cissy is nothing if not natural; and though Cissy is as true to nature in her character as Mrs. Sparsit, she "speaks like a book" in the most intolerable sense of the words. In her interview with Mr. James Harthouse, her unconscious courage and simplicity, and his hopeless defeat by them, are quite natural and right; and the contrast between the humble girl of the people and the smart sarcastic man of the world whom she so completely vanquishes is excellently dramatic; but Dickens has allowed himself to be carried away by the scene into a ridiculous substitution of his own most literary and least colloquial style for any language that could conceivably be credited to Cissy.

> "Mr. Harthouse: the only reparation that remains with you is to leave her immediately and finally. I am quite sure that you can mitigate in no other way the wrong and harm you have done. I am quite sure that it is the only compensation you have left it in your power to make. I do not say that it is much, or that it is enough; but it is something, and it is necessary. Therefore, though without any other authority than I have given you, and even without the knowledge of any other person than yourself and myself, I ask you to depart from this place to-night, under an obligation never to return to it."

This is the language of a Lord Chief Justice, not of the dunce of an elementary school in the Potteries.

But this is only a surface failure, just as the extravagances of Mrs. Sparsit are only surface extravagances. There is, however, one real failure in the book. Slackbridge, the trade union organizer, is a mere figment of the middle-class imagination. No such man would be listened to by a meeting of English factory hands. Not that such meetings are less susceptible to humbug than meetings of any other class. Not that trade union organizers, worn out by the terribly wearisome and trying work of going from place to place repeating the same commonplaces and trying to "stoke up" meetings to enthusiasm with them, are less apt than other politicians to end as windbags, and sometimes to depend on stimulants to pull them through their work. Not, in short, that the trade union platform is any less humbug-ridden than the platforms of our more highly placed political parties. But even at their worst trade union organizers are not a bit like Slackbridge. Note, too, that Dickens mentions that there was a chairman at the meeting (as if that were rather surprising), and that this chairman makes no attempt to preserve the usual order of public meeting, but allows speakers to address the assembly and interrupt one another in an entirely disorderly way. All this is pure middle-class ignorance. It is much as if a tramp were to write a description of millionaires smoking large cigars in church, with their wives in low-necked dresses and diamonds. We cannot say that Dickens did not know the working classes, because he knew humanity too well to be ignorant of any class. But this sort of knowledge is as compatible with ignorance of class manners and customs as with ignorance of foreign languages. Dickens knew certain classes of working folk very well: domestic servants, village artisans, and employees of petty tradesmen, for example. But of the segregated factory populations of our purely industrial towns he knew no more than an observant professional man can pick up on a flying visit to Manchester.

It is especially important to notice that Dickens expressly says in this book that the workers were wrong to organize themselves in trade unions, thereby endorsing what was perhaps the only practical mistake of the Gradgrind school that really mattered much. And having thus thoughtlessly adopted, or at least repeated, this error, long since exploded, of the philosophic Radical school from which he started, he turns his back frankly on Democracy, and adopts the idealized Toryism of Carlyle and Ruskin, in which the aristocracy are the masters and superiors of the people, and also the servants of the people and of God. Here is a significant passage.

> "Now perhaps," said Mr. Bounderby, "you will let the gentleman know how you would set this muddle (as you are so fond of calling it) to rights."
>
> "I donno, sir. I canna be expecten to't. Tis not me as should be I looken to for that, sir. Tis they as is put ower me, and ower aw the rest of us. What do they tak upon themseln, sir, if not to do it?"

And to this Dickens sticks for the rest of his life. In *Our Mutual Friend* he appeals again and again to the governing classes, asking them with every device of reproach, invective, sarcasm, and ridicule of which he is master, what they have to say to this or that evil which it is their professed business to amend or avoid. Nowhere does he appeal to the working classes to take their fate into their own hands and try the democratic plan.

Another phrase used by Stephen Blackpool in this remarkable fifth chapter is important. "Nor yet lettin alone will never do it." It is Dickens's express repudiation of *laissez-faire*.

There is nothing more in the book that needs any glossary, except, perhaps, the strange figure of the Victorian "swell," Mr. James Harthouse. His pose has gone out of fashion. Here and there you may still see a man—even a youth—with a single eyeglass, an elaborately bored and weary air, and a little stock of cynicisms and indifferentisms contrasting oddly with a mortal anxiety about his clothes. All he needs is a pair of Dundreary whiskers, like the officers in Desanges' military pictures, to be a fair imitation of Mr. James Harthouse. But he is not in the fashion: he is an eccentric, as Whistler was an eccentric, as Max Beerbohm and the neo-dandies of the *fin de siècle* were eccentrics. It is now the fashion to be energetic, to hustle as American millionaires are supposed (rather erroneously) to hustle. But the soul of the swell is still unchanged. He has changed his name again and again, become a Masher, a Toff, a Johnny and what not; but fundamentally he remains what he always was, an Idler, and therefore a man bound to find some trick of thought and speech that reduces the world to a thing as empty and purposeless and hopeless as himself. Mr. Harthouse reappears, more seriously and kindly taken, as Eugene Wrayburn and Mortimer Lightwood in *Our Mutual Friend*. He reappears as a club in The Finches of the Grove of *Great Expectations*. He will reappear in all his essentials in fact and in fiction until he is at last shamed or coerced into honest industry and becomes not only unintelligible but inconceivable.

Note, finally, that in this book Dickens proclaims that marriages are not made in heaven, and that those which are not confirmed there, should be dissolved.

—George Bernard Shaw, "*Hard Times*," (1912)

Chronology

1812	Charles John Huffman Dickens is born on February 7 to John and Elizabeth Dickens, at Landport, Portsmouth, England. He is the second of eight children.
1824	John Dickens is arrested for debt and sent to Marshalsea Prison. Charles works at Warren's Blacking Factory. His father is released three months later, and Charles return to school.
1824–26	Attends Wellington House Academy, London.
1831	Becomes a reporter for the *Mirror of Parliament*.
1832	Works as a staff writer for the *True Sun*.
1833	First published piece, "A Dinner at Poplar Walk," under the pen name Boz, is featured in *Monthly Magazine*.
1834	Works as a staff writer for the *Morning Chronicle*.
1836	*Sketches by Boz* is published. *The Pickwick Papers* begins to appear in monthly installments. In April, Dickens marries Catherine Hogarth, the daughter of the editor of the *Evening Chronicle*. He meets John Forster, who becomes his lifelong friend and his biographer.
1837	His first child, Charles Jr., is born. *The Pickwick Papers* is published in book form. Catherine's sister, whom Dickens deeply loved, dies suddenly at their house. Dickens becomes the editor of *Bentley's Monthly*, and *Oliver Twist* begins to appear there.
1838	*Nicholas Nickleby* begins to appear in installments. Daughter Mary is born.
1839	Second daughter, Kate, is born. *Nicholas Nickleby* appears in book form.

1840	Dickens edits *Master Humphrey's Clock*, a weekly periodical in which *The Old Curiosity Shop* appears in installments.
1841	Son Walter is born.
1842	Tours the United States with wife from January to June. Publishes *American Notes*.
1843	*Martin Chuzzlewit* begins to appear in installments. *A Christmas Carol* is published.
1844	Dickens moves to Italy. A Christmas book, *The Chimes*, is published. Fifth child, Francis, is born.
1845	He returns to England. Son Alfred is born. Another Christmas book, *The Cricket on the Hearth*, is published.
1846	Dickens moves to Switzerland. *Dombey and Son* begins appearing in monthly installments. *The Battle of Life: A Love Story* is published.
1847	The family lives in Lausanne, then moves to Paris. Seventh child, Sydney, is born. Dickens helps philanthropist Angela Burdett Coutts establish a residence for homeless women and continues to help for the next ten years. He begins to manage a theatrical company.
1848	Sister Fanny dies. *The Haunted Man* is published.
1849	*David Copperfield* begins appearing in installments. Son Henry is born.
1850	He becomes the editor of a new weekly periodical, *Household Words*. A third daughter, Dora, is born and dies within a year.
1851	*A Child's History of England* is published in *Household Words*.
1852	*Bleak House* begins appearing in monthly installments. First bound volume of *A Child's History of England* is released. Son Edward is born.
1853	Dickens gives public readings from his Christmas books.
1854	*Hard Times* is serialized in *Household Words* before appearing in book form.
1855	*Little Dorrit* begins to appear in monthly installments. The Dickens family travels to Paris.
1856	Dickens purchases Gad's Hill Place, and the family returns to London.
1857	He meets the young actress Ellen Ternan, who shortly becomes his companion.
1858	Dickens separates from his wife.

1859	*Household Words* ceases publication. Dickens establishes a new weekly, *All the Year Round*. *A Tale of Two Cities* is published there serially, then appears in book form in December.
1860	*Great Expectations* appears in weekly installments.
1862	Dickens gives a series of public readings and travels to Paris.
1863	He continues his series of readings in London and Paris. His mother, Elizabeth, dies.
1864	*Our Mutual Friend* begins to appear in monthly installments.
1865	Dickens suffers a stroke that leaves him disabled. He is also in a train accident. He decides to change the ending of *Our Mutual Friend,* which soon appears in book form.
1866	He gives thirty public readings in the English provinces.
1867	He continues his provincial reading series, then travels to the United States for readings there.
1868	In April, Dickens returns to England, where he continues to tour.
1869	He stops the reading tour on a doctor's advice.
1870	He gives twelve readings in London. Six parts of *The Mystery of Edwin Drood* appear from April to September. On June 9 Charles Dickens dies. He is buried in Poets' Corner, Westminster Abbey.

Index

A

Accuracy, 103–112, 207–214
Ackroyd, Peter, 113
Ainsworth, William Harrison, 197–198
All the Year Round, 2
Altruism, George Eliot on, 19
American Notes (Dickens)
    Henry Wadsworth Longfellow on, 152
    James Spedding on, 152–153
    Jeffrey Francis on, 154–155
    publication of, 1
    Thomas Babington Macaulay on, 152
American transcendentalism, 19
Andersen, Hans Christian, 8, 160
Aristocracy
    James Fitzjames Stephen on, 183–189
    Queen Victoria on, 195–196
    William Makepeace Thackeray on, 155

B

Bagehot, Walter, 21–38
Barnaby Rudge (Dickens)
    Algernon Charles Swinburne on, 94, 95, 102
    Edgar Allan Poe on, 144–145
    plotting in, 78
    publication of, 1
The Battle of Life (Dickens), publication of, 2
Bayne, Peter, 14, 20–21
Bentley's Miscellany, 1
Birth of Charles Dickens, 1
Bleak House (Dickens)
    Algernon Charles Swinburne on, 98
    Alice Meynell on, 108
    George Bernard Shaw on, 208
    Leigh Hunt and, 17
    optimism and, 113
    plotting in, 78
    publication of, 2
    Walter Savage Landor and, 39
Braddon, M.E., 174
Brontë, Charlotte, 159
Browning, Elizabeth Barrett, 14
Bryant, William Cullen, 13
Buildings, human imagery of, 40
Burton, Richard, 91–92

C

Caricatures
    David Masson on, 38–39
    Edgar Allan Poe on, 145–148
    Frederic Harrison on, 73–79
    Herbert Paul on, 83
    Walter Bagehot on, 22, 26–27
    William Dean Howells on, 158

Carlyle, Thomas, 5–6, 193–194
Characterization. *See also* Individuality
    Algernon Charles Swinburne on, 94–95
    David Copperfield and, 161–163, 163–170
    David Masson on, 38–39
    Edgar Allan Poe on, 145–148
    Edwin P. Whipple on, 14–17, 63–64
    Frederic Harrison on, 73–79
    of gentleman, 64–67
    George Eliot on, 18–19
    George Santayana on, 125–137
    G.K. Chesterson on, 163–170, 201–205
    hallucinations and, 48–56
    Henry James on, 41–46
    impersonality of, 20–21
    improvement in over time, 67–69
    James Fitzjames Stephen on, 183–189
    Justin McCarthy on, 58
    Sara Coleridge on, 158
    Thomas De Quincey on, 148–149
    Walter Bagehot on, 22–24
    William Makepeace Thackeray on, 196–198
Charity, George Santayana on, 125–137
Chesterton, G.K., 113–125, 177–183, 189–195, 198–205
Child-life, pathos of, 84
The Chimes (Dickens), publication of, 2
Christmas
    George Santayana on, 125–137
    pathos in, 89
    William Dean Howells on, 70
Christmas books, nostalgia and, 49
A Christmas Carol (Dickens)
    Julia C. Dorr on, 156–157
    pathos in, 89
    publication of, 2
    William Makepeace Thackeray on, 155–156
Cities, Justin McCarthy on, 58
Class. *See also* Social reform
    Algernon Charles Swinburne on, 99–100
    Herbert Paul on, 83
    political judgment and, 56–58
    Walter Bagehot on, 22–23, 32–35
    W.H. Mallock on, 71–72
    William Cullen Bryant on, 13
Coleridge, Sara, 149, 158
Collins, Wilkie, 173, 174
Comedy
    Alice Meynell on, 103–112
    George Santayana on, 131–135
    G.K. Chesterson on, 113–125
    William Dean Howells on, 158
Confessions of an English Opium Eater (De Quincey), 148–149
Conversion narratives, George Bernard Shaw on, 206–214
Creativity, William Dean Howells on, 70
The Cricket on the Hearth (Dickens), publication of, 2
Crime genre, 174–177
Criminals, William Makepeace Thackeray on, 196–198
Croker, John Wilson, 141
Cross, Wilbur L., 91

D

Daily News, 2
Dallas, E.S., 170–174
Dana, Richard Henry, on Dickens's personality, 7
David Copperfield (Dickens)
    Algernon Charles Swinburne on, 96, 97–98, 102
    Alice Meynell on, 108
    Charles Dickens's preface to, 159
    Charlotte Brontë on, 159
    G.K. Chesterson on, 164
    Hans Christian Andersen on, 160
    James Russell Lowell on, 163

Mowbray Morris on, 161–163
publication of, 2
William Makepeace Thackeray on, 160
William Samuel Lilly on, 80
Death, nature and, 13
Death of Charles Dickens, 2
Debt, 1
Democracy, G.K. Chesterson on, 182–183
De Quincey, Thomas, 148–149
Derision, Alice Meynell on, 106–107
Details, Alice Meynell on, 103–112
Dickens, Mamie, on Dickens's personality, 8–9
Dombey and Son (Dickens)
   Algernon Charles Swinburne on, 97, 100
   publication of, 2
Dorr, Julia C., 156–157

E
Eliot, George, 18–19, 181
Eliot, T.S., 113
Emerson, Ralph Waldo, 19
Emotion, 61–62, 150–151
Energy, G.K. Chesterson on, 177–183, 198–205
The English Constitution (Bagehot), 21
Escape, Margaret Oliphant on, 175–177
Evans, Mary Ann (George Eliot). *See* Eliot, George
Everyman, Scrooge as, 156–157
Evil, 113–125, 125–137
Exaggeration
   Edgar Allan Poe on, 145–148
   George Bernard Shaw on, 207–214
   George Santayana on, 131–135
   Thomas De Quincey on, 148–149

F
Factory conditions, 56
Facts, fiction and, 91
Fairy tales, 58, 177–183

Farce
   George Gissing on, 83–89
   G.K. Chesterson on, 113–125
   Margaret Oliphant on, 175–177
Fatigue, *David Copperfield* and, 164–170
Fiction, facts and, 91
Fielding, Henry, influence of, 59, 61
FitzGerald, Edward, 56
Fitzgerald, Percy, on Dickens's personality, 9
Flush (dog), 18
Forster, John, on Dickens's personality, 8
Francis, Jeffrey, 154–155
French Revolution, 193–194
The French Revolution (Carlyle), 5, 193–194

G
Gambling, 148–149
Gentleman, portrayal of, 64–67, 177–183
Gissing, George, 83–89, 150–151
Great Expectations (Dickens)
   Algernon Charles Swinburne on, 102
   Alice Meynell on, 109
   E.S. Dallas on, 170–174
   G.K. Chesterson on, 177–183
   Margaret Oliphant on, 174–177
   publication of, 2
Grotesques
   David Copperfield and, 163–170
   Edgar Allan Poe on, 145–148
   Edwin P. Whipple on, 63–64
   Frederic Harrison on, 73–79
   George Santayana on, 125–137
   G.K. Chesterson on, 113–125
   James Fitzjames Stephen on, 187–188
   Margaret Oliphant on, 174–177
   Richard Burton on, 91–92

H

Hall, S.C., 142–143
Hallucinations, psychology of artistic creation and, 48–56
Hard Times (Dickens)
    Algernon Charles Swinburne on, 99
    George Bernard Shaw on, 206–214
    John Ruskin on, 205–206
    publication of, 2
Harrison, Frederic, 72–79
Harte, Bret, 149–150
The Haunted Man (Dickens), publication of, 2
Hawthorne, Nathaniel, on Dickens's personality, 7
A Hazard of New Fortunes (Howells), 70
Headstone, Bradley, Henry James on, 44–45
Henley, W.E., 67–69
Heroism, 29–30, 177–183
Hogarth, Catherine (wife), 1
Hogarth, Georgina, on Dickens's personality, 8–9
Hone, Philip, 6, 157
Household Words, 2, 9, 56
The House of the Seven Gables (Hawthorne), 7
Howells, William Dean, 70, 158
Humanism
    George Santayana on, 131
    G.K. Chesterson on, 113–125, 163–170
    Harriet Martineau on, 58
    Queen Victoria on, 195
Humility, George Santayana on, 131
Humor
    Algernon Charles Swinburne on, 92–103
    Alice Meynell on, 103–112
    Anthony Trollope on, 61–62
    David Masson on, 38–39
    Edgar Allan Poe on, 145–148
    Frederic Harrison on, 73–79
    George Bernard Shaw on, 207–214, 210–212
    George Gissing on, 83–89
    George Santayana on, 131–135
    G.K. Chesterson on, 198–205
    Harriet Martineau on, 57
    Herbert Paul on, 83
    Margaret Oliphant on, 143
    Peter Bayne on, 20–21
    Walter Bagehot on, 22, 24–26, 36–37
    William Makepeace Thackeray on, 156
Hunt, Leigh, 17, 100
Hutton, Laurence, 90

I

Illusions, James Fitzjames Stephen on, 189
Imagery, 40, 103–112
Imaginary Conversations of Greeks and Romans (Landor), 39
Imagination
    distorting, 73–79
    Edgar Allan Poe on, 144–145, 147
    George Henry Lewes on, 50–52
    W.E. Henley on, 67–69
Individuality, 15–16, 20–21
Insight, 45, 84
Irrelevance, Laurence Hutton on, 90

J

Jack Sheppard (Ainsworth), 197–198
James, Henry, 41–46

K

Kemble, Frances Ann, on Dickens's personality, 7
Kidnapped (Stevenson), 64

L

Laissez-faire economics, 205–206, 214
Landor, Walter Savage, 39–40
Language
    Alice Meynell on, 103–112

George Bernard Shaw on, 211–212
James Fitzjames Stephen on, 188
Lewes, George Henry, 48–56
Lilly, William Samuel, 80–81
Little Dorrit (Dickens)
    Algernon Charles Swinburne on, 100, 101
    pathos in, 89
    publication of, 2
Longfellow, Henry Wadsworth, 152
Love, 150–151, 163–170
Lowell, James Russell, 163
Lytton, Edward Bulwer, 197–198

M

Macaulay, Thomas Babington, 152
Major Barbara (Shaw), 206
Mallock, W.H., 70–72, 177–183
Marriage, 163–170, 214
Martin Chuzzlewit (Dickens)
    Algernon Charles Swinburne on, 96–97
    Alice Meynell on, 109–110
    Philip Hone on, 157
    publication of, 1
    Sara Coleridge on, 158
    William Dean Howells on, 158
Martineau, Harriet, 22, 56–58
Masculinity, G.K. Chesterson on, 177–183
Masson, David, 14, 38–39
McCarthy, Justin, 58
Melville, Herman, 6
Meynell, Alice, 103–112
Milton, John, 38
Mitford, Mary Russell, 18
Modernity, George Bernard Shaw on, 207–214
Mood, Alexander Smith on, 40
Morality
    Algernon Charles Swinburne on, 92–103
    David Copperfield and, 164–170
    George Santayana on, 125–137
    G.K. Chesterson on, 198–205
    Henry James on, 42–46
    James Fitzjames Stephen on, 188–189
    Walter Bagehot on, 26–27
    William Makepeace Thackeray on, 196–198
Morning Chronicle, 1
Morris, Mowbray, 161–163
Murray, David Christie, 81–82
My Father as I Recall Him (M. Dickens), 8
The Mystery of Edwin Drood (Dickens), publication of, 2

N

Nationalism, 70–71
National Review, 21
Nature, 13, 14–17
New Grub Street (Gissing), 83
Nicholas Nickelby (Dickens), 1, 179
Norton, Charles Eliot, 46–47

O

The Odd Women (Gissing), 83
The Old Curiosity Shop (Dickens)
    Bret Harte on, 149–150
    Edgar Allan Poe on, 145–148
    George Gissing on, 150–151
    heroism in, 179
    humor in, 210
    publication of, 1
    Sara Coleridge on, 149
    Thomas De Quincey on, 148–149
Oliphant, Margaret, 143, 174–177
Oliver Twist (Dickens)
    fairy tales and, 177
    G.K. Chesterson on, 113–125, 198–205
    heroism in, 179
    plotting in, 78
    publication of, 1
    Queen Victoria on, 195–196
    sentimental radicals and, 22, 27–28
    as serial publication, 173

William Makepeace Thackeray
on, 196–198
Opposition, bias of, 53–54
Oppression
George Bernard Shaw on, 206–214
G.K. Chesterson on, 189–195, 198–205
Optimism, 113–125, 166–167
Our Mutual Friend (Dickens)
fairy tales and, 177
Henry James on, 41–46
publication of, 2

P
Passion, 41–46, 80–81
Past, representation of, 47–48
Past and Present (Carlyle), 5
Pathos
Algernon Charles Swinburne on, 95
George Gissing on, 83–89
G.K. Chesterson on, 190–195, 198–205
Margaret Oliphant on, 175–177
Paul, Herbert, 83
Paul Clifford (Lytton), 197–198
Pendennis (Thackeray), 155
Penny dreadfuls, 170–174
Periodicals, constraints from, 170–174
Perkins, F.B., 47–48
The Pickwick Papers (Dickens)
Frederic Harrison on, 78, 79
heroism in, 179
humor of, 57
John Wilson Croker on, 141
Margaret Oliphant on, 143
pathos in, 88
publication of, 1
Richard Grant White on, 142
S.C. Hall on, 142–143
W.E. Henley on, 67–69
"Pictures of Italy" (Dickens), 2
Plotting
Algernon Charles Swinburne on, 92–103

Edgar Allan Poe on, 144–145
Frederic Harrison on, 73, 78–79
Justin McCarthy on, 58
Walter Bagehot on, 28–30
Poe, Edgar Allan, 144–148
Politics, 198–205, 206–214. *See also* Social reform
The Portrait of a Lady (James), 41
Posthumous Papers of the Pickwick Club (Dickens), publication of, 1
Positivism, 72–79
Poverty
George Gissing on, 84–89
G.K. Chesterson on, 120
Margaret Oliphant on, 175–177
Pragmatism, Walter Bagehot and, 21–22
Prose style, 63, 71–72
Psychology
George Santayana on, 125–137
Henry James on, 41–46
as product of method, 48–56
Public policy, science and, 72–73
Purity, Queen Victoria on, 195–196
Pygmalion (Shaw), 206

R
Reade, Charles, 174
Realism
David Copperfield and, 161–163, 163–170
G.K. Chesterson on, 113–125
Justin McCarthy on, 58
Margaret Oliphant on, 175–177
Queen Victoria on, 195–196
use of humor and, 83–89
William Makepeace Thackeray on, 196–198
Reform
Frederic Harrison on, 73–79
George Bernard Shaw on, 206–214
George Santayana on, 125–137
G.K. Chesterson on, 113–125, 198–205
Harriet Martineau on, 56–58

John Ruskin on, 205–206
Wilbur L. Cross on, 91
Revolution, G.K. Chesterson on, 190–195
Rienzi (Mitford), 18
The Rise of Silas Lapham (Howells), 70
Ruskin, John, 19, 205–206, 207

S

Saint Joan (Shaw), 206
Santayana, George, 22, 125–137
Sartor Resartus (Carlyle), 5
Satire
    Algernon Charles Swinburne on, 99–100
    David Masson on, 38–39
    Frederic Harrison on, 73–79
Saturday Review, 183
The Scarlet Letter (Hawthorne), 7
Science, public policy and, 72–73
Sensation novels, 174–177
Sensitivity, Adolphus William Ward on, 59–60
Sentimentality
    George Gissing on, 83–89, 150–151
    Walter Bagehot on, 31, 33
Sentimental radicals, 22
Serial publications, 170–174, 174–177
Sexual passion, William Samuel Lilly on, 80–81
Shaw, George Bernard, 206–214
Shoe-blacking, 1
Skimpole, Harold, Leigh Hunt and, 17
Slavery, *American Notes* and, 152
Smith, Alexander, 40
Smollet, Tobias, influence of, 59, 60–61
Snobbishness, 180–181
Social reform
    Frederic Harrison on, 73–79
    George Bernard Shaw on, 206–214
    George Santayana on, 125–137
    G.K. Chesterson on, 113–125, 198–205
    Harriet Martineau on, 56–58
    John Ruskin on, 205–206
    Wilbur L. Cross on, 91
Sonnets from the Portuguese (Browning), 14
Spasmodic school, 40
Spedding, James, 152–153
Stephen, James Fitzjames, 183–189
Stevenson, Robert Louis, 64–67, 177–183
The Strange Case of Dr. Jekyll and Mr. Hyde (Stevenson), 64
Style, Anthony Trollope on, 63
Superficiality, Henry James on, 41–46
Suspense, Edgar Allan Poe on, 144–145
Swinburne, Algernon Charles, 58–59, 92–103

T

A Tale of Two Cities (Dickens)
    Algernon Charles Swinburne on, 95, 99, 102
    G.K. Chesterson on, 189–195
    James Fitzjames Stephen on, 183–189
    plotting in, 78
    publication of, 2
Technical estimate, bias of, 53–54
Thackeray, William Makepeace
    on *A Christmas Carol*, 155–156
    comparison to, 135–136, 180–181
    on *David Copperfield*, 160
    on *Oliver Twist*, 196–198
"Thanatopsis" (Bryant), 13
Tocqueville, Alexis de, works on America and, 16
Tone, Alexander Smith on, 40
Treasure Island (Stevenson), 64
Trollope, Anthony, 61–63
Trollope, Thomas Adolphus, on Dickens's personality, 9–10
Two Years Before the Mast (Dana), 6

U

Utilitarianism, outrage over, 22

V

Vanity Fair (Thackeray), 155, 177, 179
Victoria (Queen of England), 195–196
Villains
    Algernon Charles Swinburne on, 92–103
    Frederic Harrison on, 79
    G.K. Chesterson on, 113–125
Violence, 190–195, 196–198
Vulgarity, James Fitzjames Stephen on, 183–189
Vulgar optimists, 114

W

Ward, Adolphus William, 59–61
Whipple, Edwin P., 14–17, 63–64
White, Richard Grant, 142
Whitman, Walt, 130
The Wings of the Dove (James), 41
Wit, Alice Meynell on, 106–107
The Woman in White (Collins), 173, 174–177
Wrayburn, Eugene, Henry James on, 44–45